Exhibiting Slavery

New World Studies

Silvio A. Torres-Saillant, *Editor*

J. Michael Dash, Frank Moya Pons, and
Sandra Pouchet Paquet, *Associate Editors*

Exhibiting Slavery

THE CARIBBEAN POSTMODERN NOVEL
AS MUSEUM

Vivian Nun Halloran

University of Virginia Press

Charlottesville and London

University of Virginia Press
© 2009 by the Rector and Visitors of the University of Virginia
All rights reserved
Printed in the United States of America on acid-free paper
First published 2009

9 8 7 6 5 4 3 2 1

Library of Congress Cataloging-in-Publication Data
Halloran, Vivian Nun, 1971–
    Exhibiting slavery : the Caribbean postmodern
novel as museum / Vivian Nun Halloran.
        p.   cm. — (New world studies)
    Includes bibliographical references and index.
    ISBN 978-0-8139-2865-4 (cloth : alk. paper)
    ISBN 978-0-8139-2866-1 (pbk. : alk. paper)
    ISBN 978-0-8139-2868-5 (e-book)
    1. Caribbean fiction—20th century—History and criticism.   2. Slavery in
literature.   3. Archives in literature.   4. Slavery—Caribbean Area—History—
Sources.   5. Caribbean Area—In literature.   6. Caribbean fiction (English)—
History and criticism.   7. Caribbean fiction (French)—History and criticism.
8. Caribbean fiction (Spanish)—History and criticism. 9. Postmodernism
(Literature)—Caribbean area.   I. Title.
PN849.C3H36   2009
809.3'009729—dc22

                                                                    2009023619

THE
AMERICAN
LITERATURES
INITIATIVE

A book in the American Literatures Initiative (ALI), a collaborative
publishing project of NYU Press, Fordham University Press, Rutgers
University Press, Temple University Press, and the University of Virginia
Press. The Initiative is supported by The Andrew W. Mellon Foundation.
For more information, please visit www.americanliteratures.org.

For David Halloran,
best friend, most honest critic, staunchest ally

Contents

Acknowledgments

THE ORIGINAL RESEARCH for this book was made possible by the expert guidance of Professors Jenny Sharpe, John Skirius, and Ross Shideler at UCLA. Thanks to their willingness to let me write papers on Caribbean literature, I became interested in postmodern historical fiction about slavery.

Since arriving at Indiana University seven years ago, I completely changed my way of thinking about these same key texts because of the wonderful resources I found on campus. The first of these is the IU Art Museum, where curators Nannette Brewer and Jenny McComas helpfully answered all my questions and shared with me the museum's copies of many of the paintings and engravings I discuss in chapter 2. Their enthusiasm for their work and eagerness to share the museum's resources with a lowly assistant professor filled me with ideas and helped me focus my research.

In my own Department of Comparative Literature, I learned from colleagues who specialize in comparative arts, Giancarlo Maiorino, David Hertz, and Matei Calinescu, how to analyze the interrelationship between works of art and literature. Special thanks go to Rosemarie McGerr and Deborah N. Cohn, from the Department of Spanish and Portuguese, both of whom provided helpful advice and much encouragement. Laila Amine was an invaluable asset, providing help and guidance with the translations from the French.

Among my colleagues in other departments, I have learned the most from my professional collaborations with Professor Matthew Pratt Guterl, Director of the Program in American Studies and faculty member in the Department of African American and African Diaspora Studies. I was lucky enough to codirect a year-long faculty research seminar during 2005–6 entitled "Variations on Blackness," which received support from the College of Arts and Sciences, the Office of the Vice President for Research, and the Office of the Dean of Faculties. I first explored some of my thoughts on the role of slavery museums in contemporary culture in the essay I presented as part of this seminar. During the graduate research seminar that Professor Guterl and I cotaught, as well as in the "Variations on Blackness" conference we organized in April 2006, I fleshed out my interpretation of the interrelationship between museums and postmodernist fiction with the help of colleagues and graduate students. My thanks go out to them all.

Thanks to my aunt, Alma Benítez de Blanco, for hosting me and driving me all around Old San Juan in search of museums. We had a lot of fun finding new places neither one of us had seen before.

Finally, my husband and colleague, David Halloran, drove me from Bloomington, Indiana, to Cincinnati, Ohio, and Milwaukee, Wisconsin, so that I could spend time analyzing the various slavery-related exhibits at the Milwaukee Art Museum, America's Black Holocaust Museum, and the National Underground Railroad Freedom Center during various outings in 2005 and 2006. Without his love for the open road, I would not have been able to write this book. I thank him and hope he will continue to drive me around the country from museum to museum, and beyond.

Note on Translations

WHENEVER POSSIBLE, I have used published English translations of the original passages from the Hispanophone and Francophone texts I quote in order to make these texts more accessible to American readers. The English translations of Edgardo Rodríguez Juliá's *La noche oscura del Niño Avilés* and Patrick Chamoiseau's *L'esclave vieil homme et le molosse* that appear in this book are my own. I consulted with Laila Amine about the translations from the French; however, any mistakes or inaccuracies in the translations are solely my own.

Exhibiting Slavery

Introduction

Novels as Museums in a Postmodern Age

FOLLOWING THE 2001 passage of the so-called Taubira law, which declared slavery and the slave trade to be crimes against humanity, the French government created a national Committee for the Remembrance of Slavery made up of writers, museum curators, and historians hailing from France and its overseas departments: Guadeloupe, Martinique, Réunion, and French Guiana.[1] The committee's mandate was to increase public awareness of the history of French involvement in the transatlantic slave trade. French president Jacques Chirac appointed acclaimed Guadeloupian novelist Maryse Condé as the committee's president. Condé has written three slavery-related, postmodern historical novels: the two volumes of the diasporic family saga *Ségou*; and a neo–slave narrative about an enslaved Barbadian woman, *Moi, Tituba, sorcière . . . noire de Salem*. She is also the author of two other works of fiction portraying contemporary characters who discover and own up to their obligations toward the enslaved dead: *Les dernières rois mages*, a novel about an African American woman who appropriates her Martinican husband's African ancestor in order to downplay her own ties to plantation slavery in the United States, and the novella *Nannaya*, about a Jamaican businessman who becomes obsessed with the idea that he is descended from a notorious slave from his country's past. The committee members' disciplinary backgrounds, as well as Condé's high-profile appointment as the group's leader, attest to the considerable impact that artists and other humanists have had in framing what little public discussion there has been of this topic in France.

Further proof of art's power to commemorate the history of a people can be found in the first yearly report the committee submitted to the prime minister of France. In the report's appendix, the committee lists the various museum exhibitions held in France and its overseas departments that have addressed the themes of slavery, the slave trade, and/or abolition since 1985. That date was chosen as the starting point because it marked the three-hundredth anniversary of France's adoption of the Code Noir, or Black Code, a decree that specified how slaves were to be treated throughout the colonies from 1685 to 1789. By taking stock of the memorial activities that had been ongoing before the date of the committee's formation, this group documented a strong popular desire to learn more about the country's colonial past—its moral failures as well as its economic successes. Rather than issuing a call to conscience and atonement from on high, the Committee for the Remembrance of Slavery tapped into already-existing grassroots efforts to confront France's historical involvement in the trade in human beings. Thus, one of this committee's functions is to act as a clearinghouse for information about, and to promote further public performances of, what the cultural theorist Mieke Bal calls "cultural memorization," which she defines as "an activity occurring in the present, in which the past is continuously modified and re-described even as it continues to shape the future."[2] Implicit within both this definition and the committee's report is the sense that the work of cultural memory promotes a critical reckoning with the social, cultural, and economic cost of a nation's previous policies, rather than merely constituting nostalgia for a bygone era. This public act of taking stock serves as a precedent for shaping the future direction of governance.

Based upon the committee's recommendation, President Jacques Chirac officially declared May 10 to be a national day of remembrance for the victims of slavery. In a public speech marking the occasion in 2006, Chirac formally appointed yet another Francophone novelist, Édouard Glissant from Martinique, to chair a task force that will collaborate with the Committee for the Remembrance of Slavery to establish a National Center for the Remembrance of Slavery, the Slave Trade and Its Abolition. Glissant publicly addressed what he saw as his mission as the official chair in charge of spearheading efforts to establish this center in an editorial published in the French newspaper *Libération* on May 9, 2008. Like Condé, Glissant has found inspiration for his novels, plays, and theoretical works in the topic of slavery.[3] Chirac's two leadership appointments demonstrate his recognition of the important artistic contribution African-descended writers and other artists make to French culture. His speech also pointed to the continued existence of different kinds of bondage throughout the world, and emphasized the need for the national school curriculum to include a sustained discussion of France's history of oppression and exploitation in its colonies in the Americas, the Caribbean, and the Indian Ocean.[4] Chirac's official proclamation of a new national holiday constitutes a public performance of cultural recall; it can be interpreted as a secular act of mourning for victims of the transatlantic slave trade and of the plantation slavery system in the New World.

Taken together, Chirac's speech and the committee's report suggest that it is the government's duty to address its citizens' interest in learning more about their national heritage by encouraging cultural institutions like schools and museums to engage in introspective research about the details of a country's past actions and policies. This rhetorical connection between a country's historical involvement in the enterprise of transatlantic slavery and its contemporary public commemoration of the slave trade's victims is not new, nor is it particularly French. As arguably the largest international organization with both political credentials and cultural capital, the United Nations has led the way in the global effort to document the history of transatlantic slavery by preserving records, buildings, and other historical objects and also by honoring the achievements and contributions of the descendants of slaves. The clout of the UN's diverse constituency and its long history of sponsoring innovative cultural initiatives give this complex project its sense of internal coherence and also legitimize the aim of crafting a collective historiography.

The United Nations proclaimed 2004 as the "Year to Commemorate the Struggle against Slavery and Its Abolition." As part of its suggestions for observing what it termed the "living memory" of slavery, the General Assembly suggested three museum-related activities in the provisional agenda for its meeting in Paris in 2003: (1) to study the feasibility of establishing slave trade museums in the Caribbean, Latin America, Africa, and the Indian Ocean; (2) to promote the preservation of historical artifacts related to slavery and thereby support the museum's mission to educate the public about the history of the trade in human beings and its abolition; and (3) to train staff and develop an educational curriculum for museums to interpret the history of slavery for the public. While this and the earlier slavery-themed initiatives may appear to be a top-down imposition of the UN's moral and cultural values upon the peoples of the various regions it mentions, the international agency is actually working to consolidate the efforts of individual countries to come to terms with their respective pasts.

People in the islands of the Caribbean basin have also demonstrated an increasing interest in reevaluating the legacy of their colonial past, including their participation within the triangular trade and the slave economy. The Haitian Revolution has been a source of inspiration for twentieth-century Caribbean writers, who have commemorated it through great works of drama, fiction, historiography, and sociology. The Trinidadian author C. L. R. James's evocative history of the event, *The Black Jacobins* (1938), grew out of a play he had written by the same title. Although he is better known as a novelist and philosopher, Édouard Glissant turned to drama to honor the much-heralded leader of the Haitian Revolution in his play *Monsieur Toussaint* (1961). A fellow Martinican poet, playwright, theorist, and statesman, Aimé Césaire, published a study of the revolution's best-known leader, *Toussaint L'Ouverture: La révolution française et le problème colonial* (1962), as well as the play *La tragédie du roi Christophe* (1963), about Haiti's first self-declared monarch, Henri Christophe.

In Cuba, the anthropologist Fernando Ortiz published *Contrapunteo cubano del tabaco y el azúcar* (1940), his influential study of the tobacco and sugar industries' influence on both the slave economy and the emergent culture of that island. A little more than a quarter of a century later, another anthropologist, Miguel Barnet, fascinated academic and lay readers alike with his dramatic rendering of an old maroon's life story. Esteban Montejo lived alone in the Cuban forest for several years after running away from a plantation. *Biografía de un cimarrón* (1966) is Barnet's compilation of the ethnographic interviews he conducted with his subject. Ten years later, Cesar Leantes's historical novel *Los guerrilleros negros* (1976) used maroons as a metaphor for the Cuban revolutionaries who took to the hills and pledged their support for Castro's forces as they battled the Batista regime.

In the Anglophone Caribbean literary scene, the Barbadian novelist George Lamming addressed the pervasive effacement of the local history of enslavement and oppression in the sugar island of Barbados and criticized his fellow Bajans' penchant for commemorating British colonial icons like Queen Victoria in his autobiographical coming of age novel, *In the Castle of My Skin* (1970). His later work *Natives of My Person* (1972) chronicles an imagined Middle Passage voyage that goes wrong and never arrives at its destination. That same year saw the publication of *Die the Long Day* (1972), a fictional account of a slave uprising in Jamaica written by Orlando Patterson, a Jamaican-born Harvard sociologist who had previously written a landmark study of bondage in his island of origin, *The Sociology of Slavery* (1967).

The Trinidadian Nobel Prize winner V. S. Naipaul invoked the history of transatlantic slavery when he titled his first travel book *The Middle Passage*. Writing in 1962, he observes that, "Twenty million Africans made the middle passage, and scarcely an African name remains in the New World. Until the other day African tribesmen on screen excited derisive West Indian laughter."[5] The autobiographical narrator of Naipaul's expansive postmodern historical novel *A Way in the World* (1995) has a markedly different experience of visiting colonial Trinidad. The Naipauldian narrator remarks that even before Trinidad obtained its independence from England in 1962, the islanders of African descent felt a new interest in learning about their heritage: "In that square now there were lectures about local history and slavery. People were being told about themselves, and black feeling was high."[6] Although fictional, this reference to the Afro-Trinidadian people's appreciation of the public lecture as a means of instruction about their personal histories attests to the overall claim that the legacy of transatlantic slavery has been a subject of interest in popular culture beyond the Francophone world for quite some time.

By memorializing the pain and suffering of people forced into bondage, as well as celebrating the varied contributions made by people of African descent to the culture and society of the places to which they were transported, the United Nations and UNESCO have paved the way for a worldwide reconsideration of what can be learned from the mistakes of the past. How, then, can the modern incarnations of the public and private institutions that were originally involved in the slave trade pay their respects to the ghosts of the past while striving to avoid repeating the same mistakes? In the last two decades of the twentieth century, national and state governments, banks, transnational corporations, and universities in Europe and the United States issued official proclamations or statements of regret, and even debated offering financial reparations as a way to publicly acknowledge their historical involvement in the slave trade and the exploitation of human beings for financial gain.[7] These diverse actions constitute individual pleas for expiation for past sins. However, mere gestures of atonement have not been deemed sufficient to heal the psychic and social wounds left by this cruel labor system. Instead, the tone of the public discussion about the legacy of slavery has turned away from a discourse dominated by resentment and the idea of placing blame, and moved toward a model of reconciliation and learning from our ancestors' mistakes.

Postmodernist Novels and Museums

In recent years, it has become increasingly difficult to demarcate the boundaries between the fields of literary, cultural, and museum studies. The art historian Donald Preziosi calls attention to the influence of contemporary critical practice on the museum and concludes an article examining how museums frame modernity by asking: "What can it mean, then, to be a subject in a world in which there exist museums of anything, and where virtually anything can serve as a museum? What kind of object, then, is a museum?"[8] He does not provide a definite answer to his inquiry, but rather suggests that nothing in the world exists outside of the museum because the world, as a repository of objects, is itself a museum. There is no hard-and-fast consensus among current museum professionals about the limits of what a museum can claim to be; depending on its size, budget, and mission statement, a museum can be either a state-sponsored institution created to preserve some aspect of national heritage, a local repository for historic objects and documents, a tourist attraction, or a public site that facilitates community-based learning. However, there is a "museum effect" that shapes how objects with specific cultural roles and origins are displayed within the bricks-and-mortar institution. Svetlana Alpers's working definition of the "museum effect" demonstrates its potential to elevate ordinary objects to the status of an aesthetic icon, merely by their inclusion in the context of other works of artistic value in a museum: "the tendency to isolate something from its world, to offer it up for attentive looking and thus to transform it into art like our own."[9] Alpers points to this as a controversial result of display culture and mentions that there is no agreement within museum circles about how best to deploy or counteract this effect.

Barbara Kirshenblatt-Gimblett discusses the museum effect in an ethnographic context and argues that it is a reciprocal experience. She explains that museums do two things: first, they create a new and artificial context in which to display their featured objects, and, second, their exhibitions affect how museum visitors view themselves and approach their everyday life.[10] Speaking specifically about works of art, Ivan Karp argues that the ideology and claims to power implicit within an exhibition's design are what give rise to the museum effect: "The museum effect is clearly a force that is independent of the objects themselves. The mode of installation, the subtle messages communicated through design, arrangement, and assemblage, can either add or impede our appreciation and understanding of the visual, cultural, social, and political interest of the objects and stories exhibited in museums."[11] Karp not only points to the authorial role that exhibition designers and curators have with regard to the narratives they create about the featured objects in their exhibition, but he also argues that "stories" as such have a legitimate place within museums. Of course, visitors themselves can also resort to the use of stories or other narrative techniques in order to express their views about their museum experience by providing written feedback at specific outlets within the museum itself, such as comment boxes, or formal exhibit logs and/or walls for free expression.

In the introduction to her defining anthology *Museum Studies*, Bettina Messias Carbonell argues that visitors have a personal interdisciplinary framework of references and experiences through which they interact with museums. Carbonell cites Joseph Conrad's *Heart of Darkness* as an example of a novel that can also function as a museum: "Conrad's novel performs—and not always consciously—in a manner similar to that of an ethnographic display in a museum."[12] While Carbonell does not detail exactly how this parallel works out, her statement stakes out new territory for what fiction can accomplish vis-à-vis its readers. Although *Heart of Darkness* is a modernist novel, Carbonell traces the origins of both the novel genre and the museum back to the eighteenth century and then remarks upon the significant influence that Mikhail Bakhtin's theories about the novel have had on museology: "a number of museum exhibitions now appear inclined to emulate the 'dialogic imagination' of the novel, finding ways to criticize the museum itself and to incorporate parody and travesty of its own and other canonical genres."[13] Her comments refer to a new school of innovative museum curators and conceptual artists who engage in self-reflexive historical revisionism.

Among these, the conceptual artist Fred Wilson stands out because his 1992 exhibition Mining the Museum brought to the forefront the systematic effacement of race and/or racialized experiences as organizing principles for museum exhibitions. For this piece, Wilson restaged objects from the Maryland Historical Society's permanent collection in distinct display areas meant to imitate different types of museums.[14] Kara Walker is another visual artist working since the mid-1990s who is best known for invoking the past of slavery through black paper silhouettes depicting scenes of rape, cannibalism, and murder perpetrated by both African and European figures upon one another. The official Web site promoting Walker's retrospective show at the Whitney Museum prominently lists "testimonial slave narratives, historical novels and minstrel shows" among the inspirations for Walker's works.[15] This reference to literature within the Whitney Museum's promotional material suggests that the institution is targeting readers familiar with historical novels or slave narratives as a potential audience for the exhibition.

Both Walker's and Wilson's artwork highlight the absence of discussions of race from the permanent collections of contemporary art, culture, and history museums. Their installations share a postmodern sensibility; they deploy unexpected juxtapositions of seemingly disparate objects and also construct the physical space through which a visitor has to walk in order to see the exhibit as part of their artistic re-visions of historical discourses and iconic images. The self-reflexive and decentered narrative strategies that Walker and Wilson employ in creating their visual art are tools that professional curators also use in designing their exhibitions.

Both contemporary museology and postmodernist narrative theory reject all-encompassing grand narratives in favor of inclusive (re)presentations of multiple voices from different subject positions and experiences. The scholar Stephen E. Weil notes the influence of postmodernism upon museum theory and curatorial practices:

> Also influencing how the museum and the public interact, or at least on how they may be perceived to interact, is an idea implicit in postmodernism. It is the proposition that no text is completed except through the act of "reading" it, and that every text, accordingly, has as many versions—all equally correct—as it has readers. Translated into museum terms, that would suggest that the objects displayed in the museum do not have any fixed or inherent meaning but that "meaning making," or the process by which those objects acquire meaning for individual members of the public, will in each case involve the specific memories, expertise, viewpoint, assumptions and connections that the particular individual brings.[16]

Newly established private and public museums across the Caribbean and elsewhere reflect the values of a new postmodern museology that emphasizes the museum's role as a site where specific communities want to see their identities, traditions, and histories reflected. Weil notes that smaller, new museums are now regarded as cultural tools through which the community shares its values and histories with the world at large: "In a dozen different contexts, identity and interest groups of every kind insist that the mainstream museum is neither empowered nor qualified to speak on their behalf. Increasingly, such groups are creating their own museums from which to speak in their own voices and address what they consider to be their own issues."[17] African Americans, Native Americans, and people of Caribbean descent are among those groups opening up museums throughout the United States to showcase their respective cultural and artistic heritage.

Writers, artists, filmmakers, historians, museum curators, musicians, business executives, and government officials from around the world were trying to make sense of the legacy of transatlantic slavery on both a small scale, within their respective communities, and more broadly, in the virtual stage of the World Wide Web as the twentieth century drew to a close. Their efforts have been guided by what they have learned from Holocaust trauma scholars who have investigated the connection between memory and healing. In 1988, Dr. James Cameron founded America's Black Holocaust Museum to promote awareness of African American history in general, as well as to document his tragic firsthand experience of racism as the lone survivor of a Ku Klux Klan lynching in Marion, Indiana. A longtime civil rights advocate, Dr. Cameron was inspired by his visit to Yad Veshem Holocaust Memorial in Israel to set up a formal museum that would simultaneously educate its visitors about the past and also honor the victims of racism and oppression. Located in Milwaukee, Wisconsin, America's Black Holocaust Museum performs the memorial function in two ways: First, it celebrates the late Dr. Cameron's life through an acknowledgment of his substantial contribution to improving the well-being of African Americans everywhere after narrowly escaping his own lynching. Second, the museum addresses all aspects of African American history, but it makes an explicit connection between the profit-driven European violence against, and forced repatriation of, millions of Africans through the Middle Passage journey, and the targeted and systematic extermination of millions of Jews throughout Europe that constituted the Shoah.

The inauguration of the United States Holocaust Memorial Museum in Washington, D.C., in 1993, redefined the role that American society wants its museums to fill as cultural institutions. The museum's primary focus is to depict the Holocaust as a specific dark chapter in world history; however, its main goal is not only didactic (teaching about dates, figures, and specific events) but also memorial (honoring the survivors and commemorating those people who were victimized and died). The Holocaust Memorial Museum's architecture and design create an atmosphere evocative of life in the prison camps because this is an institution that expects to make both an intellectual and a visceral impression on its visitors. The theater on the second floor that shows films of survivors telling their stories and the Hall of Remembrance constitute spaces that allow visitors to experience a sense of catharsis—where they can safely grieve for and mourn those millions who suffered and died during their time of captivity.

Slavery-themed museums that have opened their doors after the United States Holocaust Memorial Museum have also set out to combine their didactic mission of educating the general public about the slave trade and plantation economy with a memorial function of honoring the dead. In 2002, the Museo de Nuestra Raíz Africana in San Juan, Puerto Rico opened, and two years later, the National Underground Railroad Freedom Center in Cincinnati, Ohio, followed suit. Their respective exhibits about the Middle Passage also reflect the Holocaust Memorial Museum's efforts to honor the past victims of crimes against humanity and to shed the cold light of history upon the events leading up to such a tragedy. While not all of these institutions have been able to design their buildings from the ground up as was the case in Washington, D. C., the slavery museums in Cincinnati, San Juan, and Milwaukee contain among their permanent exhibitions life-size dioramas of the Middle Passage depicting the horror to which slaves were subjected down in the hold of slaving vessels during their journey to the New World. A quiet and dimly lit space usually follows such emotionally affecting displays in each museum; it is set aside for private reflection and meditation. These newly emergent trauma museums anticipate that audiences who have walked through these disturbing exhibitions will experience a moment of catharsis or emotional release that should be both welcomed and respected. Thus, trauma museums have come to play a new role in American and Caribbean society, functioning as secular venues for the consecration of human suffering, past and present.

The emerging global interest in the preservation and consumption of cultural heritage(s) and history/(ies) has occurred simultaneously with an era of market liberalism, privatization, and a huge boom in technological advancement, all factors that have influenced the theory and practice of cultural conservancy. National parks, museums, libraries, and other cultural institutions in the United States and Europe have had to reimagine their own roles as contributors to, rather than reflections of, a broad historical narrative of international economic transactions, such as the transatlantic slave trade. No longer content to be considered staid institutions housing relics from the past, these official state apparatuses have begun transforming themselves into more user-friendly, interactive repositories of both historic artifacts and general information about them.

The new, explicitly historical programming in place at state-owned libraries, national or public parks, galleries, and museums of all genres throughout the United States and the islands of the Caribbean emphasizes a sense of community identity in its narrative component. As part of the Department of the Interior, the National Park Service receives federal funding for its Museum Management Program, which is in charge of coordinating the administration and preservation of the national collections housed throughout the various parks.[18] These different venues inform their visitors about how a specific group of people lived, worked, and fought with one another at some earlier point in time, while they also prompt the audiences to reexamine their own personal involvement with cultural production, political activism, and consumerism. Despite their claims of being "national" or "American" in scope, the smaller, private museums receive little to no government funding. This allows them to exercise autonomy over what and how they exhibit objects, but it also means that they must rely heavily on contributions from charitable foundations and private donors to remain in business.

The great impetus and appeal of slavery-themed museums is the possibility they offer to reach mass audiences with all the visceral impact that accompanies an actual journey and physical encounter with the material remnants of the historical past. These projects are capital-intensive, and the need to meet rising expenses amplifies the pressure to draw large audiences. As a result, many museums have come to rely on corporate sponsorships, as well as technical innovations in their curatorial practices. The twentieth anniversary exhibit of the Black Holocaust Museum, for example, is sponsored by Northwestern Mutual Foundation, while the permanent exhibitions at the National Underground Railroad Freedom Center receive funding from charitable foundations associated with banks, the aviation industry, and even Oprah Winfrey. These economic arrangements inherently bring with them the risk of corporate co-optation and of charges of "Disneyfication," which, in turn, suggest a betrayal of the legacy of the enslaved peoples they hope to memorialize and a trivialization of the entire subject of human bondage.

Andrea Witcomb, a museum studies scholar and curator, reports that museum professionals are divided as to the positive or negative effects of the recent proliferation of small-scale museums and the demonstrable transformations that some larger institutions have undergone. Witcomb tries to find a middle ground between the opposing camps in her own

discussion of new museology, remarking that "both critics and support-
ers of recent changes see a collapse of a distinction between culture and
commerce and discern a new role for museums within a post-industrial,
postmodern society."[19] This view implies that museums have changed
their modus operandi in order to adapt to, and remain relevant within,
an increasingly nonhierarchical society. The anthropologists Corinne A.
Kratz and Ivan Karp see the museum's influence as extending beyond
their geographical community: "Reproduced, adapted and transformed
globally, museums are not just a place or institution but have become
a portable social technology, a set of museological processes through
which such statements and claims are represented, embodied, and debated."[20] This way of interpreting museums suggests that these institutions have undergone such a large-scale conceptual transformation as to
transcend the mere bounds of the physical and reach the ethereal status
of being almost a state of mind or a way of thinking about the human
experience.

Along similar lines, Faith Davis Ruffins, a historian and curator,
points to how the rise of new media has sought to address the public's desire for more information about slavery: "by the 1990s the public interest aroused through other media, novels as well as films, began to affect museums, especially in terms of audience interest in and
demands for exhibitions on slavery."[21] In her piece, Ruffins does not
name the novels that motivated readers to seek further information and
entertainment from museum exhibitions. I contend that a new school of
Caribbean postmodern novels portray the institution of slavery as a mul-
tilayered socioeconomic phenomenon by explicitly showcasing real and
imagined historical "objects" within their pages, rather than trying to
explain away its negative impact on individual characters. In this study,
I analyze a wide range of novels from the Francophone, Anglophone,
and Hispanophone traditions. I give their titles here in the original language, with English translations in parenthesis when available: Reinaldo
Arenas's *La loma del ángel* (*Graveyard of the Angels*); Alejo Carpentier's
El reino de este mundo (*The Kingdom of this World*) and *El siglo de las
luces* (*Explosion in a Cathedral*); Patrick Chamoiseau's *L'esclave vieil
homme et le molosse*; Michelle Cliff's *Free Enterprise*; Maryse Condé's
two-volume family saga *Ségou* (*Segu*) and *Moi, Tituba, sorcière . . . noire
de Salem* (*I, Tituba, Black Witch of Salem*); Fred D'Aguiar's *Feeding
the Ghosts* and *The Longest Memory*; David Dabydeen's *A Harlot's
Progress*; Caryl Phillips's *Cambridge, Crossing the River* and *Higher
Ground*; and Edgardo Rodríguez Juliá's *La noche oscura del Niño*

Avilés and *La renuncia del héroe Baltasar* (*The Renunciation*). These texts whet their readers' appetite for historical information and prompt them to undertake their own personal quests to find what meaning the legacy of transatlantic slavery can have in their lives.

In a North American context, Alex Haley's best-selling family-saga *Roots* also attracted huge viewing audiences when it was adapted into a television miniseries during the 1970s. Two widely popular novels about slavery, Alice Walker's *The Color Purple* and Toni Morrison's *Beloved* were both adapted to the silver screen (in 1985 and 1998, respectively), as was William Styron's short story "Shadrach," about an aged freed slave who returns to the plantation where he was born so he could be buried with his kin (1998). For years, British and American readers have had access to English-language translations of Hispano- and Francophone slave-themed novels by Reinaldo Arenas, Alejo Carpentier, Maryse Condé and Edgardo Rodríguez Juliá in bookstores throughout the United States and Canada.[22] Online booksellers like Amazon.com have also made Spanish and French translations of American novels about slavery available through their country-specific sales portals.

Likewise, Brazilian popular culture has reflected that country's interest in its own history and on the legacy of slavery within its borders through countless historical soap operas, or *telenovelas,* set during the eighteenth and nineteenth centuries, but mass-produced in the 1970s and 1980s. These were then dubbed into Spanish and shown across Latin America and the U.S. Latino television markets. Brazilian filmmakers like Carlos Dieges have celebrated the slaves' resistance against enforced bondage. His 1963 film *Ganga Zumba* focuses on the exploits of Zumbí, the founder of Palmares, a maroon community that played off the Dutch and Portuguese colonists against each other and ensured its own survival for more than two hundred years. Dieges returns to Palmares as an emblematic symbol of resistance to oppression in his 1986 film *Quilombo*.

Although museums and historical novels cater to an audience willing to spend a defined period of time learning about the past and being entertained in the process, both media must somehow meet the challenge of putting their freeborn audience members in touch with the oppression and indignity of bondage when approaching the inhumane legacy of slavery. To meet their dual goals, postmodern novels and museums resort to interdisciplinary displays of historical facts and events: museums turn to curatorial explanations accompanying the objects on display, such as dioramas, works of visual art, audio recordings, or even

Web sites, whereas novels showcase their chosen "artifacts" within their plotlines and include in-text debates about an object's provenance, stylistic or architectural features, or aesthetic value. Postmodern museums and novels eschew static, overdetermined grand narratives in favor of interactive exhibitions presenting a variety of viewpoints, thereby allowing individual readers/visitors to customize their consumption of information to suit their particular tastes. The emergence of virtual museums, like PBS's online museum that was set up in connection with the series *Slavery and the Making of America* and that features "exhibits in the museum . . . curated by four student groups from across the country," attest to the growing public interest in the historical past of slavery as a crucial period in the development of both a national, and a region-specific cultural identity in the United States.[23]

Unlike box office or sales figures, which measure the relative success or failure of commercial edutainment vehicles like costume-drama movies, television series, or fiction and nonfiction books, ticket sales and the number of family memberships at slavery museums cannot accurately quantify or give the full measure of the intellectual and emotional impact of exhibitions addressing various aspects of life in chains. In the islands of the Caribbean, slavery exhibitions have gained prominence within larger art, history, or plantation museums, where they function as both tourist attractions and repositories of official documents related to a nation's origins.

In the early years of the twenty-first century, the museum as a hybrid and interdisciplinary institution has made a move toward situating displays about the history of slavery in the United States and the Caribbean islands within a broader, more international context. Traveling exhibits aim to highlight the active correspondence and communication that existed transnationally between New World slaveholding territories and the European metropolises, as well as regionally, between those ports in the Caribbean islands and the coasts of North and South America. Artistic references to slavery and its legacy continue to be relevant in regional and inter-American popular culture, and even in political life, thus prompting me to ask: How can museum exhibitions about transatlantic slavery spur a more open public dialogue about past policies that legitimated exploitation and institutionalized racism? Can public displays of artifacts and works of art related to slavery contribute to a sense of community-wide reconciliation instead of reinforcing the impulse to assign blame?

Despite the museum's goal of making history come alive for visitors, it is ultimately up to the individual to decide what relevance the exhibitions and the facts contained therein have to his or her own everyday life. Like postmodern narrative, the new museum exhibition does not provide historical or narrative closure for the visitors but, rather, encourages them to investigate the theme further on their own either by returning to the exhibition at a later time, or by conducting their own supplementary research. At its best, the museum disseminates knowledge thoughtfully and provocatively, by creating an environment where one can engage with the past while pleasantly spending a morning or afternoon of leisure. At its worst, the museum experience amounts to nothing more than a walk through a tried-and-true display of big names or famous objects in history that does not challenge anyone's assumptions about the period or the topic at hand.

Both the postmodern historical novel and the new slavery-themed museum ask their respective audiences to participate actively in the narrative process by filling in the gaps they perceive to exist between their preexisting knowledge about the historical objects on display in an exhibition and the ideology of the official documents that accompany and even define the same. By refusing to draw any overt connections whatsoever between disparate discourses of and about slavery included within their covers, postmodern historical novels about slavery achieve the effect of a historical exhibition at a museum: they are provocative and suggestive, but ultimately lacking an overarching narrative or ethical perspective. Many museums offer self-guided tours that include a curatorial recording available through tape recorder or podcast. However overdetermined the facts may be, museum visitors nonetheless retain the ability to edit the narrative by fast-forwarding, skipping, or turning the recording on or off as they see fit.

Postmodern historical novels make the act of reading about fictional slaves' lives entertaining while prompting readers to question just how much they actually know about the specific history of the trade in human beings. Their lack of narrative closure demands that the reader, like the museum visitor, assign an ethical and aesthetic significance to the various discursive and rhetorical displays he or she has seen while engaged in the reading act itself. Historical novels can be generally classified into two distinct types: traditional and postmodern. In *The Historical Novel*, Georg Lukács outlines the defining characteristics of the texts I consider to be "traditional" historical novels like *Guerrilleros negros*, *La mulâtresse Solitude*, *Roots*, *Jubilee*, *Gone with the Wind*, *The Autobiography of Miss Jane Pittman*, *The Chaneysville Incident*,

The African, Die the Long Day, Dessa Rose, The Color Purple. and Madison Smartt Bell's Haitian Revolution trilogy. The events they depict take place in an era prior to the author's birth; they value realism as a narrative style, and do not contradict the official historical record. These texts' primary narrative mode is realism, and their plots accord with the version of events contained within the historical record. Readers of traditional historical novels want a clear narrative arc; they like the comfort of predictable historical outcomes, and relish the poignancy of reading about the plight of individual characters caught up in events that are larger than themselves. Empathy is the strongest impulse these texts encourage, as opposed to the critical distance necessary to evaluate the relevance that reading about the victims of slavery has to those who have inherited its legacy. This reading experience has more in common with the act of watching a period drama on the movie screen than it does with a visit to a museum exhibition about slavery.

In his study on the minor genre, Lukács does not address postmodern historical fiction, but he proposes the category of the "classical" historical novel as that which grew out of Romanticism and was strongly influenced by Swift. While I do not dispute that there is a distinct type of historical novel that falls within these parameters, in this study I am concerned exclusively with analyzing late twentieth-century Caribbean fictional texts that reflect a distinctly postmodernist sensibility. Postmodern historical novels do not strive to create verisimilitude through the portrayal of a hyperreal past, as I explain in chapter 3. Instead, much like museum exhibitions, they take a more interactive approach and avoid providing narrative closure to the tales they tell. Texts like *Graveyard of the Angels, The Kingdom of This World, Explosion in a Cathedral, L'esclave vieil homme et le molosse, Segu, I, Tituba, Black Witch of Salem, Free Enterprise, Feeding the Ghosts* and *The Longest Memory, A Harlot's Progress, Cambridge, Crossing the River Higher Ground, The Renunciation,* and *La noche oscura del Niño Avilés* place the burden of achieving that chronological coherence upon their readers, who must consult reference volumes outside of the text to fill in the gaps in their historical knowledge. Through their transparent use of postmodernist pastiche, anachronism, apocryphal history, and the fantastic, these historical novels highlight the need for a process of incorporating the memory of the past into visions of the present.

These postmodern novels about slavery do not adhere to the narrative constraints that Lukács delineated in his study; generally, they feature entire historical eras or problems rather than specific events or figures. These narratives strive to simultaneously create and undermine the concept of documentary authenticity—the novels pass themselves off as other kinds of texts, like letters, court transcripts, journal entries, historiographic treatises, and "official" reports of all kinds. As apocryphal or alternative histories, these novels invent, rather than merely revise, the historical record, thus creating a new version of the past as it never was. The self-conscious narrative incongruities in these texts call attention to themselves not because of their unusual nature, but because of the strange juxtaposition or context in which they exist.

While museums cannot introduce apocryphal detail into their exhibitions about history with the same impunity that postmodern historical novels can, their exhibitions about historical events, people, and ideas can include anachronistic details, such as contemporary works of art on a historical theme. I explore these areas of overlap in chapter 2, which analyzes how postmodern fiction showcases actual works of art in a similar manner to art museums, and in chapter 3, which explores how novels function as ethnographic museums. Museums can also provide a variety of imaginary "interpretations" of historical events and traditional customs, and create composite characters to serve as proxies for everyday life and habits, as I explain in a discussion of living history and plantation museums in chapter 4.

Caribbean writers from Cuba, Martinique, Guadeloupe, Jamaica, St. Kitts, Guyana, and Puerto Rico portray the large-scale displacement of European, African, and Native American peoples brought about by the Atlantic slave trade as the birth of a fragmented, postmodern New World subject, whose national and racial identities come into conflict with one another and give rise to new, hybrid ethnicities. All the novels I analyze suggest that the slave trade severed the causal relationship between birth, national identity, and citizenship. These texts invent apocryphal histories that deviate from, but do not ultimately alter, the course of actual historical events rather than looking to the past as a source of recoverable knowledge. As a group, these works depict slavery more as an occasion to frame a discourse about self-fashioning an ideology than as an accurate, or realistic, reenactment of historical events. Rather than conveying any concrete, historically verifiable information about slavery, these novels create a "museum effect" by *exhibiting* slavery through the use of quotations or vignettes, which I compare, in chapter 2, to museum dioramas or exhibitions.

The depictions of slave life in these texts deviate from the conventions of realism because of: (1) their largely anachronistic insistence on the literacy of their slave protagonists, (2) their emphasis on their protagonists' freedom during the time of the narrative, and (3) their references to supernatural elements. While not all of the novels under analysis here feature individual slave protagonists, those that do detail the wide breadth of their character's knowledge of art, history, and other humanities. Unlike actual American slave narrators, like Frederick Douglass and Harriet Jacobs, who either learned to read and write after reaching the North or else dictated their tales of woe to abolitionist scribes, the majority of the enslaved protagonists in Caribbean postmodern novels generally claim to have become literate before they were enslaved. These characters also maintain diaries while living in chains, reject the label "slave" as it is applied to them, and feel qualified to comment at length upon international politics.

The second narrative characteristic these novels have in common is an emphasis on their slave character's freedom during the time of the narration, a pattern that indicates the authors' general reluctance to reduce the horrors of life under bondage to a scene or two of pathos within the pages of each novel. This is due, in part, to postmodernism's preference for self-referential, nonverisimilar narrative, but it also reflects a sense that the truth of the past can only be understood intellectually, not felt viscerally as it was by those who endured it. In this, the novels differ considerably from the trauma museum model of targeting the audiences' heartstrings as well as their minds as sites for creating a powerful impact. Postmodern, freed slave-narrator protagonists like Caryl Phillips's Cambridge and Fred D'Aguiar's Mintah highlight their own status as literary constructs by explicitly acknowledging that they are the creation of writers who have never lived in a world in which one human being could own another. Since there is no direct political change that can be achieved with their fictional narratives, these writers invoke history as a model for the more introspective goal of individual self-determination and categorization in a world of fragmented subjectivity.

Through the slave narrator, postmodern historical novels about slavery also carve out a textual space within which readers can vicariously carry out the work of mourning for the long-dead slaves who actually lived and died under bondage. By staking out a fragmented subject-position from which to write against the grain of the legal definition of persons of African descent as nothing more than chattel, these postmodern slave narrators establish their own claims to humanity. Postmodern neo–slave narratives include both an account of the slave's birth as well as one of their (eventual) deaths, thereby achieving an artificial level of narrative closure unavailable to the historical slave narrators whose tales of survival depended for their success on the ex-slaves' presence as proof of the veracity of their account. The novels, then, act as mimetic representations of historical slave narratives, by providing contemporary readers an intimate glimpse of a historical world of which they have no direct experience. Nineteenth-century British and American readers of historical slave narratives were separated from the day-to-day world of slavery by geography, whereas contemporary readers are temporally divided from historical slaves and separated through the veil of fiction from the protagonists in the novels. The grief evoked by the death of the slave characters is a simulacrum—it is not authentic because the dead characters are not real, yet the need for mourning is more deeply felt toward fictional characters than toward individual historical slave narrators who died a long time ago. The world occupied by neo-slave fictional characters is more familiar to contemporary readers than the nineteenth-century culture described by historical slave narrators in their autobiographies.

The third and final element the selected novels share is their inclusion of the fantastic within their respective worldviews. In this respect, I argue that the Caribbean novels I discuss here have been directly influenced by two literary predecessors: The first is the Latin American narrative styles of the marvelous real and magical realism, popularized during the 1940s and after by Alejo Carpentier and later made famous by Gabriel García Márquez. The second literary influence is the rise of speculative fiction as a genre defined as the African American variant of science fiction, practiced most famously by Octavia Butler and Samuel R. Delany. While the novels I examine in this study do not strictly adhere to the conventions of either of these literary genres, they are indebted to the contributions both made to challenging assumptions of the inherent interrelationship between history and realism in literature. These novels all question our perception of reality and how much we can really understand the worldview of the past.

The overall thesis guiding this comparative study is not merely that postmodern historical novels function as museums in general, but that each specific type of museum they function as at any given time affects how the texts link the legacy of slavery to the readers' present time. There is no inherent hierarchy of museum-effects within these Caribbean novels, just as no real-life art, history, or natural history museum has a monopoly on portraying the essential "truth" about transatlantic slavery. The six chapters that follow feature close readings of how the novels I mentioned earlier function as different types of museum.

Both novels and museums that dramatize slave life aim to convey a balanced sense of how some portions of the population in any given country supported slavery while others fought to end it. No matter how moved a twenty-first century reader/visitor feels by either a text or an exhibition about slavery, his or her opinions about the morality of the practice are always already obsolete because the outcome has been decided. Visitors/readers can justify learning more about this aspect of the human experience because to forget it means to not validate either the pain and suffering or the endurance that it took to survive under such conditions. Through exhibitions showcasing artwork, historical artifacts, and other objects associated with slavery and the slave trade, museums and historical novels construct a space in which visitors/readers can overcome their sense of belatedness and self-righteousness by acting like witnesses to the past. Effective exhibitions or novels about slavery allow contemporary readers/visitors to commemorate the loss of life and human dignity involved in the operation of slave economies through the work of mourning. By witnessing the cruelty of the past through viewing artifacts, records, or documents, visitors/readers affirm the continued relevance of these objects and their stories to the present.

1 Books as National (Literary) History Museums

IN OCTOBER 1992, the Museum of the Americas opened its doors in San Juan, Puerto Rico, to coincide with the five-hundredth anniversary of Colombus's "discovery" of the New World.[1] Located on the site of the former barracks of the Spanish colonial army, el cuartel Ballajá, the Museum of the Americas houses three permanent exhibits, The Indian in America, Popular Arts in America, and Our African Heritage, and hosts a variety of traveling exhibitions throughout the year. The museum is the brainchild of Dr. Ricardo Alegría, a noted anthropologist, and archaeologist who has dedicated his professional life to the systematic documentation, preservation, and promotion of Puerto Rican culture at home and abroad. In 1955, Dr. Alegría founded the influential Institute of Puerto Rican Culture, which oversees parks, museums, arts, and musical programs throughout the island.

Although he is no longer involved in the day-to-day administration of either the institute or the museum, Alegría's ongoing influence and research is most evident in the exhibition Our African Heritage, which opened in 2000 and is located on the second floor. Like other examples of colonial Spanish architecture, the barracks building features an interior courtyard. The first door on the second-floor hallway opens to a small antechamber full of displays, which is followed by a much longer hall containing artifacts from West African cultures and traditions, documents pertaining to the European slave trade on the African coast and across the Atlantic, old maritime maps, newspaper clippings of ads offering rewards for runaway slaves, and abolitionist pamphlets, among other things. Paintings and sculptures made by both African and Puerto Rican artists adorn the space, and shackles and chains dating back two to three centuries accompany wall-mounted displays discussing the Middle Passage journey and slavery as it was practiced in Puerto Rico.

All the artifacts displayed in Our African Heritage are from Dr. Alegría's personal collection. The information on the labels that accompany the various displays is excerpted from a manuscript he is preparing about the legacy of slavery on the island. The exhibition itself, then, can be legitimately considered as either the outline, or even the first draft, of Alegría's latest history book. Michael Belcher, a museum design expert, has pointed to the inherent parallels between museum exhibitions and books: "This mixture of objects, text and other interpretive aids has often been likened to a three-dimensional essay or book, whose prime function is to inform and educate."[2] According to the museum employees I asked during a recent visit, the audience who "reads" or sees Alegría's "three-dimensional" book about Puerto Rican slavery is made up primarily of schoolchildren who come to tour the museum with their teachers during official field trips.[3] I was told that foreign tourists comprise the next-largest group of visitors since Old San Juan is a staple on the cruise ship circuit and the island heavily promotes the historic charms of the colonial city in its tourism brochures and advertisements. All of the informational material that accompanied the displays is written in Spanish, which heightens its educational value to schoolchildren but makes the same information inaccessible to tourists who do not speak the language. So, while the exhibition is clearly geared toward a local audience of Spanish speakers eager to learn more about their own culture, it does not seem to attract Puerto Rican adults in large numbers. The lack of informational materials in English, meanwhile, means that the museum is failing in its mission to educate much of the the audience that does visit on a regular basis: tourists. These people have to rely primarily on the visual images—paintings, maps, book illustrations, shackles, chains, pottery, and portraits—in order to decipher what particular story the exhibition is trying to tell. To some extent, Alegría's book-as-museum has yet to be translated for this audience.[4]

The first display that greets visitors as they enter the Our African Heritage exhibition is a wall of books, a display that physically demonstrates the significant prevalence of the idea of blackness as a theme within the canon of Puerto Rican literature, broadly conceived. Called "The Theme of Blackness in Puerto Rican Literature," this display includes at least twenty-seven volumes of poetry, folklore, historiography, drama, novels, abolitionist tracts, and even works of literary criticism dating from the early nineteenth until the twenty-first centuries. While it may seem odd to see so many books on display outside of a library, books are considered perfectly appropriate sociocultural objects to be included in a history museum exhibition, as the anthropologist James Deetz explains: "The basic building block of any exhibit, whether in a small table case or in a full recreation of an early community, is the individual artifact. The term 'artifact' is somewhat vague, and while a house can be thought of as an artifact as well as a thimble can, normal usage restricts 'artifact' to smaller objects, usually portable: furniture, ceramics, firearms, toys, clothing, books and tools, for example."[5] More than shedding any light on past attitudes toward bondage or exploitation, the sheer number of literary and scholarly books on view in this display attests to the increasing interest in the history of slavery and the emergence of "blackness" as a valuable cultural identity in twenty-first-century Puerto Rican society.

The curatorial statement that accompanies the book display frames the discussion of blackness positively within the national discourse of Puerto Rican identity. Dr. Alegría's short essay proclaims that there is a long-standing tradition of including black Puerto Ricans within the national literature: "Our literature has sought to offer information about black Puerto Ricans, their history, customs and traditions."[6] Although it is meant to be inclusive, this statement demonstrates that Puerto Ricans of African descent have occupied a subaltern position within the island literary canon; they appear as objects to be discussed rather than as self-defined black subjects who write about their own experiences and points of view. Despite this enthusiastic affirmation of the value of contributions made to Puerto Rican culture by people of African descent, Alegría acknowledges that lingering traces of racism still remain within the larger social fabric: "Regrettably, signs of racial prejudice still remain in our nation principally motivated by a lack of knowledge." The discrimination to which Alegría refers continues despite the widespread promulgation of a national myth of origin that celebrates a heritage based on the union of the European colonists, indigenous natives, and African slaves. The anthropologist Jorge Duany explains that such nationalistic rhetoric is disempowering to Puerto Ricans of African descent: "This traditional conception considers Africans the third root of Puerto Rican identity not only in chronological terms but also ranked according to their avowed contribution to the Island's contemporary culture."[7] Regardless of whether he ever finishes his book on the history of the black presence in Puerto Rican culture, this permanent exhibition in the Museum of the Americas, as well as the establishment of the Museo de Nuestra Raíz Africana, constitute Ricardo Alegría's widest-reaching efforts to combat the ignorance and cultural amnesia that feeds racism and prejudice on the island.

Among the books not included in the literature display at the Museum of the Americas are *La renuncia del héroe Baltasar* (1974) and *La noche oscura del Niño Avilés* (1984), two apocryphal historical novels about fictitious eighteenth-century slave rebellions in Puerto Rico written by Edgardo Rodríguez Juliá. Space considerations probably are to blame for this exclusion, as well as the fact that their floridly baroque prose and extravagant flights of fancy may make these texts inaccessible to the general public whether or not they read Spanish.[8] Nonetheless, I contend that these novels would fit perfectly within the rubric of "The Black Theme in Puerto Rican Literature" because they take the archive and, by extension, the museum, as their central motif. Both *La renuncia del héroe Baltasar*, translated into English as *The Renunciation*, and *La noche oscura del Niño Avilés* question how, and to what extent, the archive exists to hide documents and the "truths" these may contain from the prying eyes of academic researchers and private citizens alike.[9] Thus, by dramatizing the process of constant discovery of new evidence about the past, *The Renunciation* and *La noche oscura* emphasize the constructed, fragmented, and necessarily imperfect nature of our knowledge of the past.

Like the Museum of the Americas, both *The Renunciation* and *La noche oscura* assume that there is a lay, local, public audience that is eager to listen to academic experts share information about their country's origin. These are metafictive texts that highlight their own status as virtual archives or repositories of (fictitious) historical documents; they suggest that the nation-state is a fundamentally unstable sociopolitical construct developed out of an incomplete understanding of past events. Thus, *The Renunciation* and *La noche oscura* reject the absolute standards of racial or national purity implied by rigid categories corresponding to race and ethnicity and, instead, look back to a supposedly simpler time before the different groups of people who now make up the Puerto Rican "race" intermingled and became one blood. As we saw from the important place books occupied within the Our African Heritage exhibition, works of literature also can contribute to the establishment of a national foundation myth through references to real or imagined documents, as well as to elements of popular culture, like folktales and legends, which affirm their shared sense of belonging to one distinct "imagined community," to use Benedict Anderson's term.

Estelle Irizarry convincingly demonstrates that Rodríguez Juliá based *The Renunciation* on a popular local legend collected and transcribed by the renowned Puerto Rican folklorist Cayetano Coll y Toste.[10] As a hybrid genre combining historical and literary elements, the *leyenda folklórica,* or folk legend, seems ideally suited as a source for Rodríguez Juliá's postmodern historical novel, which itself parodies the genre of academic historiography. According to legend, Baltasar Montañez was a young man who supposedly survived a precarious fall after his horse was startled and ran down a cliff. Montañez is said to have uttered a prayer as he fell and, as a result, was miraculously saved. He then erected a chapel at the site of the accident that still stands today, the Capilla del Cristo, or Christ Chapel. Like the Museum of the Americas, the chapel is a regular stop in the colonial city tour circuit of San Juan.[11] Surviving the fall is what earned Montañez the title of "hero," as suggested in the Spanish version of the novel's original title.

While Coll y Toste's description of Montañez in his legend makes no reference to the unlucky rider's race, Rodríguez Juliá's fictive retelling of this event fully enmeshes the character's racial identity within the larger political dramas of eighteenth-century Puerto Rico. His version of Baltasar Montañez is an enslaved black cane cutter whose father had supposedly led a failed slave rebellion in his own youth. *The Renunciation* portrays the incident involving the horse not as an accident, but as a carefully orchestrated event staged by the island colony's Spanish Catholic bishop in order to raise Baltasar Montañez's profile as a leader among the slave population. By controlling the younger Montañez, the prelate hopes to eradicate the memory of Montañez senior and thereby quell the angst of the slave masses and consolidate his power over Puerto Rican politics.

Rodríguez Juliá's version of this folktale introduces new complications in the basic plot. Whereas in popular lore Montañez himself was said to have uttered a prayer as he fell, in Rodríguez Juliá's novel, the person calling out for divine assistance was none other than the secretary of state for the colony of Puerto Rico, Tomás Prat, a character based on an actual historical figure. The older white man's prayer saves the young black slave, thus allowing the bishop to arrange a strategic marriage between the "hero" Montañez and Prat's teenage daughter in 1753 as a public act of gratitude to God. The bishop elevates the newly married young man to his father-in-law's place as secretary of state, no doubt hoping to create the impression that upward mobility and the eventual intermixing of races is a real possibility for the island's population of free blacks and slaves. All these machinations are performed in order to prevent another uprising like the one previously led by Montañez's father.

Rodríguez Juliá's appropriation of the folk hero Baltasar Montañez constitutes the kind of intertextuality that Brian McHale, citing Umberto Eco, calls "transworld identity." In *Postmodernist Fiction*, McHale uses the term to describe the movement "between characters in their projected worlds and real-world historical figures,"[12] but he extends the concept so that it also applies to a writer's use or appropriation of fictional characters originally created by a different author. McHale considers transworld identity to be a hallmark of most historical fiction; he argues that more traditional novels try to downplay or minimize these overlaps between reality and fiction, while postmodernist historical novels pause on the rupture or areas of intersection between two fictive worlds, or between history and fiction, in order to draw attention to their own status as constructed narratives.

Since the novel makes no direct allusion to Coll y Toste, most non–Puerto Rican readers of *The Renunciation* would have no way of knowing that the protagonist was not merely invented by Rodríguez Juliá, but based upon an actual historical figure. This means that the novel's museum function is limited; it cannot be said to be exhibiting this character as a historical "artifact" to anyone other than a select group of native readers who would recognize Montañez as such. As Mieke Bal points out, "Cultural memory can be located in literary texts because the latter are continuous with the communal fictionalizing, idealizing, monumentalizing impulses thriving in a conflicted culture."[13] Thus, outsiders who are not fully part of the community of meaning implicit within the text cannot engage in the production of cultural memory through reading in the same way that insiders can. Like the Spanish-language annotations to the book display in the Museum of the Americas, *The Renunciation* reinforces the ideas and assumptions that Puerto Ricans have of themselves as a people, and of the importance of their colonial-era architecture, even as it demands that race relations and the history of slavery occupy a more central role in these articulations of a national character.

Although I am distinguishing between those readers who fully understand the folkloric underpinnings of Rodríguez Juliá's fiction and those who do not, I am mindful of the dangers of such an interpretive strategy. In *Tropics of Discourse*, the historian Hayden White warns literary critics against establishing a hierarchical ranking of the readers a given text attracts. He uses the bondage-inflected tropes "master" and "slave" to describe what he considers as the academic propensity to fetishize read-ing practices: "it is understandable how, given the notion of the text as 'everything . . . or . . . nothing,' criticism would be driven to try to distinguish rigidly between what might be called "master readers" and "slave readers," that is to say, readers endowed with the authority to dilate on the mysteries of the texts and readers lacking that authority. Not surprisingly, then, much of contemporary criticism turns on the ef-fort to establish the criteria for determining the techniques and the au-thority of the privileged reader."[14] Heeding White's warning, I now turn to a discussion of three Caribbean postmodern historical novels about slavery that avoid distinguishing between "master" and "slave" read-ers but appeal explicitly to as broad a readership as possible. Reinaldo Arenas's *La loma del ángel* (1987; translated into English as *Graveyard of the Angels*), Patrick Chamoiseau's *L'esclave vieil homme et le molosse* (1997), and Maryse Condé's *Moi, Tituba, sorcière . . . noire de Salem* (1986; translated into English as *I, Tituba, Black Witch of Salem*) func-tion like national history museums: they explicitly display and label their literary "artifacts"—characters borrowed from the work of other writ-ers as well as quotes from previous texts about slavery—for all readers to see as they tell a tale of the "black presence" as a theme in their re-spective national literatures.[15] Through repeated instances of transworld identity and metafiction, these three texts proclaim the existence of a national literary canon about slavery that stands in contradistinction to the collected works that Dr. Alegría displays in his museum. These post-modern works maintain an uneasy relationship to the archive as system of knowledge that holds on to its secrets.

These novels' explicit exhibitions of other writers' characters and/or excerpts from previous texts draw their readers into a metafictive debate about the nature and relevance of national literatures, canon formation, and intertextuality as categories through which to evaluate and under-stand the lingering influence of the past in shaping the course of the pres-ent. Published at least a century after the abolition of slavery throughout the Caribbean, *L'esclave*, *Graveyard of the Angels*, and *I, Tituba* address the need for contemporary writers, readers, and people in general to confront the legacy of slavery from an individual, national, and transna-tional perspective.[16] Using parody and intertextuality, *Graveyard of the Angels* and *L'esclave* create a literary genealogy that establishes a direct line of descent between earlier nation-specific Caribbean fiction about slavery and their own late twentieth-century portrayals of the same his-torical circumstance.

Like both physical and online slavery museums, *I, Tituba, L'esclave,* and *Graveyard of the Angels* portray episodes of slave life through their selection of literary and historical objects to display for their respective audiences. Where Alegría tried to give his grand work of Puerto Rican history three dimensions by transforming and incorporating it into his museum, Arenas and Condé incorporate mediating intertextual and deconstructive reading strategies into their narratives to give their readers the illusion that they have access to the truly valuable information hidden in the archive, defined broadly as the literary and documentary history of the islands as written from the perspective of the social and economic elites. The literary artifacts featured within each novel's pages are representative of a larger national literary tradition, both Caribbean and American. By exhibiting them within their pages, these three novels prompt their readers to consider just how much they know about the history of Caribbean slavery and about local abolitionist efforts to emancipate those in bondage.

Unlike research libraries, archives, or repositories of information, which merely warehouse books and other materials for the specialized use of academics and officials, novels that function as national history museums exhibit their collection of other books through epigraphs and allusions so as to convey a range of attitudes about the past and place them in the context of recent cultural debates. Arenas's *Graveyard of the Angels* parodies the most famous nineteenth-century Cuban abolitionist novel, Cirilo Villaverde's *Cecilia Valdés* (1882). Condé's text uses the trope of oral literature, or "oraliture," to manipulate the conventions of the slave narrative genre embodied in the United States by Harriet Jacobs's *Incidents in the Life of a Slave Girl* (1861) and in the Caribbean by Mary Prince's *The History of Mary Prince: A West Indian Slave* (1850). Patrick Chamoiseau's *L'esclave* follows the general trajectory of novels of marronage, or runaway slaves, as practiced by his mentor, Édouard Glissant.

By openly exhibiting their borrowed characters or excerpts within their pages, *Graveyard of the Angels, L'esclave,* and *I, Tituba* trace a literary genealogy of fictive depictions of life under bondage in Cuba, Martinique, and Barbados. Through the use of narrative devices such as transworld identity, metafictive reflections on the art of writing, and repeated direct appeals to the readers, these three novels emphasize the temporal displacement that distances contemporary readers from the historical events they read about. The novels' very artificiality calls into question their ability to convey either historical accuracy or emotional

truth, but this transparency also encourages readers to view the experience of reading about the past to be a form of "edutainment."

Graveyard of the Angels uses transworld identity through the inclusion of fictionalized versions of three influential Cuban writers as minor characters in the novel: the aforementioned Cirilo Villaverde; Lydia
Cabrera, a twentieth-century folklorist who collected and preserved oral
narratives from the Afro-Cuban community in her volume *Cuentos negros de Cuba* (1840); and also Reinaldo Arenas himself.[17] *L'esclave* uses
transworld identity by appropriating a title character from one of the epigraphs from Glissant, "an old man who does not know anything about
'poetry,'" and places him in a completely new setting, which involves
a showdown against supernatural creatures. *I, Tituba, Black Witch of
Salem* claims to be an oral tale or song passed down from one generation
of Barbadian people to another. However, Condé uses transworld identity when she appropriates Hester Prynne, the protagonist of Nathaniel
Hawthorne's *The Scarlet Letter*, as well as an excerpt from the actual
testimony the historical figure Tituba gave during the Salem witch trials.
I, Tituba exhibits these foreign texts as exotic objects that represent their
country and time of origin for a Caribbean audience, while *L'esclave* and
Graveyard of the Angels both proudly display their literary objects as
homespun treasures that add to the glory and prestige of their respective
islands.

Written at the interstices of multicultural societies by hybrid, postcolonial, diasporic, or newly creolized subjects, each novel celebrates
individual choice as the only determinant in the fluid notion of identity
while, together, these texts also acknowledge the relational nature of
cultural identities claimed by members of each imagined community.
Almost all the enslaved characters within *Graveyard of the Angels*, *I,
Tituba*, and *L'esclave* are one-dimensional "types," rather than fully developed characters. Through metafictive reflections on the power of the
"author" over his or her "subject," *I, Tituba*, *L'esclave*, and *Graveyard
of the Angels* convey the ruthless violence that one group of people
wielded against another by killing off the characters they borrow from
other sources.

By eschewing verisimilitude and psychological depth and instead
highlighting the slave characters' relative anonymity within the narratives in which they appear, these novels demonstrate for their readers
the dehumanizing effect of the institution of slavery as a system of clas-
sification that attempted to relegate its victims to a status somewhere
between the human and the animal. Postmodern historical novels about

slavery suggest that the condition of living *as a slave* is unimaginable to contemporary readers except through the mediation of fiction and other media representations of suffering. Every glimpse into the condition of slavery the texts offer the readers is provisional, tinged with a consistent skepticism about the adequacy of empathy as a primary response. Later in this chapter, I explore the specific impact of this conceptual barrier on neo–slave narratives.

Both Chamoiseau's and Arenas's texts confront what they perceive as their reading audience's lack of interest in the genre of antislavery or abolitionist literature, unlike Edgardo Rodríguez Juliá's *The Renunciation* and *La noche oscura*, which assumed readers would want to know more about a part of their past that has been neglected in the history books. Arenas and Villaverde both contributed to Cuban letters from afar, by writing and publishing in exile in the United States. In *Graveyard of the Angels*, Arenas assures the reader that although *Cecilia Valdés* is now regarded as one of the best examples of Cuban antislavery literature, to use William Luis's term for abolitionist fiction, it "[is] really much more than that."[18] Cirilo Villaverde famously rewrote and expanded *Cecilia Valdés*[19] in an effort to achieve a greater degree of verisimilitude and realism, as he reflects upon the process of revision in the prologue to the longer version of the story. We can thus read Arenas's version of the tale literally as "more" than real, or hyperreal, precisely because it is aware of its own limitations, its inability to create or produce an authentic critique of slavery so long after its abolition. In "Simulacra and Simulations," Jean Baudrillard defines the hyperreal as "the generation by models of a real without origin or reality."[20] In revising Villaverde's revision of *Cecilia Valdés*, Arenas produces a text that is a metafictive meditation upon the process of reading, more than on the act of writing itself. As such, his revision is a gesture of mourning for the great artists whom Arenas immortalizes within the pages of his novel, Cirilo Villaverde, Lydia Cabrera, the painter Goya, and even himself.

For his part, the narrator of *L'esclave* confesses: "We are no longer moved by stories of slavery. A small percentage of the literature deals with it. That's why here, in a *land bitter with sugar*, we feel submerged by the knot of memories that sours us with forgetting and with howling presences."[21] By using the first-person plural pronoun "we," the narrator implies that he shares his Caribbean audience's distaste for novels about slavery. However, the tone of this passage is clearly ironic. Not only does the narrator confront the weight of collective memory by telling the story that follows, but he also speaks of his desire to write such a tale about slavery: "I fell prey to an obsession, the more surprising, the more familiar, of the kind that only manifests itself through Writing. Writing. I know that one day I will write a story, this story, filled with great silences of our combined histories, our tangled memories. That of an old slave running through the great forest; not towards freedom but towards the immense testimony of his bones."[22] Character development is subordinate to stylistic flair in this passage. The narrator is enthralled by the very act of writing rather than feeling compelled to come to terms with the past. Although he initially recalls the experiences of maroons in the forest, ultimately, the narrator is more concerned with finding the right kind of language to express himself than he is with correcting an omission in the historical record.

Arenas's and Chamoiseau's novels try to find new ways of talking about slavery not subordinated to the fact-based historiography of textbooks. Chamoiseau's and Arenas's historical novels invoke an earlier tradition of realist Caribbean fiction as the inspiration for their own belated portrayals of slavery, without adopting their traditional narrative methods. Rather than merely celebrate the heroism of individual slaves who successfully broke free from their chains, *Graveyard of the Angels* and *L'esclave* use parody and metafiction to emphasize the textual nature of our contemporary understanding of events in the past. Chamoiseau and Arenas also criticize revisionist attempts to speak for the oppressed; their use of anonymous slave "types" in the background of their plotlines highlights the dehumanizing effect that the system of chattel slavery had on countless individual lives. Maryse Condé, however, avails herself of those same literary tools precisely to draw attention to the figure she feels was most exploited by both the rhetoric and the practice of chattel slavery: the black woman.

While *Graveyard of the Angels*, *L'esclave*, and *I, Tituba* all are set during slavery in their respective islands, each features a purposefully anachronistic worldview rather than echoing the realist version of slavery created by the literary objects they reconceptualize within their pages. Arenas and Chamoiseau openly impose a late twentieth-century perspective onto events that purportedly take place in the nineteenth century, while Condé's version of colonial Salem leads her to compare the African and Jewish diasporas, as well as to question first- and second-wave white American feminist discourse.

As a first-person tale narrated by a slave, *I, Tituba* parodies the romantic language of both nineteenth-century American sentimental novels and contemporary Harlequin fiction. Tituba spends more time describing her various lovers and their sexual encounters than she does chronicling the abuse she suffered at her mistress's hands, as actual nineteenth-century female slave narrators like Mary Prince from Antigua or Harriet Jacobs from the United States did in their accounts. Likewise, both *Graveyard of the Angels* and *L'esclave* avoid describing the plight of slaves' lives in their respective islands in much detail. Slave characters are present but mostly as "types," not individuals. This reluctance to dramatize the plight of slaves has two sources. First, implicit within the silence surrounding slaves' daily life in these narratives is the recognition that the trauma they endured is almost unimaginable to an audience living more than one hundred years after their emancipation. Second, since transatlantic chattel slavery is no longer a pressing concern against which the authors must take a dangerous moral and political stand, they seem to feel that simply transforming these characters into symbols of contemporary oppression would once again efface the specific suffering and endurance of the enslaved.

Marianne Hirsch proposes the term "postmemory" to describe the secondhand memory of trauma developed by people who were not the original sufferers, but who have internalized traumatic events from the past by repeatedly viewing images of them or hearing or reading about them. Hirsch explains, "Postmemory characterizes the experience of those who grow up dominated by narratives that preceded their birth, whose own belated stories are displaced by the stories of the previous generation, shaped by traumatic events that they can neither understand nor re-create."[23] In this configuration, postmemory is a condition or state of consciousness that second- and third-generation descendents of trauma victims are born into, and it exists outside the individual in the community as a sort of echo of the historical trauma at work in the present. Chamoiseau's, Condé's, and Arenas's awareness of their own belatedness as antislavery writers prevents them from attempting to empathize with the daily horrors of life under bondage even as they reimagine the period of slavery within their texts. However, by prominently featuring excerpts from the work of their predecessors as either characters or epigraphs, these three writers direct their readers to those seminal works, thereby allowing them the opportunity to go to the discursive roots of the stories that shaped the authors' postmemory of the trauma of slavery.

I, Tituba, *L'esclave*, and *Graveyard of the Angels* recognize that in order to overcome the emotional and intellectual pain associated with delving into the past of slavery, writers and readers must pause and mourn—both for the deaths of the actual enslaved people who died so many years before the novels' publication and for the lost opportunity to take a stand against this moral evil when it would have mattered. In their erudition and self-reliance, slave characters in these metafictive novels have more in common with twentieth-century fractured subjects than they do with either seventeenth- or nineteenth-century slaves, whose humanity was systematically denied and whose every action was policed.

My close readings of these novels' function as national history museums is mediated through the lens of new museology, an emerging field of museum studies influenced by postmodernist theory that has been behind the recent push to expand the notion of what kinds of materials should be included within museum exhibitions. Andrea Whitcomb suggests that the move to combine featured objects with supplementary materials from a variety of media constitutes the museum industry's effort to change the public's perception of the museum as an elite institution removed from everyday life; by incorporating elements from contemporary popular culture into their exhibits or displays, such as new technologies, museums following this ideology reach out to their audiences in ways that they recognize and appreciate: "At a practical level, exhibitions now include non-objects—particularly mock-ups, audio-visual technologies and interactive computer information points. They also use other media such as film, television footage, magazines and newspapers. At a discursive level, these inclusions can be understood, from a certain postmodernist perspective, as making the museum continuous with modern media forms."[24] In order to successfully communicate their messages to an audience, both museum exhibitions and postmodern historical novels have to find ways of making the past seem not only interesting, but relevant to everyday life. Further supporting this comparison of the self-referential function of both novels and museums is the sense of the museum exhibition as both a work of art in itself, and a vehicle for communicating information. The museum design expert Michael Belcher explains: "Indeed, exhibitions *are* pieces of functional design, with the purpose of doing a specific task. However, at their best they also satisfy the most generally accepted criteria of an art form."[25] Belcher goes on to list the exhibition's ability to surprise its viewers and to have an emotional impact upon them as some of those criteria.

Self-referential artworks questioning the ideology implicit within museum practices themselves have been on the rise in the American art world and museum scene since the late 1980s. Conceptual artists have

been creating and exhibiting installations that explicitly target the elitist foundations of the Western museum as it amassed and displayed its
collections. Fred Wilson has been recognized and praised by art critics and museum critics for his innovative work restaging museums' permanent collections to highlight the absence of discussions of race as a
guiding principle in contemporary curatorial practices. One such exercise in metamuseology, Wilson's 1992 installation Mining the Museum
was the result of a collaboration between the Contemporary, a new art
museum in Baltimore, and the Maryland Historical Society. Using the
entire third floor of the Historical Society as his exhibition space, and
the Historical Society's permanent collection as the source of his objects,
Wilson staged three distinct display areas as mini-museums of different
genres. Lisa G. Corrin, the exhibition's curator, described their emphasis as: "ethnographic, Victorian 'salon,' and the minimalist space of a
contemporary gallery."[26] Corrin cites Mining the Museum as one of the
few exhibitions that openly talks about race to pose a direct challenge to
museums as cultural institutions.[27]

   Both Mining the Museum and the novels under discussion in this
chapter, *Graveyard of the Angels*, *L'esclave*, and *I, Tituba*, function as
self-conscious imitations, or simulacra, of other cultural objects. Wilson's
exhibition pretends to be three different kinds of museums, while each
novel functions as a national history museum through its display of literary artifacts related to slavery.

   By actively incorporating either quotes or entire characters from
their predecessors' works into their narratives, Arenas, Condé, and
Chamoiseau engage their forebears in a metafictive dialogue about literature's changing ability to act as a catalyst to political action. Condé
elevates her protagonist from the dustbin of history, where she was a
mere footnote to the Salem witch trials, into the limelight by letting
Tituba tell her own story. As Condé appropriates characters brought
into prominence by the historical record and by best-selling works of
fiction, the novel co-opts their existing literary reputation and increas-
es its potential readership. In this way, Condé's novel writes itself into
the literary tradition from a critical perspective, and introduces a wide
audience of people unfamiliar with Caribbean letters to her own post-
feminist, revisionist view of American history. Like Condé, Chamoiseau
borrows a literary character as constructed in someone else's novel and
gives him new life in his text. He also makes reference to his previous
success as a novelist, specifically by attributing his own extradiegetic
achievements, like the publication of the novel *Texaco*, to his fictional

alter-ego. Some of the historical figures Arenas mentions retain their actual distinguishing characteristics or mannerisms in *Graveyard of the Angels*, while others, like Cirilo Villaverde, become involved in utterly absurd and anachronistic situations. Arenas's playful reference to them suggests that his text is more a cultural critique of twentieth-century Cuban society under Fidel Castro's rule than an attempt to revise in any way the official colonial historical record about slavery.

Slavery in Martinique

The literary objects that *L'esclave* exhibits in its role as a national history museum are excerpts from the work of the Martinican novelist and theorist Édouard Glissant, and also from an apocryphal memoir, *Toucher*, supposedly written by the narrator himself. The title of that apocryphal work refers to the writer's obsessive guilt about having touched or desecrated the title character's bones, which he considers sacred or supernatural. The extent of the novel's curatorial work of these objects takes place on the title page, which proclaims that the novel is supplemented by "un entre-dire d'Édouard Glissant." The term "entre-dire" was coined by Mauritian poet Edouard Maunick and refers specifically to intertextuality between works of Francophone literature, such as the epigraphs from Glissant that inspired Chamoiseau. However, nowhere within the pages of the novel is there a word of explanation to the reader as to what the "entre-dire" with Glissant consists of, or how it works. Unattributed epigraphs appear in italics on the left-hand page preceding each chapter but are not identified until the index page at the end of the book.[28] By waiting until the end to give the title of the two texts from which he quotes, Chamoiseau forces the reader to consider Glissant's words as isolated fragments instead of as parts of a larger work. In this way, Chamoiseau limits the parameter of the dialogue or "entre-dire" in which he wants the implied reader to engage.

Unlike *Graveyard of the Angels*, which parodies an entire nineteenth-century abolitionist novel, each of the chapters of *L'esclave* expands upon a given fragment of Glissant's work through the genre of the epigraph. Since they address the same themes, subjects, or characters as the quotations from Glissant's *L'intention poétique* and *La folie celat*, Chamoiseau's individual chapters render Glissant's words uncanny or unfamiliar, by forcing the reader to compare the two in light of each other. Epigraphs from the apocryphal book *Toucher* also appear in italics at the beginning of each chapter, and are discussed in more detail in chapter 6. As in the case with the "entre-dire," the mystery of their authorship and authenticity is not resolved until the last chapter, when the first-person narrator claims to have written *Texaco*, Patrick Chamoiseau's previously published novel, thereby further blurring the line between the writer and the written in this novel.

The epigraphs from *Toucher* are metafictive instances in which the author/narrator/writer quotes himself instead of his literary forebear, Glissant, as he tells the story of the old slave. Since *Toucher* exists only in the fragments in which it is quoted, Chamoiseau's use of it as epigraphs, and its proximity on the page to the quotes from Glissant's texts, suggest that the context of a quote is unimportant as long as it is somehow reframed in another text. This authorial manipulation of the way the text appears on the page undermines the notion that there can be only one reading of any given text, as William Luis argued of *Graveyard of the Angels*. However, whether seriously or in jest, the juxtaposition of excerpts from real and imaginary texts in the midst of chapters in a larger work constructs a particular, although not necessarily reliable, reading of the novel as a meditation on guilt, obsession, and, finally, on the nature of writing itself.

L'esclave adds another instance of doubling by featuring oral literature within its pages through the figure of the plantation's storyteller, le Papa-conteur, who transforms both himself and the world around him by the sheer power of the words in his stories. Listening to the storyteller is the one collective activity in which the title character participates with the nameless slaves that live alongside him on the plantation. As H. Adlai Murdoch has argued in his discussion of Chamoiseau's earlier novel, *Solibo Magnifique*, "the figure of the conteur functions discursively as a sign of communal opposition to the hierarchies of slavery and colonialism grounded in a violence both verbal and political; indeed it is in this moment of differential transformation that the basis of Chamoiseau's discursive praxis may be located."[29] As a listener to the oral tale, the old man is the reader's double, but even in this correspondence there is an implied negation, since the reader never actually hears (or reads) the stories the storyteller shares with the slaves. The old man's understanding of the world around him is tinted by his knowledge of these stories, and he maintains in his memory a well of readily available references that constitute an intertextual canon of "oraliture," to use one of Glissant's own terms.

Along with fellow Martinican writers Jean Bernabé and Raphaël Confiant, Patrick Chamoiseau has argued that in order to establish a Caribbean literary tradition distinct from that of Europe, it is not enough for Caribbean authors simply to write plays, poems, stories, and novels; they must also incorporate the Creole language into their writing to be true to themselves and attract a Caribbean reading audience. Such a focus on reading practices and strategies is just the sort of critical discourse that Hayden White had in mind when he warned against creating "master readers" and "slave readers." For this group of writers who were to form the core of the *créolité* movement, the use of the Creole language renders the text indecipherable to non-Caribbean readers without the aid of extratextual devices such as glossaries. Chamoiseau, Bernabé, and Confiant therefore privilege Caribbean readers above all others, and imply that the literature of the Caribbean exists only in the *correspondence* or *communion* between readers and writers even if they do not openly acknowledge in their manifesto that there are both Caribbean readers and works of Caribbean literature already in the present time. Chamoiseau, Bernabé, and Confiant begin the manifesto "In Praise of Creoleness" with the bold proclamation that "Caribbean literature does not yet exist. We are still in a state of preliterature: that of a written production without a home audience, ignorant of the authors/readers interaction which is the primary condition of the development of a literature."[30] The *créolité* writers' emphasis on the rootedness and shared national space of their ideal reading audience is proof of their political agenda to promote regional pride as a catalyst for nationalism and a demand for independence from France. The historical power structure of the "peculiar institution" of slavery undergoes an ironic reversal when applied to the *créolité* writers' manifesto. Bernabé, Chamoiseau, and Confiant bemoan the lack of Caribbean "master readers" who can fully understand all the references and cultural contexts at work in their own novels, even as their own books have sold well at home and they have enjoyed international acclaim and financial rewards from the sale of these same texts to "slave" or slavish readers in Europe, America, and around the world.

Whereas the *créolité* writers seem to discount or devalue the economic impact of the international success of their work, Antonio Benítez-Rojo, the Cuban novelist and theorist, celebrates the monetary rewards of the commercial relationship between foreign or "slave" readers and Caribbean texts. He contends that Caribbean literature not only exists, but that it has an inherent popular appeal for different kinds of readers: "I believe Caribbean literature to be the most universal of all. I will go a step further and argue that the more Caribbean a text is—the more complex and artistic its state of creolization—the more readers it will find in the world. Some publishing houses have already understood this reality, and they are going to do a good business."[31] Although Benítez-Rojo contradicts himself in claiming that Caribbean literature is at once the "most universal of all" literatures as well as uniquely identifiable *as* Caribbean, he raises an interesting point about its popularity. While it may be argued that Western publishing houses profit from the work of Third World writers when they aggressively market their novels, it is also true that the more books they sell, the more cultural capital Caribbean literature accrues. Therefore, when Reinaldo Arenas refers to Cirilo Villaverde in his New York–published *Graveyard of the Angels* and Patrick Chamoiseau quotes extensively from fellow Martinican writer Édouard Glissant in *L'esclave*, published in Paris, each writer engages in self-exoticism even as they establish their credentials as "master readers" of their own country's literature. Their texts proclaim their Caribbeanness as a marker of sophistication, all the while taking advantage of publishing opportunities in the metropolis.

L'esclave establishes a hierarchy among the slave characters it features: the eponymous protagonist is both aloof and self-sufficient, while the nameless others engage with one another regularly and partake of a hybrid cultural life improvised by the entire slave community in the plantation. Rather than protesting the master's unjust treatment of his peers by cooperating with other slaves and participating in slave revolts or insurrections, the title character runs away and tests himself against supernatural creatures in the forest. When he apparently succumbs during one of these trials, no one other than the reader and the narrator witnesses his death.

Slavery in Cuba

Unlike *I, Tituba*, Arenas's text does not try to follow the conventions of the slave narrative genre, although the novel is admittedly a parody of abolitionist fiction in general, and Villaverde's novel in particular. Instead, *Graveyard of the Angels* uses excess as a narrative strategy through which to underscore modern readers' emotional disconnect from the moral evils of the past. Slave characters die by the hundreds in *Graveyard of the Angels*, whether as a result of silly accidents or wanton displays of a master's cruelty. The sheer exaggeration of the numbers of daily casualties suggests that only through statistics can late twentieth-century readers comprehend the scale of abuse and torture involved in slave economies in the Caribbean islands and the North and South American continents. The hyperbolic and inflated statistics at once

indicate our collective inability to value individual life and the ineffi-
cacy of communal empathy when faced with mass catastrophe. White
Cubans do not fare much better than their Afro-Cuban counterparts in
this novel, thereby implying that life in general was more precarious in
centuries past than in an age of highly trained medical professionals and
computer technology. The overall effect is one of numbness to the pain
and suffering of previous generations, which gives rise to mourning for
the missed opportunity to have acted on their sense of moral outrage and
stood up against and resisted this system and the deaths it caused. The
complex legacy and the economic inequities that persist in the modern
world offer no easier answers, but the novel suggests that cold moral
outrage at a distance from these sorts of issues is no better.

Unlike the *créolité* writers, Reinaldo Arenas does not question the existence of his audience, Caribbean or otherwise, and addresses the reader
directly in his prologue: "I am not offering the reader the novel Cirilo
Villaverde wrote—which is obviously unnecessary—but the novel I
would have written had I been in his place." It is important to note
here that Arenas's novel and its English translation were both published
simultaneously in 1987, thereby doubling the potential pool of readers. *Graveyard of the Angels* constitutes Arenas's personal revision of
the Cuban literary canon, which does not necessarily include his own
works within its ranks. The earlier writer published several drafts of
Cecilia Valdés in New York until the definitive version appeared in print
in 1882. Although Arenas's novel is considerably shorter than its nineteenth-century namesake, Arenas argues that *Graveyard of the Angels* is
not a summary of *Cecilia Valdés* but, rather, an interpretation of it. He
argues in the preface that his text is an imaginative work in its own right
and not merely a criticism of Villaverde's work. *Graveyard of the Angels*
is a parody of the earlier work and constructs a genealogy of "illustrious
antecedents" for himself and his novel that juxtaposes "the most illustrious authors of all time," Aeschylus, Sophocles, Euripides, Shakespeare,
and Racine, and four Latin American writers of varying renown: the
internationally acclaimed Borges and Vargas Llosas, and the lesser-
known authors Alfonso Reyes from Mexico and Virgilio Piñera, also
from Cuba. Unlike Reyes and Piñera, however, whose work parodies the
ancient Greeks, Reinaldo Arenas set his sights on a Cuban predecessor
who wrote about problems in his own country, thus emphasizing his
commitment to reexamine a distinctly national literary tradition.

Whereas Villaverde's novel sought to bring about social change during his lifetime by criticizing the institution of slavery as a social evil,

Graveyard of the Angels depicts both slavery and the discourse of abolition as literary constructs and criticizes the way writers impose their own sensibilities upon the subject matter of their text. Arenas signals the difference between his novel and Villaverde's by exaggerating what particularly interests him from the original text, the incestuous relationship between the legitimate heir of the plantation family's fortune and his younger half sister, the daughter of a mulatta slave and the family patriarch, and extending it to apply at all levels of society. He downplays most of the abolitionist didacticism of Villaverde's nineteenth-century text but includes that writer as a character persecuted for teaching poor black children to read through the use of his novel *Cecilia Valdés*. So, while slavery has been abolished in Cuba, Arenas's novel suggests that illiteracy continues, not necessarily because young black children are not taught to read but, rather, because they are not necessarily "master" readers familiar with the Cuban texts that preceded the "triumph" of the Cuban revolution.

The literary critic J. Michael Dash argues that Caribbean literature cannot be read in isolation, but must be considered in what he terms "a New World context" that transcends regionalism. In *The Other America*, Dash illustrates the international appeal of Caribbean literature when he remarks that "the Czech novelist Milan Kundera has championed the work of Chamoiseau, although temperamentally, he is closer to the life-enhancing, manic laughter of Confiant."[32] By insisting on Kundera's role as advocate for Chamoiseau on the world stage, as well as remarking upon the similarities between Kundera's prose style and that of fellow *créolité* writer Raphaël Confiant, Dash negates the arguments about the Caribbean's isolation and its state of preliterature that Chamoiseau and Confiant advance in "In Praise of Creoleness." Dash, himself a Caribbean "master" reader of Caribbean literature who came to prominence by translating Édouard Glissant's fiction and theory, comments on the popularity of parody in Caribbean letters: "This parodic vein in Caribbean writing . . . calls language and the literary act into question and reduces everything to matter. This view of the world as absolutely material, absolutely carnal, undercuts any idealistic dualism separating the literary from the real, consciousness from matter, mind from body. It is not surprising that this tradition should result in a rejuvenation of language, making it more immediate and sensory."[33] The parody in *Graveyard of the Angels* and *L'esclave* makes language "more immediate and sensory," but it also renders narrative increasingly abstract. As language describes "carnal" or "material" events in these novels, the narrative incorporates more fantastic or supernatural elements and gradually excludes any reference to the (novelistic or extradiegetic) world at large. Thus, *Graveyard of the Angels* and *L'esclave* "call . . . the literary act into question" as a matter of form precisely because they incorporate these texts into their own diegesis.

The narrative strategy both Chamoiseau and Arenas pursue in these novels is one of continuous interruption. Arenas's "Preface" is the first of many direct appeals to the reader; it becomes particularly important only because *Graveyard of the Angels* features a character named "Reinaldo Arenas," as mentioned earlier, who simultaneously is and is not the implied author of the text. At other times, entirely fictional characters comment upon their own status within the novel as a work of literature. Nemesia Pimienta is a case in point: she is the lovelorn black female companion of the heroine, Cecilia Valdés. The third-person omniscient narrator in *Graveyard of the Angels* reveals Nemesia's thoughts about her dependence on the author since she is a secondary character whose troubles occupy a relatively small portion of the narration as "not even the author of the novel in which she is an insignificant element was interested in her tragedy."[34] Her chapter ends in an ellipsis.

Nemesia's complaint against the "pitiless author of the novel" could conceivably refer *either* to Villaverde or to Arenas, or even to both of them simultaneously. Since this segment is narrated in the third person, it could be read as Arenas's condemnation of Villaverde's treatment of his minor characters. Then again, it could be Arenas's criticism of his own style, or mere narrative play. Whatever the referent, the "author" becomes a sinister presence in this text when Nemesia compares the act of narration to physical violence, especially given the context of slavery, since she is a black female character silenced or stifled by a white man who controls the wor(l)d.

By equating the white male writer with the white slave master, *Graveyard of the Angels* criticizes not only the cruel mistreatment of the slaves that took place in Cuba during the time of slavery, but also the patronizing abolitionist rhetoric that sought to correct this injustice. Villaverde is as guilty of not treating his black characters fairly, in the narrator's view, as were the Spanish colonizers for continuing to safeguard the prosperity of the slave economy. *Graveyard of the Angels* does not describe life in nineteenth-century Cuba in encyclopedic detail as does *Cecilia Valdés*; instead, it parodies the rigid social classifications and standards that ignored the racial intermingling that characterized plantation life in nineteenth-century Cuba. For Arenas to join

Villaverde in denouncing slavery would be anachronistic since he is writing a little more than a hundred years after abolition in Cuba, but the former's critique of the privileges associated with either light or white skin still applies in spite of Castro's political rhetoric of national unity and equality.

Nemesia's chapter in *Graveyard of the Angels* illustrates the intrusion of contemporary attitudes and mores into what claims to be a fictional historical narrative. Brian McHale provides a more useful interpretation of this type of metafiction when he argues that "a character's knowledge of his own fictionality often functions as a kind of master-trope for determinism—cultural, historical, psychological determinism, but especially the inevitability of death."[35] Arenas' portrayal of the all-controlling author can be read as a commentary on Cuba's tradition of repressive government, dating from colonial times to Castro's revolution, especially since both Cirilo Villaverde and Arenas himself had to leave the island to escape political persecution. In exile at different periods in history, Villaverde and Arenas have been written out of the Cuban literary canon by the governmental authors of Cuban reality.

Entirely fictional characters are not the only ones at the mercy of the implied author in this novel. As I mentioned earlier, Cirilo Villaverde, the author of *Cecilia Valdés*, shows up as a character in an eponymous chapter. Unlike poor Nemesia, who succumbs to the power of the implied author and abruptly disappears from the text, one of the historical Cirilo Villaverde's own fictional creations in *Cecilia Valdés*, the plantation matriarch Doña Rosa, runs Arenas's fictional character out of town because of his literacy activism. Bursting into his classroom, Doña Rosa throws three barrels full of dangerous animals (poisonous snakes, hairy spiders, and land crabs) against Villaverde's desk. The author/teacher runs away in fear, and the only clue to his fate comes as Doña Rosa and her family are on their way home from their violent expedition. They hear shrieking in the distance and wonder if Villaverde has finally met his match; instead of resolving the doubt, Doña Rosa's husband, Don Cándido, breaks the narrative spell by concluding: "that's for the curious reader to decide."[36]

Much as the *créolité* writers express in their manifesto years later, Arenas's fictional Villaverde believes there are too few Caribbean readers (both "master" and "slave" readers, according to White's formulation) for his work, a circumstance he attributes to the low rate of literacy on the island. The implied author leaves Villaverde's fate up to the reader to decide; thus, Arenas reverses the power dynamics of the earlier instance of metafiction in the Nemesia chapter. Here, the author cedes agency to the reader, putting him or her in a position to assign their own individual sense of closure to this chapter.

By calling the authorial position into question in *Graveyard of the Angels*, Arenas emphasizes his double role within the narrative as both a reader of the antislavery works of the past, and a writer defined by the literary style of his day: postmodernism. However, William Luis reads these two acts of narrative violence as Arenas's affirmation of the multiplicity of interpretation possible for any text. According to his reading of *Graveyard of the Angels* as a current antislavery work, Luis argues that Arenas's undermining of the authorial position within the novel is due to his desire to amend or rewrite the historical record: "By undermining the author as the only interpreter of his work, *Graveyard of the Angels* opposes all monolithic and unidimensional understanding of Villaverde's work but also of history. . . . Within the context of the time in which Arenas writes his novel, he strives to decentralize an understanding of history in which historians and functionaries of the Castro government are the only functionaries of Cuban history and culture."[37] Luis's emphasis on Arenas's revisionism misses the mark because *Graveyard of the Angels* does not add in any way to our knowledge of the past as it was, but only of our own contemporary assumptions about the importance of events that occurred a long time ago. The target of Arenas's parodic vision is exactly the "antislavery narrative tradition" Luis discusses in his own work. Instead of refusing to privilege any one reading of a text above another, the overtly explicit instances of metafiction in this novel call attention to the fact that *Graveyard of the Angels* is itself a reading of, and commentary upon, Villaverde's abolitionist text. The third-person narrator does not claim to inhabit the same time or space (nineteenth-century Cuba) as the characters s/he describes and therefore emerges as a figure closer to the reader than to the fictional Arenas or Villaverde.

Slavery in Barbados

The protagonist's life in Maryse Condé's *I, Tituba* begins and ends in Barbados, despite the fact that, like her historical counterpart, the protagonist of the novels gains international notoriety during her stay in Salem Village, in the American colony of Massachusetts. Thus, out of the three novels discussed in this chapter, this is the only one that discusses the institution of slavery from a transnational perspective. Like *L'esclave*, *I, Tituba* invokes the Middle Passage journey as the defining historical symbol for transatlantic slavery. However, unlike Chamoiseau's old man who arrives in Martinique never to leave it again, Condé's Tituba embarks upon her own journey through the triangular trade by voluntarily entering bondage in order to accompany her enslaved husband to his new place of servitude in the British colonies in North America. After her participation in the celebrated witch trials, and a period of service to a Jewish merchant, Tituba returns to the island of her birth and takes up with maroons in the hills.

Through the plot of her novel, Maryse Condé portrays different experiences of life in bondage that correspond to the history and geography of each place she mentions: (1) plantation slavery in a Caribbean sugar island, both in the fields and the big house; (2) personal servitude within a small rural household in an American colony; (3) personal service within a large urban estate in an American colony; and (4) precarious freedom within a maroon village in the hills of a Caribbean sugar island. *I, Tituba* also depicts the eponymous protagonist's loss of freedom through incarceration. Tituba first goes to jail when she is accused of witchcraft in Massachusetts. Later, back in Barbados, she is jailed on charges of conspiracy to participate in a slave insurrection and is sentenced to death by hanging. By subjecting her enslaved main character to a further loss of freedom through incarceration, Condé suggests that modern-day correctional facilities are little different from plantations of yore.

While invoking the past of slavery in order to criticize modern-day criminal justice practices may attract some readers' attention in this novel, *I, Tituba* functions as a national history museum when it uses transworld identity to exhibit three different kinds of literary artifacts related to slavery in Barbados within its pages: (1) fictional characters from American literature, including Tituba herself and Nathaniel Hawthorne's character, Hester Prynne; (2) metafictive references to a Barbadian folksong about Tituba; and (3) historical court transcripts from the Salem witch trials. The first and third literary artifacts are examples of non-Barbadian ways of knowing because both the contemporary and historical American texts constitute the preservation of a story by means of the written word, which makes its dissemination among strangers possible. Like the *créolité* writers, Tituba-the-narrator claims that there is a long-standing history of oral storytelling within Barbados that facilitates the transmission of knowledge among different villages and between the generations of people and to which the folk song about her belongs through the second literary object on display. Whereas the narrator/implied author in *L'esclave* spoke for, and about, the old slave who liked to listen to stories by the fireside in Martinique, Condé navigates the line between both narrative traditions by authoring a novel that purports to be a communication from beyond the grave spoken by a dead slave.

The English translation of *I, Tituba* includes an interview with Ann Armstrong Scarboro in which Condé discusses the two literary precursors for her own depiction of Tituba, Arthur Miller's play *The Crucible* (1953) and Ann Petry's novel for young adults *Tituba of Salem Village* (1964). Condé also mentions Nathaniel Hawthorne's *The Scarlet Letter* (1850), the historical novel in which the adulteress Hester Prynne originally appeared. The addition of such paratextual documents means that the English translation of Condé's novel functions like a national history museum with a larger exhibit area, so to speak, than that of the original French text.[38] Condé tells Ann Scarboro that, in her view, neither Miller's nor Petry's portrayals of Tituba depict her as an individual free from gender or racial stereotypes. Condé's comments imply that there are no credible portrayals of enslaved women of color within the American literary canon, even when African American women writers like Petry dedicate entire novels to a little-known historical figure like Tituba. Condé's versions of Hawthorne's, Miller's, and Petry's characters are more ideologically charged than the original ones; within the narrative, their function is to illustrate or embody the limited potential of American first-wave feminism as a liberatory philosophy for women of color.[39]

Condé's Hester Prynne kills herself in jail while she is pregnant rather than compromise her feminist ideals, whereas Hawthorne's tragic heroine embodies his version of rugged individualism by enduring public scorn in jail and refusing to surrender to ostracism. Hawthorne's Hester achieves a sort of domestic fulfillment, living out her days at the outskirts of town and raising her daughter, Pearl. Neither option is really open to Condé's Tituba, a woman of color in a slave-owning society who is more outspoken than Miller's acquiescent servant or Petry's broken slave, who is grateful to be purchased by the local weaver after the witch trials.

The eponymous heroine is the first-person narrator of *I, Tituba* and points to the tale's popularity among those she considers "master" readers of Barbadian history: "My real story starts where this one leaves off and it has no end. . . . [T]here *is* a song about Tituba! I hear it from one end of the island to the other, from North Point to Silver Sands, from Bridgetown to Bottom Bay. It runs along the ridge of the hills. It is poised on the tip of the heliconia."[40] Like the storyteller's yarns in *L'esclave*, the "song" to which Tituba-the-narrator alludes is not duplicated within the novel: no fragment of this fictional folk song appears anywhere in Condé's text. The narrator Tituba is not merely the historical subject of the apocryphal song; as a ghost freed from the constraints of time and place, she is its primary audience as well. The non-Barbadian reading audience can know of the song's popularity but, as outsiders, they are not privy to its secrets much in the same way that non–Puerto Ricans would not necessarily know the origins of the Baltasar Montañez legend in *The Renunciation*. By privileging a Barbadian audience for oraliture over the American (or French) audience for the written text that constitutes the novel, the narrator affirms the value of native and populist ways of knowing as an alternative to the elitism and exclusion of the historical record.

The novel's use of the transcript from Tituba's actual interrogation during the Salem witch trials serves as a case in point. Although the words are duplicated verbatim, albeit in French, the novel's plotline undermines any truth value that the coerced confession might have had. Everyone from John Indian to Hester Prynne advises Tituba to say whatever is necessary to save herself. Likewise, when Tituba returns to Barbados, she domesticates, or creolizes, her experiences in the Massachussetts colony by translating her testimony in the tribunal, which had been recorded on the transcript, into an oral narrative: "The maroons listened to me as they sat in a circle. There weren't very many, not more than fifteen with their wives and children. And I relived my suffering, my hearing before the tribunal, the unfounded accusations, the false confessions, and the betrayal by those I loved."[41] In this way, the fictional Tituba incorporates the Salem witch trials into the folk history of Barbados, which at this point in time was also a British colony. Like the song people tell about her after her death, readers do not have access to the specific oral narrative Tituba shares with the maroons. After this reference, the novel changes into dialogue to record the maroons' questions about Tituba's tale. Her answers to these inquiries provide the only hint readers have of how her tale of woe was interpreted by the "native" audience.

Tituba's oral narrative and the inclusion of the historical testimony within the novel suggest a comparison between this text and the literary genre of slave narratives written either by former slaves like Frederick Douglass and Harriet Jacobs, or transcribed by white abolitionists, as in the case of Mary Prince, from Antigua. Dwight A. McBride analyzes what he calls "the theater of abolitionism," the rhetorical production of abolitionist discourse through propaganda and eyewitness accounts of cruelty that both allowed for ex-slaves to testify to their suffering through the lecture circuit as well as made those same black bodies understandable only through the abolitionist prism of abjection and pain. McBride's theoretical analysis applies as much to the modern reader of historical and fictional slave narratives as it did to nineteenth-century audiences: "the slave serves as a kind of fulfillment of the prophecy of abolitionist discourse. The slave is the 'real' body, the 'real' evidence, the 'real' fulfillment of what has been told before. Before the slave ever speaks, we know the slave; we know what his or her experience is, and we know how to read that experience. Although we do not ourselves have that experience, we nevertheless know it and recognize it by its language. This is because the language that the slave has to speak in, finally, is the language that will have political efficacy."[42] Late twentieth- or twenty-first-century readers of historical fiction ascribe the same type of "political efficacy" to the firsthand testimony of a fictional slave, especially when Tituba's tale appears at first to follow all the narrative conventions of the slave narrative genre: the "I was born" beginning, descriptions of cruel mistresses and masters, references to humiliating and painful punishment, and accounts of broken family bonds. However, while the parallels are there, this genre is not one of the three types of literary objects on display in *I, Tituba*'s function as a national history museum.

While it has an initial buy-in from readers, the novel then moves into uncharted territory by chronicling Tituba's life, not among a group of fellow abolitionists, but within a community of runaway slaves who plan violent attacks on nearby plantations. This shift of paradigm involves an entirely different kind of "political efficacy" than did those ex-slaves appealing to the hearts and wallets of religious do-gooders. Tituba's later disavowal of the maroons' guerrilla-type tactics in favor of an isolated, yet peaceful, coexistence with the natural landscape entails yet another political discourse, environmentalism, which is abruptly cut short by her execution. At this point, Tituba's idiosyncratic choices assert her individuality so strongly that her tale moves beyond the limits of abolitionist rhetoric; she ceases standing in for Caribbean slaves in general and represents no one but herself.

This brings up a problem in reading *I, Tituba* as a Barbadian museum of national history. Although there is proof that Tituba Indian was a slave originally born in Barbados and transported to Salem, Massachusetts, and she was indeed the first person to testify about her

involvement in witchcraft at the trials, the historical Tituba does not occupy a prominent place in Barbadian history. There is no reference to her
in the Barbados National Museum and Historical Society, which was
originally founded in 1933. The museum not only houses various permanent exhibitions related to the history and heritage of Barbados, but
it has also developed a significant archive of historical documents, the
Shilstone Memorial Library. This institution has made great strides in
adapting to the ever-changing technological landscape of both museum
and library sciences.[43] Currently, the museum is collaborating with other
CARICOM countries to develop an archive relating to the Caribbean
slave trade. The focus of this proposed archive is the collection of written documents and images, rather than transcripts of oral narratives.

I, *Tituba*'s strident assertion of the oral storytelling tradition in
Barbados downplays the country's actual literary canon about the history of slavery. Unlike *Graveyard of the Angels* and *L'esclave*, whose exhibitions open up their respective countries' literary canons to outsiders, *I,
Tituba* forecloses the possibility that outsiders could have a meaningful
engagement with other Barbadian written texts. Among the works that
non-Barbadian readers would not learn about would be the novels of
George Lamming. His debut novel, *In the Castle of My Skin* (1953), vividly depicts instances of "postmemory" in which the trauma associated
with the older generations personal experience of slavery was so strong
that it resulted in cultural amnesia, or a tacit denial that slavery had ever
been practiced in Barbados. *Natives of My Person* (1972), Lamming's
most recent publication, is a historical novel about a clandestine slaving expedition setting sail from England that encounters trouble after
picking up a cargo of African slaves and never reaches its Caribbean
destination. The Barbadian poet Edward Kamau Brathwaite has drawn
inspiration from the history of colonialism and slavery in the Caribbean
and translated it into both scholarly treatises, like *The Development of
Creole Society in Jamaica, 1770–1820* (1971), which features a long discussion entitled "Folk Culture of Jamaican Slaves," and his poetry. His
1994 collection of poems, *Middle Passages*, is only the most obvious example of a poetic oeuvre that repeatedly addresses the plight of the slave,
the Amerindian, and others. Brathwaite is one of the more high-profile
Barbadian writers who promote the use of "nation language," or the
Creole language spoken in Barbados. However, he has always published
his poetry in written form, thus demonstrating none of the hostility that
Condé's Tituba seems to feel toward that medium of expression.

More recently, Austin Clarke has gained prominence in Canada and the United States. His memoir, *Pig Tails 'n Breadfruit* (1999), chronicles his childhood in Barbados, where Clarke fondly recalls eating "slave food." In 2004, Clarke published a historical novel about slavery, *The Polished Hoe*, which parodied the detective novel genre as a way to illustrate the traumatic aftermath of surviving life under bondage. Unlike Tituba, Clarke's female protagonist takes out her suppressed anger at being violated by the white plantation owner who fathered her only child by killing the elderly man with the very tool she had previously used to tend to his field. I mention these texts only to establish that the Barbadian cultural landscape is not particularly hostile to the written tradition.

Unlike both the *créolité* writers and Arenas, Maryse Condé does not write as a cultural insider when she tells the story of slavery in Barbados in *I, Tituba*: she hails from Guadeloupe and writes this neo–slave narrative in French. In her emphasis on the importance of oraliture, Condé reveals her Francophone preoccupation with Creole culture and the *créolité* movement within the French overseas departments more than any particular engagement with twentieth-century Barbadian culture. Her French prose does not try to approximate the cadences of Bajan nation language so, once again, "slave" readers who are outsiders would not learn much about this particular cultural movement from reading *I, Tituba*.

Maryse Condé's penchant for depicting the universal truths about slavery in her fiction, instead of depicting its regional variations, may be what made French president Jacques Chirac name her to the presidency of the French committee for the remembrance of slavery. Her international outlook makes her especially well suited to lead a group of fellow artists and scholars in their efforts to account for France's role in this global enterprise. In contrast, Chamoiseau and Arenas both find inspiration for their work in previous novels about slavery written by insiders about their respective islands. In their postmodern texts, the peculiar institution serves as a literary trope to be reworked as a meditation on contemporary issues of cultural self-definition, citizenship and nationality. *L'esclave* and *Graveyard of the Angels* outline a national literary canon for Martinique and Cuba, respectively, and include themselves within it, despite the political obstacles entailed in such claims.[44] In a creolizing move, *L'esclave* and *Graveyard of the Angels* broadly disseminate aspects of this history of slavery so that twentieth-century readers, wherever they may reside, can become familiar with it and claim it as part of their own cultural legacy. Arenas's and Chamoiseau's texts also seek to redefine the time of slavery in Martinique and Cuba as a distinct chapter in each country's lived reality, the legacy of which still shapes economic, social, and racial dynamics of day-to-day life. By providing a national context in which to understand their novels, *Graveyard of the Angels* and *L'esclave* function as national history museums by showcasing the literary history of their respective islands.

2 Art Museums

Visual (Inter)Texts

THEMATIC EXHIBITIONS at art museums regularly display visual and three-dimensional art objects as representative of larger sociopolitical conflicts or movements that characterized a particular era. During the summer of 2005, the Milwaukee Art Museum hosted an exhibition in its Decorative Arts Gallery entitled About Face: Toussaint L'Ouverture and the African American Image, curated by Glenn Adamson.[1] Ceramic arts—pitchers and jugs—bearing the iconic image of the prominent leader of the Haitian Revolution, Toussaint L'Ouverture, are at the heart of this exhibition. It may be surprising for modern audiences to consider how nineteenth-century ceramics functioned as a vehicle for political propaganda, but the curator uses this particular artistic form of expression as a lens through which to question and analyze how the domestic realm was shaped by hot-button political issues of the day, like the possibility that large-scale slave insurrections would spread to American shores. In a move reflective of the exhibition's status as a work of postmodern new museology, which privileges the fabric of culture as an interwoven pattern of intersecting artistic and domestic realms, the portrait pitchers are displayed in the context of four different political discourses. According to the official exhibition description published by the Milwaukee Art Museum, these are: "historical representations of Toussaint," "abolitionist propaganda ceramics," nineteenth-century "derogatory racial images," and "pots made by African-Americans."[2] Included among the first of these categories are works of literature from the early nineteenth to late twentieth centuries, such as William Wordsworth's sonnet "To Toussaint L'Ouverture" (1803), Édouard Glissant's play Monsieur Toussaint (1961), and the first volume of Madison Smartt Bell's trilogy of traditional historical novels chronicling the events of the Haitian Revolution, All Souls Rising (1995).

The literary "objects" were displayed in the museum alongside selected portraits of the Haitian leader from the *Toussaint L'Ouverture* series (1938) done by the twentieth-century African American painter Jacob Lawrence. The Amistad Research Center commissioned the *Toussaint L'Ouverture* paintings as a fund-raiser.[3] Lawrence's history series encompassed multiple panels, more than forty in the case of the Toussaint portraits, accompanied by his own written captions, which reflect his interpretation of the time period and the historic figure. Thus, these works comprise a multimedia narrative about Toussaint as an iconic figure. This exhibition's juxtaposition of visual and textual historical narratives, whether defined primarily as paintings or as literary texts, suggests that the tale of a slave's rebellious heroism cannot be contained within a single medium.

Much as the nineteenth- and early twentieth-century historical novels discussed in the previous chapter constitute a spectral canon of Caribbean literary history that haunts and informs postmodern novels' depictions of slavery, contemporary historical fiction about life in bondage also contains repeated references to paintings, etchings, engravings, and portraits done by European and Caribbean artists between the seventeenth and nineteenth centuries. Whereas Patrick Chamoiseau's, Reinaldo Arenas's, and Maryse Condé's references to the work of their literary forebears are fraught with the anxiety of influence as it plays out in the novel genre, the frequent allusions to the visual arts in Reinaldo Arenas's *Graveyard of the Angels*, Alejo Carpentier's *Explosion in a Cathedral*, Michelle Cliff's *Free Enterprise*, David Dabydeen's *A Harlot's Progress*, and Edgardo Rodríguez Juliá's *La noche oscura* constitute interdisciplinary meditations on the power of different media to (re)present human suffering for the consumption, edification, or entertainment of others. The novels not only mention, but overtly appropriate, the following visual texts: J. M. W. Turner's seascape *Slave Ship (Slavers Throwing Overboard the Sick and Dying, Typhoon Coming On)* (1840); Goya's series of anti-French etchings, *Estragos de la guerra/The Disasters of War* (1820) and an unspecified portrait of Spain's Ferdinand VIII; William Hogarth's paintings/engraving series *A Harlot's Progress* (1732); François de Nomé's *Explosion dans une église* (sixteenth century); and José Campeche's portrait of a deformed child born in Puerto Rico, *El Niño Juan Pantaleón Avilés* (1808).[4] These hybrid texts enact and perform the interrelation between art, history, and fiction through allusion, quotation, description, and interpretation.

The novels display their featured artwork for their readers by mentioning the title and artist of the works within their pages. *Graveyard of the Angels, Explosion in a Cathedral, La noche oscura del Niño Avilés, A Harlot's Progress,* and *Free Enterprise* then curate these featured pieces in one of three ways: (1) they directly discuss the artwork's aesthetic qualities, (2) they weave the life stories of the human subjects depicted within the images into their larger plot, or (3) they incorporate references to, or explanations of, the historical background of the events depicted within the visual work into their plot. The novels emphasize the artwork's authentic existence outside of, and beyond, the fictive text. This break in the suspension of disbelief calls for an in-depth analysis of the changing role images play within the historicized and fictionalized discourse about slavery at the end of the twentieth century, versus the immediate impact of the commodification of human beings at the height of the international slave economy. Like the artworks, these historical novels reflect the mores and attitudes of the time in which they were written; any sociocultural relevance contained within these texts can only apply to the temporal continuum in which they are published, namely, the late twentieth century.

A broad temporal divide separates the publication of *Graveyard of the Angels, Explosion in a Cathedral, La noche oscura, A Harlot's Progress,* and *Free Enterprise* from the creation of the artworks to which they make reference. This gap in time accomplishes two different tasks: first, by exhibiting artworks from historical and cultural discourses completely removed from slavery or the New World, the novels map the horror of slavery as it played out in specific geographic locations onto a larger, global tradition of oppression, violence, and warfare. Contrasting paintings of actual European conflicts with both apocryphal and historically informed fictional depictions of the Caribbean experience of life in bondage suggests that transatlantic slavery is not an isolated expression of human cruelty, but another in a long series of violent interactions between people of different backgrounds. The second task this disruptive perspective facilitates is a metacritical meditation upon the function of art in popular culture by opening up a textual space in which the relative merits or flaws of a given work of visual art can be either debated or mimetically dramatized. This decentered notion of time as artifice underscores the status of the "peculiar institution" as a schizophrenic undertaking that sought to naturalize man-made changes to the landscape, labor force, and the redistribution of geopolitical power in New World territories.

These five novels all create an apocryphal version of history as it never was by treating portraits, engravings, and paintings as cultural commentaries on, or reflections of, historical phenomena that took place at a time different from that of the artworks' composition. They mediate the reading audience's experience of visual pieces—of painting and etchings—either through providing a real or imagined backstory within the narrative to accompany the events depicted in the work of art, or else by juxtaposing overt references to works of art not directly discussed within the plot of the novel itself to create what one may call interdisciplinary pastiche.[5] By appropriating the cultural currency of these assorted paintings and engravings without including reproductions of the visual texts themselves within the pages of their respective texts, Arenas, Carpentier, Rodríguez Juliá, D'Aguiar, Dabydeen, and Cliff effectively direct readers outside of and beyond the literary texts, asking them to prolong or duplicate the museum experience created within each novel by finding the visual supplements to the historical and fictive material about which they have been learning. The considerable technological advances that have taken place since the publication of these five texts now make it possible for twenty-first-century readers to take an interactive approach to the reading experience and do what the novels could not at the time of their publication: surf the Web to create their own, individual, virtual museums that function as multimedia supplements to the fictive text by finding links to all the artworks and artists mentioned, as well as to historical figures and events, earlier canonical books, places designated as World Heritage Sites, and so on.

This thematic grouping of Caribbean postmodern texts facilitates—in fact, almost demands—such an interactive approach to reading in order to breach the distances across time, space, and even economic circumstance. The resultant effect of these textual juxtapositions, the visual and the written, is a dynamic, multisensory reading experience in which readers derive enjoyment and satisfaction not only from the words on the page, but also from their own search for the images described secondhand within the fiction.

Art and History

La noche oscura, A Harlot's Progress, Feeding the Ghosts, Free Enterprise, Explosion in a Cathedral, and *Graveyard of the Angels* recast a predominantly European canon of visual artistic expression as a commentator upon, as well as a contributor to, the process of global historiography and the ongoing fictionalization of historical events. While neither novels nor works of art hold the same claim to accuracy as sources of information about slavery as do primary documents like captain's logs from the slave ships, plantation records, or bills of sale, they nonetheless capture a particular ethos of the popular opinion at a given time regarding morally and politically charged issues that influence the perspective from which we construct our historical knowledge about the past. Their common emphasis on the universality of art and the ability of different genres of artistic expression to enhance each other's portrayal of human suffering propel these five postmodern Caribbean novels about slavery out of a strictly postcolonial context and toward a global understanding of the interconnected networks of immigration, commerce, and cultural exchange.

Rather than asserting the primacy of either the visual or written medium, these five novels insist on their, and the artworks', joint status as independent texts that nonetheless comment upon and complement one another. As predominantly belated documents, produced after the time of the events they chronicle, neither the novels themselves nor their allusions to visual arts can effect any direct change of political doctrine, practice, or economic policy since they have all been resolved in the intervening years between the development of transatlantic slavery and its abolition. However, the newness and, in some cases, the utter anachronism of the juxtapositions between art and literature featured in these novels attest to their overwhelming desire to establish an explicit and enduring connection between the present and the past. They act more indirectly, affirming the significance of our understanding of the legacy of slavery on current debates regarding cultural values and sociopolitical conflicts.

La noche oscura, A Harlot's Progress, Free Enterprise, Explosion in a Cathedral, and *Graveyard of the Angels* exhibit various actual paintings within their fictional stories. First, the novels themselves (re)read history through the lens of visual artworks. Prominent characters in both *Free Enterprise* and *Graveyard of the Angels* discuss the aesthetic merits of or interpret the works of art explicitly mentioned within each novel's pages, such as Turner's *Slave Ship* or Goya's portrait of Ferdinand VII, thus giving their readers a sort of "guided tour" of the art objects and making each text function as an art museum. In contrast, *A Harlot's Progress, Explosion in a Cathedral*, and *La noche oscura* reject the role of museum guide; these novels interject artwork with no direct connection to slavery into their fictional, and sometimes apocryphal, depiction of life in bondage in the Caribbean islands or Africa without offering any didactic explanation of the implications of this strategic placement.

Carpentier's *Explosion in a Cathedral* describes the scene depicted in Monsú Desidério's painting of the same title through various characters' points of view, thereby demonstrating that a visual text can give rise to multiple interpretations. However, this novel makes no overt attempt to elucidate the connection it suggests between events in the Caribbean during the Haitian Revolution and its aftermath and the Napoleonic invasion of Spain around the turn of the nineteenth century; it merely mentions, in selected chapters, the titles of specific engravings in Goya's series *Disasters of War.* Rodríguez Juliá's *La noche oscura* spends more time describing imaginary paintings created by secondary characters within the narrative than it does discussing José Campeche's actual 1808 portrait of the title character, El Niño Avilés. Likewise, Dabydeen's *A Harlot's Progress* ignores the aesthetic dimension of the artwork mentioned in the title, telling instead the fragmented backstory of the little African boy depicted in only one panel within Hogarth's allegorical engraving series and then projecting a bleak view of what the rest of his life might have been like in England.

Whereas the Museum of the Americas in Old San Juan operates as Dr. Ricardo Alegría's "three-dimensional book," *La noche oscura del Niño Avilés*, *A Harlot's Progress*, *Free Enterprise*, *Explosion in a Cathedral*, and *Graveyard of the Angels* function as art museums in miniature, not only exposing readers/visitors to the works of art they mention, but also suggesting interconnections, actual or imagined, between the world of art and the sociopolitical and economic circumstances surrounding the production and consumption of artwork. The level of reader involvement these texts demand surpasses that of the intertextual novels in the previous chapter; these five books require their readers to engage in a more complex multisensory activity—the researching, viewing, and interpretation of art—than was called for in simply becoming "master" readers of the transnational Caribbean literary canon. As they "exit" or finish reading these texts, readers/viewers/visitors leave with a broader appreciation of European art, Caribbean history, the transformative powers of fiction, and the interaction of all three discourses in contemporary life.

Reading these novels and looking at these works of art can bring the same catharsis, provoke the same questions, and inspire further inquiry and research much in the way that a visit to an art museum—physical or virtual—does, with the added benefit of perhaps prompting readers to make that visit after all. To facilitate my reading of the museum effects present within these five postmodern novels, I have organized the rest of the chapter as a "tour" of the various artworks previously mentioned. In the sections that follow, I curate, so to speak, the works of art each novel exhibits to its readers by providing some historical background of the paintings' or engravings' subject matter and composition, and remarking upon their critical and popular reception when appropriate. I also explain how the novels themselves display the artwork they reference by situating the various allusions within the context of the plot. Finally, I draw a connection between the visual and written texts and their respective roles within the larger work of mourning, which, I argue, all the novels discussed in this study carry out through their interface with the reader. This connects the past and the present through the twin lenses of artistic interpretation and the collective memory of trauma and suffering.

This chapter has four sections corresponding to the world-renowned works of Turner, Hogarth, Goya, and also the lesser-known portraiture of the Puerto Rican painter José Campeche. The subject matter of all artwork discussed is the abject spectacle of the grotesque: death, disfigurement, and destruction are front and center.

J. M. W. Turner's *Slave Ship (Slavers Throwing Overboard the Sick and Dying, Typhoon Coming On)* (1840)

In this dramatic seascape, J. M. W. Turner memorializes the massacre of 132 slaves being transported from Africa to the Caribbean aboard the slave ship *Zong*, who were thrown overboard while still alive. The ship's captain and his backers later sued the insurance company to recuperate their losses. James Walvin, a leading historian of British slavery and the black British presence in England, has called the *Zong* case "the most grotesquely bizarre of all slave cases heard in an English court" because it did not contest the legal definitions of either slavery or freedom but, rather, accepted the premise that slaves were indeed chattel.[6] The facts of the case highlight some of the primary problems with the European side of the international slave trade.

In 1781, Luke Collingwood, the captain of a British slaver, committed a navigational error during the Middle Passage voyage: whether through sheer incompetence or because he, like Antonio Benítez-Rojo, also regarded the Caribbean archipelago as a series of "repeating islands," Captain Collingwood mistook Jamaica for Hispaniola, which caused some considerable delay to the trip. An illness already had afflicted both the crew and the cargo of the *Zong*, killing several officers and spreading widely among the slaves. Citing both concerns about the spread of disease and the need to conserve water for the remainder of the journey, Collingwood ordered his men to throw 132 of the sickest slaves over-board. The captain apparently operated out of the premise that by sac-rificing some of the human cargo in order to spare the health and well-being of the remainder, he ensured that the owners of the vessel could receive compensation for their loss from their insurance companies.

Acording to Walvin, British insurance law at the time decreed that insurers would not compensate owners for the loss of slaves who died through "natural causes" such as disease, old age, and complications from childbirth but would cover the cost of those slaves who were killed in order to stop a rebellion on board. After the massacre, Captain Collingwood and his crew were prosecuted in England for insurance fraud, not murder, despite abolitionist Granville Sharp's insistent pleas.[7] As Turner's painting of the *Zong* massacre almost six decades later dem-onstrates, this act of cruelty and the outrageous nature of the legal case horrified the British public and raised awareness of the need to reform slave laws and end the slave trade. This trial marked the beginning of or-ganized resistance to, and calls for the end of, British involvement in the slave trade and its use of slave labor in the West Indies. Both the *Zong* incident and Turner's painting of it continued to fascinate the British public even after the government finally emancipated slaves in its West Indian colonies.

From its inception, Turner's painting was an exercise in histori-cal reenactment since it was not contemporaneous with the events it chronicled: Captain Collingwood made his fateful decision to jettison the human cargo in 1781, before the British abolished the slave trade in 1807. Turner, for his part, did not finish *Slave Ship* until seven years after England had emancipated the African-descended slaves in its West Indian colonies in 1833. The painting briefly reached an abolitionist au-dience from 1840 to 1843 while it was exhibited in conjunction with the meeting of the Africa Civilization Society or World Anti-Slavery Convention at Exeter Hall.[8] A Web site entry for *Slave Ship* available through the Museum of Fine Arts, Boston, which holds the painting in its permanent collection, points out that when the painting was origi-nally exhibited at the Royal Academy, it was accompanied by an ex-cerpt from "The Fallacies of Hope" (1812), one of Turner's own poems.[9] Thus, Turner himself relied on multiple media, painting and poetry, in order to fully express his outrage at the inhuman treatment of slaves by their European masters. However, neither Turner's painting nor his un-finished poem had the opportunity to effect direct change on the British

Empire's own involvement in the slave trade since both were composed *after* the practice was officially banned. At most, Turner's works could only hope to inspire people in countries that were still participating in the slave economy, such as France, Spain, and the United States, to follow England's lead, while also mobilizing the British sentiment in favor of the naval suppression efforts in which they were engaged.

The historical massacre aboard the *Zong* and Turner's famous painting fascinates the Jamaican novelist Michelle Cliff, who has incorporated references to both in *Free Enterprise* and her first novel, *Abeng*. Cliff mentions her ongoing preoccupation with this tragic event in an interview with Judith Raiskin: "There's a whole chapter in my novel [*Free Enterprise*] based on one painting, which is by Turner called 'Slavers Throwing Over the Dead and Dying.' It's illustrating a very famous case of a ship called the *Zong*, which is described at the end of *Abeng*, where they threw over slaves from a trading ship to collect insurance money on them and Turner illustrates it."[10] *Abeng* is a coming-of-age tale set in Jamaica during the middle of the twentieth century, whereas *Free Enterprise* takes place almost entirely in the United States during the mid- to late nineteenth century. Neither work dramatizes the massacre aboard the *Zong*, but, instead, each portrays the transmission of historical information about this event as a tale that is told privately, between women. Miss Winnifred, an older white woman, tells young Clare, the light-skinned protagonist of *Abeng*, the tale to illustrate the horrors of the Middle Passage as the epitome of colonial cruelty against the subjugated peoples of the Caribbean. The lines of ethical transmission once again show that the power system continued to be dominated by whites, and point to the moral ambiguity that allowed the suppression of the slave trade to become the impetus for expanded European colonialism in Africa.

Free Enterprise also features a similar set of female characters discussing the events of the *Zong* massacre, but whereas the female characters discuss the *Zong* face to face in *Abeng*, women do not speak as freely with each other in person in *Free Enterprise*, but communicate primarily through correspondence. The older female character, Mary Ellen Pleasant, is a fictionalized version of a real, free-born black abolitionist from San Francisco who claimed to be one of John Brown's coconspirators for the raid on Harpers Ferry. Cliff's Pleasant shares the story of the *Zong* with a younger, light-skinned Jamaican woman, an entirely fictional character whom Pleasant addresses as Annie Christmas. This particular exchange is decidedly one-sided: Christmas reads Pleasant's missives, but does not reply. The novel also includes yet another set of interfeminine epistolary discussions about the artistic merits and flaws of J. M. W. Turner's famous painting: Mary Ellen Pleasant corresponds with Alice Hooper, another fictional version of an actual person, the wealthy, white American art patron who purchased Turner's *Slave Ship*. Although these characters' meeting does not contradict any known fact about either woman or the painting's provenance, this fictional scenario nonetheless acts as an apocryphal supplement or corrective to official history because it imagines two well-meaning, highly educated women from different backgrounds and positions on the color line engaging in a two-pronged debate about aesthetics and about the possibility for meaningful cross-cultural understanding. Rather than offer any particular insight into the American experience of slavery, *Free Enterprise* insists on the global scope of it as an exploitative economic practice.

Cliff's staging of this pseudodebate between two female amateur art critics resonates with twentieth-century concerns about how an artist's race influences the creation and/or interpretation of the visual images s/he creates depicting life in chains.[11] Each woman's discussion of Turner's painting is framed by their references to other male figures of public renown: Pleasant's letter mentions the painting's previous owner, John Ruskin, and also alludes to William Makepeace Thackeray's thoughts on the artwork, while Hooper finds parallels between the painting's visual evocation of the sea and the maritime settings of the work of the American novelist Herman Melville and the British Romantic poet Samuel Taylor Coleridge. This is a strange turn for a novel that so adamantly insists on women's power to communicate and use language as a tool to wield power and effect change. Apologizing to her guest for having asked her to explain the history of the Middle Passage to the assembled dinner guests because of her status as the only black member of their company, Alice Hooper writes: "I should have spoken about the *Zong*. About the white flash of typhoon at the center of the work, surely comparable, in foreboding and whiteness, to Melville's white whale and Coleridge's albatross—emblems of that belief which allowed and supported something like the slave trade. The belief which endangers the white race as well as the African."[12] Rather than constituting a gesture toward establishing a literary archaeology of the kind seen in the previous chapter, Alice Hooper's allusions to *Moby Dick* (1851) and *The Rime of the Ancient Mariner* (1798) represent interesting end pieces against which to consider Turner's painting. These intertexts also hint at *Free Enterprise*'s most characteristic tone: a sense of belatedness. Hooper's interpretation of the picture symbolically associates the typhoon's white-ness in the background with the immense guilt weighing or dragging down the white race because of its involvement with the slave trade, but her letter to Pleasant was supposedly written in 1874, almost ten years after the end of the American Civil War and almost one hundred years after the *Zong* massacre took place. In one last instance of belatedness, Hooper only sends the letter of apology *after* the dinner party, once Mary Ellen Pleasant has recovered from the shock and outrage she felt at being singled out to speak about slavery merely because she was the only guest of color, rather than immediately apologizing to her guest for the offense.

While Hooper's allusions to male artists and intellectuals demon-strate her familiarity with their works, Mary Ellen Pleasant's references to Ruskin and Thackeray are primarily personal and mediated by her disapproval of their imagined values. In her letter to Annie Christmas, Pleasant reports that the art historian who eventually spoke about the painting at Hooper's dinner cited Thackeray's response to *Slave Ship* as typical of the painting's critical reception: "Thackeray ridiculed it, he said; that I remember."[13] The tone of that assertion is somewhat ambiva-lent; it is unclear whether Pleasant disapproved of Thackeray's supposed reaction to the painting, or if she remembered the comment because she objected to the art historian's reference to it. The novel does not elabo-rate further on Thackeray's evaluation of the painting, nor does Pleasant admit to having read his review.[14]

Upon learning John Ruskin had displayed *Slave Ship* in his own par-lor but eventually grew too distressed by the subject matter to see it every day, Pleasant bitterly retorts, "I am sorry it caused Mr. Ruskin so much pain."[15] Her condescending remark implies that she thinks only people of African descent can truly empathize with the anguish and hor-ror depicted in the painting itself, despite it being the product of a white British painter's brush. Pleasant insists upon claiming an ethical and emotional superiority to the white audience of the painting.[16]

This racialized view of what constitutes an appropriate emotional response to artwork belies Pleasant's earlier notion that her race does not grant her more authority to "signify" the events of the *Zong* before the assembled company. In *The Signifying Monkey*, Henry Louis Gates Jr. argues that a black cultural identity can be performed linguistically through the use of specific rhetorical strategies: "The language of black-ness encodes and names its sense of independence through a rhetorical process that we might think of as the Signifyin(g) black difference."[17]

The white art patron's request that Mary Ellen Pleasant, as the sole black woman among the assembled group of white guests, provide the group with a historical retelling of the events surrounding the British massacre of enslaved Africans transported aboard the *Zong* allowed for no expression of individual personality unmarked by the prism of transatlantic slavery.

Free Enterprise's narrator emphasizes the continuing relevance of historical events to contemporary life in the United States by directly addressing the reader. These metatextual gestures place a frame around the viewers in the text, reaffirming the importance of art to cultural debates. Only with some outside research can the twenty-first-century reader verify the connection that the fictional text makes between the real work of art fictionalized within this novel, Turner's *Slave Ship*, and the historical events that led up its composition, the *Zong* massacre. Unlike the self-aware narrator of Reinaldo Arenas's *Graveyard of the Angels* discussed in the chapter 1, Cliff's intrusive third-person narrator separates him or herself from the novel's implied author, as well as from the characters whose lives she describes; in addressing the audience, the narrator is both cynical and combative. Like the About Face exhibition in the Milwaukee Art Museum, Cliff's text calls into question the ethics of buying and selling overtly political art as a mere aesthetic commodity. At one point, Hooper asks Pleasant in a letter whether her purchase of the painting makes her complicit in the larger slave economy. The narrator does not answer, but concludes the novel's discussion of Turner's painting in the context of the life of its American owner thus: "Alice Hooper also passed on. The painting by J. M. W. Turner, *Slavers Throwing Overboard the Dead and Dying, Typhoon Coming On*, went in 1899 to the Boston Museum of Fine Arts, where it hangs today. Go see it. Take the kids."[18] Rather than encouraging the reading audience to connect with their fictive counterparts through the shared experience of gazing upon the very painting that aroused such conflicting emotions among them, the sarcastic final suggestion, "Take the kids," conveys the narrator's contempt for anyone who would minimize the scale of human suffering depicted in the painting by treating it as a mere novelty. Cliff's narrator leaves open the possibility that even at this distance in time from the events depicted in Turner's painting, her white audience's ignorance about the importance of the *Zong*, as well as their monetary contribution, however indirect, to support the work's continued exhibition still makes them complicit with, and therefore culpable for, the financial network that facilitated European imperialism in both the New and the developing worlds.

Through its allusions to historical figures who critiqued Turner's *Slave Ship* as both an abolitionist statement and a freestanding work of art, *Free Enterprise* argues that the arts do more effective political work when they are accessible to many than when they exist as mere status symbols attesting to their owner's wealth. As a historic object in public view, Turner's *Slave Ship* functions as a primary source documenting abolitionists' reliance on the affective power of visual imagery as an effective propaganda tool, like the portrait pitchers or Wedgwood china featured in About Face.

The temporal displacement between the painting's composition and the unfolding of the violent events it depicts parallels the distance in time between *Slave Ship*'s appearance upon the world stage and its spectral presence in Michelle Cliff's *Free Enterprise*, a novel that is also haunted by ghostly projections of a "future" that postdates the events it describes. Both fictive and visual texts juxtapose the graphic depiction of human suffering and objectification with the discourse of the international abolitionist movement, thereby emphasizing that while this heinous act may have gone unpunished in the court of law, it did not go unwitnessed. However, as was the case with Reinaldo Arenas's implied criticism of abolitionist fiction's lack of agency in Cuba in *Graveyard of the Angels*, Cliff's *Free Enterprise* does not paint abolitionists, black or white, in a strictly positive light, but overtly portrays the tensions felt by both constituencies as they joined forces to bring down the "peculiar institution" in the United States.

Museums figure in yet another, more obscure way in Michelle Cliff's *Free Enterprise*; not only does the narrator explicitly mention the Boston Museum of Fine Arts within the text, but the writer herself admits to traveling to museums in the western United States in order to learn more about the lives of African Americans living on the frontier. Cliff tells her interviewer that she specifically chose the Great Plains Black Museum as a destination because she had read about it.[19] The influence of her visit to Malcolm X's birthplace in Omaha, Nebraska, can be felt in the novel through Mary Ellen Pleasant's parroting of Malcolm X's speech and her meeting with the still-unborn leader in a San Francisco coffeehouse. So, while Michelle Cliff may not be a professional art critic, this interview attests to her personal enthusiasm for museums in general, and for black-themed museums in particular. For their part, both

David Dabydeen and Edgardo Rodríguez Juliá have written nonfiction books of art criticism on the oeuvre of the painter whose artworks they fictionalize, William Hogarth and José Campeche, respectively.[20] David Dabydeen has also curated the BBC's online exhibition of black art in Britain, thereby reaching an exponentially larger audience of readers/viewers interested in visual depictions of an African presence in Britain beyond Hogarth's work.[21]

Despite their forays into art history, these novelists do not strive for either historical accuracy or verisimilitude in their discussions of these actual paintings/engravings within their fictional works but, rather, invent wild backstories for the subjects portrayed therein. Rodríguez Juliá and Dabydeen use the paintings' titles within the titles of their own novels, thereby signaling that the works of both visual art and fiction claim a similar level of artistic achievement. *A Harlot's Progress* and *La noche oscura* function as art museums by dramatizing the life behind the paintings or engravings. These novels can be said to "curate" the works of art they address by situating them and their subjects within a larger historical framework, in this case, the world of slavery and the slave trade during the eighteenth century, and recasting the works of art as part of a larger discourse on nationalism, citizenship, and the question of belonging.

William Hogarth, *A Harlot's Progress* (1732)

Dabydeen's *A Harlot's Progress* takes its title directly from a series of paintings, later sold as limited-edition engravings, by the eighteenth-century English artist William Hogarth. Through the engravings that make up *A Harlot's Progress* (1732), Hogarth condemned what he saw as the growing decadence of British society. The series visually narrates the story of a young country girl, Moll Hackabout, who moves to the city (plate 1), where she becomes a high-class prostitute who keeps a monkey as a pet and has a young, black boy wearing a turban and pearl earrings as her servant (plates 2 and 3). Moll eventually falls out of favor with her rich visitors and ends up doing manual labor in jail (plate 4). Her body ravaged by venereal disease (plate 5), Moll dies at a young age (plate 6). Dabydeen blends elements from Hogarth's engravings, such as the image of the monkey, with his own fictionalized depiction of the now-aged and moribund little black page of old, referred to as "Mungo" within the narrative. The novel blurs the boundaries between the worlds of overseas commerce and domestic prostitution, emphasizing their shared attributes: cruelty, enslavement, and profiting at the expense of the degradation of others through unceasing physical labor.

In *Hogarth's Blacks: Images of Blacks in Eighteenth Century English Art*, Dabydeen reads the high frequency with which black subjects appear in the painter's oeuvre as historical proof of the existing racial diversity of eighteenth-century English society.[22] Establishing that there was a visible historical presence of black bodies in England is important for Dabydeen's Marxist feminist reading of Hogarth's *A Harlot's Progress*; in his scholarly treatise on the painter, Dabydeen compares the exploitation of women and the working poor in eighteenth-century England to the inhuman conditions to which Africans were subjected in bondage in the West Indies. While Hogarth never directly portrays images of transatlantic slavery per se in his paintings or engravings, Dabydeen contends that his repeated use of black subjects is a constant reminder of the negative impact the trade in human beings had in the shaping of British society at home. By emphasizing England's complicity in the slave trade both at home, before the Somerset decision, and abroad, Dabydeen asks his readers, as well as the art lovers who gaze upon Hogarth's engravings, to question their own assumptions of England as a land of freedom.

Featuring scenes of aristocratic debauchery narrated from the black servants' point of view, *A Harlot's Progress* suggests that England, like the prostitute Moll, sullied its own reputation by pandering to its populace's lust for easy wealth through the heedless exploitation of foreign others. The novel provides an alternative historical context in which the reading and viewing audience can understand the moral tale Hogarth spun visually. Through the prism of Mungo's jumbled thoughts on his deathbed, Dabydeen's text juxtaposes references to African tribal life chaotically interrupted by slave catchers, a cabin boy's sexual subjugation at the hands of his captain, and cruel and wanton exploitation of lower-class servants within city households. *A Harlot's Progress* dramatizes the commercial aspect of art as a commodity by making several overt references to Hogarth's other engravings as well as to *A Harlot's Progress*.

Mungo's (unspoken) version of his life story constitutes the first-person portion of the book. In it, the ex-slave meditates upon the idea that the luxury status of Hogarth's *A Harlot's Progress* paintings perpetuates English society's commodification of him as an African boy: "For though Mr. Hogarth's art was not affordable to many, a dozen ballads and a dozen pirated versions of his pictures appeared, cheap enough for mass purchase. Once I was affordable only to the very rich, a slave worth countless guineas, but because of Mr Hogarth, I was possessed, in penny image, by several thousands."[23] Mungo's suggestion that the purchase of art implicates visitors in the criminal economy depicted within the canvas echoes the sentiments expressed during the Mary Ellen Pleasant–Alice Hooper mock debate in Cliff's *Free Enterprise* about the ethical dilemma of owning *Slave Ship* as an investment. Dabydeen's indictment of the masses in this scene rightly questions the value of images of debauchery, pain, and degradation as either entertainment or art, given their role as decorations for private households. It also suggests that the use of visual depictions of blacks in bondage in abolitionist propaganda was just as exploitative of the enslaved subjects as was the use of such images in advertisements for slave auctions or of notices of runaway slaves because all such images deny the individuality of the person in question in favor of promoting a degraded group identity.

The novel *A Harlot's Progress* juxtaposes these two contrasting images of England's innocence or culpability vis-à-vis domestic slavery through its two main protagonists: the aforementioned Mungo, and Mr. Pringle, a white British abolitionist who wants to write down Mungo's life story and publish it as a slave narrative.[24] The novel engages in postmodernist pastiche by portraying art simultaneously as a historical document of the generous treatment ex-slaves received as domestic servants in Britain, which only Mr. Pringle takes literally, and also as a false record of events, from Mungo's point of view. Dabydeen's *A Harlot's Progress* demands more than mere familiarity with Hogarth's work for it to be clearly understood; it also requires its readers to know about the slave narrative tradition, and to be aware of how those written in England by white abolitionists taking dictation from, and editing the words of, freed "Africans" differ fundamentally from the American accounts of torture and escape written in the North by runaway bondsmen from the South.

A Harlot's Progress posits itself as a hybrid neo–slave narrative, interspersing the italicized text of Mr. Pringle's ghostwritten account of what he projects Mungo's life to have been like within the larger text of the ex-slave's hallucinations about the destruction of his African home. Mungo prefers not to speak to Mr. Pringle about his past, and therefore the abolitionist must turn to the engravings themselves, and read in them the truth his subject will not allow him to know or tell. To make sense of this combined narrative, readers must consciously keep these two authors and their respective plots separate, rearranging them chronologically if they are to fully comprehend the novel's relationship to the painting after which it is named.[25]

Using Hogarth's artwork as historical "proof," David Dabydeen imagines an Enlightenment-era England where slavery was legal and slaves were bought and sold on English soil. Dabydeen's novel suggests, therefore, that while art might serve as a political tool to voice the artists' views on the moral dilemmas affecting his or her society, later critics can turn to it to reconstruct important social debates of the time. Yet, by presenting an accurate version of England's past as a slave-trading and slave-holding nation within a postmodern narrative that rejects chronological time and imagines the "lives" of fictional characters from paintings, *A Harlot's Progress* puts the burden on its readers to sort out which events in the novel are based on historical facts and which are completely imagined. Dabydeen's novel poses provocative questions, but he is careful to avoid making the same mistake he depicts Mr. Pringle as committing: imposing a rigid, overarching ideological interpretation on what life in bondage was (or must have been) like. By affirming Mungo's right to his silence, *A Harlot's Progress* emphasizes that neither well-intentioned empathy nor distance in time can ever fully allow outsiders to comprehend the experience of being treated as property.

José Campeche, *El Niño Juan Pantaleón Avilés de Luna Alvarado* (1808)

Edgardo Rodríguez Juliá's *La noche oscura* engages in interdisciplinary pastiche by depicting the subject of an actual portrait of a deformed infant born without arms done by the Puerto Rican painter José Campeche in the early years of the nineteenth century. The novel's prologue changes the date of the actual child's birth to coincide with the timing of an actual British invasion of San Juan Bautista, the island's capital, in 1797.[26] Rodríguez Juliá further conflates fact and fiction by suggesting that the name "Niño Avilés" refers to two distinct characters—the deformed baby depicted in the painting and an unrelated adult male who was the spiritual leader of the fictitious slave rebellion and supposedly presided over the establishment of the nonexistent maroon colony of New Venice on the island of Puerto Rico that same year.[27]

Ramón Soto-Crespo has argued that Campeche's painting is a metaphor for the unfinished or incomplete nature of the Puerto Rican nation-state in Rodríguez Juliá's narrative. Soto-Crespo points to *La noche oscura*'s use of this painting as creating a hybrid space between fiction and art criticism: "Yet there is no daring transgression of generic boundaries between fiction and art criticism in the novel; rather, *La noche oscura* attempts a confluence by trying to fill a forgotten conceptual gap between history and painting. Not any type of history or any type of painting, but the history and painting of historical origins and of incomplete national identity formations."[28] While I agree with Soto-Crespo's analysis of Edgardo Rodríguez Juliá's references to painting in general in his metafictive meditation about Puerto Rican national identity, the subject of the painting seems to be at odds with that assertion, although the melancholy gaze upon the young child's face does accord with the overall sense of sadness or mourning that Soto-Crespo finds in the novel.

Museum scholars have pointed out that portraits of illustrious (or merely wealthy) men usually play this iconic role of embodying the nation within historic houses turned museums, historical societies, and even national history museums. While Soto-Crespo pauses to examine how Edgardo Rodríguez Juliá reads Campeche's portraits of influential eighteenth-century figures, such as the island's governor, he assigns more importance to José Campeche's status as a free-born mulatto painter who chose to remain in Puerto Rico rather than accept offers to paint for the royal courts of either Spain or England than he does to the young boy's status as anything other than a scientific curiosity.[29]

La noche oscura addresses the sudden reappearance of the "truth" of the past in the present through the "discovery" of a trove of historical documents, including a set of paintings. The novel's prologue gives 1913 as the year two long-lost historical documents were found that attest to the existence of this now-forgotten maroon colony in Puerto Rico: a triptych narrating the story of the colony's foundation through images, supposedly painted by José Campeche's nephew, a fictional character called Silvestre Andino, as well as a set of papers that describe the scenery illustrated in the paintings and comment upon the canvases. As Reinaldo Arenas does later in *Graveyard of the Angels*, Rodríguez Juliá engages in transworld identity by including Campeche as a character within the novel's opening pages, although this fictional version of the artist never directly addresses the audience like Arenas's Goya.[30]

The prologue, thus, creates a museum effect: it exhibits a (fictional) artwork curated by an equally fictitious expert. Alejandro Cadalso, another fictional character and the ostensible author of the prologue, dated 1946, argues that of the two sets of documents, the paintings comprising the triptych present the most authentic historical account of the foundation of Nueva Venecia: "Through dark, symbolic visions and minutely detailed realist landscapes, real miniatures, the canvas narrates the history of the singular crew and its founder, el Niño Avilés. But that's not the end of the relationship between the documents and the miniatures; the former are, for the most part, detailed descriptions of, and commentaries about, the latter. While the word complements the image, deciphering visions and animating landscapes, Andino's brush dares to tell us the myth of the cursed city." By emphasizing the complementary relationship that exists between the fictional history paintings and the apocryphal written accounts of the colony's foundation, *La noche oscura* nonetheless affirms the importance of art as a source of historical knowledge and information.

Carlos Rincón interprets the novel's multiple references to portraits and landscapes as a "visionary pastiche" of eighteenth-century visual and narrative rhetorical conventions. He considers Rodríguez Juliá's use of metaphor, and the repeated references to "the body, the libido, desire" as the organizing principles in the narrative, which allow *La noche oscura* to function as both "a *re-vision* of paintings attesting to the modernity of the society they represent, and a *re-writing* of non-existing historical documents."[31] I would add that this is precisely what constitutes the novel's curatorial function according to the precepts of conventional museology, which favors the didactic text as a mediator between the art patron and his/her own experience of the work of art.

Although Cadalso claims to have seen Andino's art personally, his report of what the triptych shows is secondhand; he cites the following description from yet another source to which the novel's actual reader has no access, the apocryphal *Historia de un descubrimiento*, supposedly written by José Pedreira Murillo, the person who originally "found" the long-lost documents: "a triptych that represented 'a strange landscape of canals and islets from which rose majestic edifices resembling beehives.'"[32] By comparing the city's fortresses to beehives, Pedreira and, implicitly, Cadalso and even Rodríguez Juliá impose a naturalistic interpretation on the runaway slaves as a group of undifferentiated social creatures whose insectlike devotion to a singular leader and his/her vision almost certainly ensures their quest for freedom will fail.

As a virtual art museum, the novel simultaneously postpones and makes immediate the readers'/viewers'/visitors' experience of the work of art; first, by alluding in its title to Campeche's 1808 painting of El Niño Avilés, which actually exists and can be found; and second, by describing the "historical" scenes the fictional triptych depicts without actually showing them in the body of the text. In both the prologue and the novel as a whole, the fictive triptych displaces Campeche's portrait

of the deformed infant in terms of "historical" relevance, thereby emphasizing the relative importance of maroon communities to large-scale
independence movements throughout the Caribbean and Latin America.
In contrast, the image of the child's incomplete, or lacking, body serves
as a metaphor for the absence in Puerto Rico's own history of a successful, organized, large-scale rebellion against slavery and Spanish imperialism. Along these lines, Carlos Rincón interprets *La noche oscura*'s
imaginative use of Campeche's last portrait more broadly, as a metaphor
for Puerto Rico's monstrous or incomplete transformation into an independent nation.

While Rincón's and Soto-Crespo's readings of Rodríguez Juliá's allusions to, and appropriations of, Campeche's paintings in *La noche oscura del Niño Avilés* both suggest that the title character's physical de-
formity corresponds to Puerto Rico's political status as a commonwealth
freely associated with the United States (*estado libre asociado*), neither
critic takes into consideration that all the figures depicted in Campeche's
portraits are white and, by extension, Spanish. I contend that Rodríguez
Juliá's most political commentary on the state of the nation in Puerto
Rico comes not from his allusion to Campeche's portraiture alone, but
from his overall portrayal of all concerned parties—Spanish bishops,
government leaders, and soldiers as well as African slaves—as uncre-
olized outsiders trying to re-create a sense of their previous lives elsewhere in this swampy Caribbean island.

Like the prologue's implied author, Cadalso, the novel's actual writer,
Edgardo Rodríguez Juliá, considers painting a medium more apt than literature for conveying historical knowledge and a sense of a burgeoning
nationalism. Rodríguez Juliá begins his monograph on the work of the
Puerto Rican painter José Campeche by echoing the Gospel of John in
his praise of painting: "Before literature, there was painting. Campeche's
oeuvre gives our nationality an image that precedes literary testimony;
we will have to wait until the mid-nineteenth century for our culture to
become action."[33] Rodríguez Juliá interprets Campeche's art as indelibly
creole, "creole painting—art, therefore, between two cultures,"[34] bridg-
ing the worlds of Spanish colonial forces (military and ecclesiastical) and
a mulatto elite class despite the painter's overwhelmingly Eurocentric
choice of subject matter: portraits of Spanish officials. Despite his claims
for the mestizo hybridity of Campeche's painting, Rodríguez Juliá acknowledges that the big aporia at the center of Campeche's oeuvre is
the absence of any images of blacks when he remarks: "in Campeche's
paintings slaves only appear once."[35] *La noche oscura* further cements

its status as interdisciplinary pastiche when it attempts to remedy Campeche's oversight by peopling its pages with multitudes of runaway slaves. However, as I argue in chapter 4, not even Rodríguez Juliá fully includes either slaves or black characters within a distinctly Puerto Rican imaginary since the narrators of the text continuously refer to them as "the Africans." *La noche oscura*, thus, strives to bring readers/viewers/ visitors closer to the history of human bondage in the island without establishing an unmediated emotional connection to the primary actors of the drama of slavery.

In his compelling article, Soto-Crespo points to yet another way in which Edgardo Rodríguez Juliá's fiction incorporates references to Campeche's work: through a series of five pornographic drawings that the narrator of *The Renunciation* discusses and explains for his audi- ence. Soto-Crespo describes the drawings as "miniaturized fictional paintings attributed to the fictional painter Juan Espinosa"[36] and argues that they "replicate the form of Campeche's religious paintings"[37] with- out specifying which of Campeche's paintings embody this form. Unless the novel's audience is entirely made up of Caribbean "master" readers, the correspondence between the fictional works of art and the real ones will not be as overwhelming as was the explicit allusion to Campeche's work in the title of Rodríguez Juliá's second novel, *La noche oscura*.

Another remarkable way in which *The Renunciation* functions as an art museum is through the narrator's own curatorial work. The novel is divided into three distinct academic lectures supposedly given by a univer- sity professor who is an authority on Puerto Rican history. In the second of these lectures, the professor emphasizes the importance of documents he uncovered while he was conducting archival research and that attest to the changing emotional state of the historical figure he writes about, Baltasar Montañez: "One of these sources, little known and even less commented on, is a collection of drawings by Juan Espinosa. . . . They lie today in the Municipal Archives of the city of San Juan. No doubt the reason for their scholarly neglect, the reason they have not been studied, or even very often mentioned, is their scabrous and shocking subject matter, for they contain graphic scenes of the orgies which Baltasar cele- brated in the private apartments of the Palace of State."[38] This statement constitutes the rationale for the professor's discussion and exhibition of these same drawings before the assembled audience. The novel contains the professor's description and analysis of the five individual drawings in the rest of the chapter, alongside his discussion of other fictional primary documents that support his narrative of the events in Montañez's life.

This portion of the professor's talk approximates a "portable exhibition," which Michael Belcher defines as "those small, self-contained exhibitions which may be transported to a site, erected and, after a period of display, removed and probably be brought back to base for use again if required. . . . [P]ortable exhibitions are generally quite small and may comprise as little as a few graphic panels."[39] The novel simultaneously criticizes governmental institutions like the municipal archives for not sharing their collections with the general public, as well as rectifies this sin of omission by "exhibiting" the naughty neglected artworks alongside the professor's curatorial commentary.

SLAVERY APPEARS mostly as historical background in the novels by the two Cuban writers Alejo Carpentier and Reinaldo Arenas. This narrative remove creates an insulating emotional distance between the reader and the anonymous slave masses that functions like Mungo's and Mary Ellen Pleasant's willed silences in the works previously discussed and, like them, has the effect of foreclosing avenues for mourning for the slaves. Rather than directing readers' pity toward a historical injustice far removed in time, *Explosion in a Cathedral* and *Graveyard of the Angels* employ anachronistic juxtapositions between different European and Caribbean historical discourses and epochs to create an artificial conflation of distinct historical events and there locate pathos.

A different type of temporal dissonance arises when we consider the paratextual elements of the English translation of Capentier's novel. The literal English translation of the text's original Spanish title is "The Age of Enlightenment." Titling the English translation *Explosion in a Cathedral* after the seventeenth-century oil painting by François de Nomé, which recurs throughout the novel as a leitmotif, downplays the significant effect on the novel's plot of Enlightenment philosophy and the revolutions it spawned. The title also wrongly suggests that it is the most important artistic reference contained within the novel. While one of the young protagonists is certainly obsessed by the image, the novel as a whole is a richly textured tapestry that also contains multiple references to the work of Goya, as well as implied descriptions of surrealist landscapes like those of Dalí. Thus, the English title is an anachronistic and reductive paratext that creates a set of expectations that the novel itself will not meet.

François de Nomé's *Explosion dans une église*

Nomé's painting is primarily an architectural landscape that operates within two distinct visual planes. The stillness and symmetry of the arches and columns on the left side of the painting draw the eye toward the painting's center, a bastion of peace, tranquility. The kinetic energy unleashed by the explosion depicted on the right side of the painting is embodied by the fragments of the columns suspended in midair. Both sides of the painting are bathed in a warm light. The violent beauty of the crumbling architectural detail is highlighted by the apparent absence of smoke or dust from the explosion. Like the more orderly left side, the chaos of the right side of the canvas also draws the eye toward the distant center, which appears to serve as a desired refuge to the human figures depicted running toward it. Despite the great detail depicted in both sides of the foreground, the center dominates and unifies the perspective, reasserting a sense of harmony into what at first appears to be a tense standoff between order and disorder.

The presence of François de Nomé's painting in the household creates tension between Sofía and Esteban, the two cousins who are the novel's protagonists, precisely because it appears to stop time in its tracks. Esteban becomes mesmerized by the painting's uncanny ability to immobilize a catastrophe, while Sofía feels repulsed by how the artificiality of the medium endlessly postpones the completion of the action it most literally depicts, the fall of the cathedral's columns. Like the epigraphs from Goya, which will be discussed shortly, the painting *Explosion dans une église* is a European work of art. The narrator mentions that the piece hails from Naples but is the work of a French painter; this artist is not actually named within the narrative because neither Sofía, her older brother Carlos, nor Esteban know who painted it. As young men and women who come into possession of the family estate through the recent death of the patriarch, none of these characters are full consumers of the cultural capital they have inherited. Because of this narrative blind spot, readers who wish to fully decode the supplement of the novel by following up its extradiegetic allusions must act like art sleuths: first, they need to determine whether the painting described exists and, if so, take steps to track it down on their own so they can see it for themselves. Having done that, they must decide whether their own interpretation of the visual material accords more with Esteban's or Sofía's appraisal of the same. The narrator does not settle the argument one way or another by suggesting a third or objective reading of this visual text.[40] This unresolved conflict highlights the painting's status within the novel primarily as an aesthetic object, a decorative flight of fancy rather than a historical document that happens to be artistic in nature.

Carpentier's *Explosion in a Cathedral* presents itself to readers as a self-contained art museum by using the epigraph as a tool to exhibit historical European paintings and engravings whose relationship to the plot of the novel is distant at best. It stages its own tour of these works by rearranging the order in which they appear within their original contexts, thus prompting curious readers to conduct their own research beyond the fictive texts to find out what connections, if any, exist between the incidents depicted in the visual text and those narrated in each selected chapter. The virtual museum tour proceeds through mimesis: the young protagonists, Sofía and her cousin Esteban, are the readers' stand-ins as they travel throughout the Caribbean and witness the aftermath of both the French and Haitian revolutions. They are the orphaned heirs of a middle-class merchant in Cuba who meet and befriend Victor Hughes, a historical figure who worked as an agent of the French government. Sofía and Esteban travel with him as Hughes takes control of the island of Guadeloupe, winning it back from the British, who had invaded it during the Haitian Revolution. He abolishes slavery, but Napoleon later reimposes it on the island in 1804. Enthralled by this magnetic leader, Sofía and Esteban follow him as he moves around the different slave colonies in the Caribbean. Eventually the cousins leave for Spain, where they get caught up in the Spanish uprising against the invading French forces, and fade out of the narrative altogether. Plotwise, the novel's conclusion brings together the chaos of the events following the Haitian Revolution and France's renewed attempts to exercise its imperial control over its Caribbean colonies and its invasion of Spain.

Through its emphasis on what visual art can show, the novel highlights the impossibility of literature to depict the pain and suffering of others empathetically or authentically. Most literally, the novel enacts its own admission of the failure of representation by not establishing any noticeable correspondence between the events that transpire in chapters prefaced by epigraphs and the images to which Goya assigned the titles. Slaves are present in the background of the events that transpire in *Explosion in a Cathedral*; but they speak no lines nor are they in any way distinguishable from one another, unlike in Carpentier's earlier novel about the Haitian Revolution, *The Kingdom of This World*. This narrative distance between the protagonists and the slave masses ensures that neither Sofía and Esteban, nor the readers themselves, learn many details about the historical reality of daily life under bondage in the Caribbean.

Francisco de Goya, *Estragos de la guerra* / *Disasters of War* (1820)

Like Dabydeen does with Hogarth, both Arenas and Carpentier turn to the work of the Spanish painter Francisco José de Goya y Lucientes (1746–1828), especially to those paintings and engravings that decry royal tyranny and social injustice, in order to write the violence of slavery in Spain's New World colonies back into Spanish history. The thirteen epigraphs that appear at the beginning of selected chapters correlate with the titles of some of the sketches in the series *Disasters of War*, engravings Goya made as a protest against the Napoleonic invasion of the Iberian Peninsula and Spain's overseas possessions in the New World from 1808 until 1814. This instance of intertextuality constitutes an extradiegetic juxtaposition that implicitly suggests historical parallels between the slaves' uprising and demand for both personal freedom and national independence in Haiti, and the Spanish populace's desperate attempts to fight the loss of national sovereignty and freedom at the hands of the French imperial forces. Because the epigraphs refer to events that postdate those chronicled in the specific chapters of the novel, they constitute what the critic Catherine Wall has called "futuristic anachronisms," while the use of the painting as a leitmotif linking the violence and anticlericalism of a past historical time with the events that will unfold in some future constitutes a somewhat less jarring temporal disruption because of its transparent role as an aesthetic commodity within the household.[41]

Carpentier creates a space for mourning the death, torture, and mistreatment of these slaves through his repeated use of epigraphs corresponding to the titles of Goya's engravings. By interjecting references to the atrocities the French committed in Spain, *Explosion in a Cathedral* implies that they were also capable of much worse abuses in their own colonies against subjects whose humanity they did not recognize. The implied author of the novel attributes to Goya all but one of the epigraphs that appear in the novel, but does not indicate that they correspond to titles of the engravings; the novel appears to give equal weight to the text from the Spanish painter and that of the excerpt from the book of Job, the only other epigraph in the novel. This absence creates discursive dissonance by highlighting the titles of the epigraphs without making any reference to the images themselves.

This is yet another instance in which readers who want to fully make sense of the epigraphs must perform the role of art historians and sort

through the catalogue of Goya's works until they find the corresponding visual material. Then they must rearrange the order of the images
contained within the *Disasters of War* series so they correspond to the
implied author's arrangement, and not to the order in which Goya produced them and in which they were printed. Readers who undergo this
long process learn more about art than they ultimately do about the history of slavery in any of the affected Caribbean slave states at the turn
of the nineteenth century.

Carpentier follows the Spanish painter's own example of privileging
the written text so as to limit the possible interpretations of individual
images that constitute a visual narrative or pseudojournalistic account of
war decades before the birth of the photographic essay by using Goya's
titles as epigraphs within his novel. In the concluding chapter, Esteban
and Sofía become caught up in the Napoleonic invasion of Spain and
presumably die, a convenient plot twist that allows the two historical
French military campaigns that have framed the Cuban family saga to
intersect: the reimposition of slavery through French West Indian territories after the Haitian Revolution and the impulse to spread the French
empire's reach by claiming the Spanish throne. As representatives of the
Enlightenment, they literally disappear into the Spanish countryside
just as the Enlightenment principles that spurred the Revolution and
formation of the Grand Army are subsumed in the conventional imperial campaign Napoleon conducts in the Iberian Peninsula. Though
the events narrated in this final chapter correspond more directly to the
wave of Spanish nationalistic feeling and chaos of May 2 and 3, 1808,
which Goya famously depicted in paintings of that name, the novel's
denouement features yet another reference to a specific engraving within
the *Disasters of War* series, *It Happened Like This*, which depicts the
murder of a priest against his church's altar railing as looters walk by
laden with bags full of gold candleholders and crucifixes.[42] In the closing
pages, however, Esteban and Sofía join the throngs of Spaniards rising
up against the French army. The critique against anticlericalism implicit
in the engraving shows that no life is sacred in times of war.

Francisco de Goya, *Fernando VII with Royal Mantle* (1814)

Whereas Carpentier colonizes Spanish art through his appropriation of
Goya's work in the service of Cuban historical fiction, Reinaldo Arenas
literally reanimates the ghost of Spanish colonialist rule of Cuba by simultaneously parodying the Spanish royal family and their prominent

court painter in his novel. Like *Explosion in a Cathedral*, *Graveyard of the Angels* also features a painting by Goya that has no explicit connection to slavery at all—the 1814 portrait of *Fernando VII with Royal Mantle*, now housed in the Museo del Prado, in Madrid. Arenas's reference to this painting is not as political as Carpentier's allusions to European art. Instead, *Graveyard of the Angels* parodies the image contained within the painting itself, claiming it has deadly supernatural powers. The narrator traces the painting's fatal effects to its astoundingly faithful reproduction of its subject's facial features: "an outsized, diabolical mouth, huge, pointed ears, a gigantic triple chin, sparse, ashen hair, a spectral, depraved face, a harrowing nose, or bulging sinister eyes."[43] Since all who see the painting reportedly die because of the toxic effect of beholding "such horror and malignity" at once, the narrator assures the "curious and impertinent reader" that his account of the painting is not only accurate, but also authentic because he is "the artist, its creator—Francisco de Goya y Lucientes."[44] In yet another instance of transworld identity in this novel, Goya-the-narrator celebrates the integrity of his own artistic vision by emphasizing how his portrait does not hide the truth of the monarch's ugliness. He also points to the cruelty with which Spain governed its New World territories from afar, by shipping the painting around from colony to colony so as to kill those who did not follow royal decrees with sufficient strictness. This last plot point is a clear allusion to Carpentier's *Explosion in a Cathedral*, where the novel tracks how the use of the guillotine as an instrument of punishment gradually spreads from one Francophone Caribbean island to another in the wake of the Haitian Revolution.

The only survivors of the wrath of the Spanish Crown in the chapter titled "The Philharmonic Society Ball" are the two hundred black musicians who blind themselves on purpose so as not to perish by inadvertently glancing at the portrait. The passage never discusses the musicians' legal status—the blackness of their skin serves as their only identity marker in a novel where all characters are caricatures of exaggerated social types found within the nineteenth-century Cuban slavocracy. Like *Explosion in a Cathedral*, *Graveyard of the Angels* portrays slaves collectively as an undifferentiated mass. The black musicians, for example, are impervious to the dangerous effects of visual art as a commercial venture, but must nonetheless ply their musical art in order to survive.

Arenas's allusion to Goya's painting in *Graveyard of the Angels* contributes to the general pattern of excess—in wealth, in violence, and in indulgence—that is at the heart of his critique of both the Spanish colonial rule of the island from its conquest until the end of the Spanish-American War in 1898, as well as his own opposition to the repressive Communist government led by Fidel Castro. The novel's repeated use of transworld identity suggests that artists live on through their work, but that their public personas belong to all who may claim them. In outing himself as Goya "the artist," the narrator does not give up his claim to firsthand knowledge of Cuban history. By imagining a Spanish artist's concern with the Cuban sociocultural crisis of conscience, *Graveyard of the Angels* emphasizes the lack of a great Cuban visual artist during this particular period to bear witness to the atrocities perpetrated under the system of slavery as well as under colonial control. This continued dependence on the artistic resources of the European motherland stands in for the dependent relationship that slaves have with their masters in slave-holding societies.

Because of the passage of time separating twenty-first-century readers from the composition of these works of art, they have now accrued symbolic importance as both aesthetic objects and historical documents: they depict a world no one alive now can remember. Viewers feel personally attached to the subject of paintings or illustrations, be it a person or a place, without necessarily feeling a connection to the artist him- or herself. The paintings and engravings themselves function as historical snapshots of what was going on in the Caribbean islands in the early nineteenth century.

3 Ethnographic Museums

The Literary Diorama

As I ARGUE in chapter 1, Maryse Condé's *I, Tituba*, Patrick Chamoiseau's *L'esclave*, and Reinaldo Arenas's *Graveyard of the Angels* use intertextual citations to place themselves within the framework of a national literary tradition and/or history in Barbados, Martinique, and Cuba, respectively, regardless of their authors' birthplace. In contrast, the postmodern historical novels about slavery discussed in this chapter—Fred D'Aguiar's *The Longest Memory* (1995), Caryl Phillips's *Crossing the River* (1993) and *Higher Ground* (1995), and both volumes of Maryse Condé's epic family saga *Segu* (1984 and 1985)—are part of a large diasporic project that purposefully rejects the geographic specificity of national boundaries in favor of a more inclusive, transnational understanding of slavery as a phenomenon instituted on a large scale by the European colonial domination of the American continents and the Caribbean islands. These novels efface their geographic specificity as Caribbean literary products through their insistence on the importance of their African characters and settings.[1] This act of narrative distancing effectively creates a liminal space in which the Caribbean writers and those few Caribbean subjects who appear as characters in the narratives function as mere spectators of, or witnesses to, the historical drama of slavery as it plays out on distant shores.

The Longest Memory, *Segu*, *Crossing the River*, and *Higher Ground* make use of representational strategies, such as the diorama and the panoramic mural, usually employed by ethnographic museums to convey to their audiences a snapshot of life in faraway places. The French painter J. L. M. Daguerre, who later invented the photographic technique of the daguerreotype, developed the diorama in 1821 as a novel way of displaying large-scale paintings as a spectacle for paying audiences.[2] Daguerre displayed his paintings in a building erected especially for the purpose, and through the manipulation of light and the rules of perspective, as well as the movement of the seating, the paintings gave the illusion of space and three-dimensionality and change. Ethnographic museums have since adopted the term "diorama" to describe those of their installations that use painted backgrounds and trompe l'oeil to heighten the realism of scenes and objects within a given display.

Dioramas used within museum settings blur the boundaries between truth and fiction; they facilitate an experience of total sensory engagement for visitors in order to convey the illusion of authenticity. Although they are purely the work of the imagination, the painted backgrounds within dioramas complement the physical and/or cultural objects featured most prominently within the display, be they animals or objects, giving them a specific context in which to be regarded. In short, the juxtaposition between actual object and imaginary background creates a visual narrative. Dioramas give museum visitors the impression that they are seeing the featured object in its natural or proper setting instead of displayed in isolation within a sterile environment. This impression is clearly false, since the museum is indeed a neutral setting far removed from where the animal or clay pot was obtained. By reminding visitors that the items they see displayed around them are not inherently artistic or historically significant but, rather, have specific functions and values within their societies of origin, dioramas are an important tool to counteract the "museum effect" described in the introduction.

In this chapter, I use the term "literary diorama" to refer to mostly descriptive narrative set pieces in novels by Phillips, Condé, and D'Aguiar that paint a picture of tribal life and domestic customs in Africa. These extended forays into description in postmodern fiction can serve as the "authentic" background against which readers evaluate individual scenes, characters, or circumstances in the novels. Often these literary dioramas employ excessive detail to give the illusion that they are simple slices of life taken from a larger reality. *Higher Ground, Crossing the River, The Longest Memory*, and *Segu* present overdetermined set pieces composed of specific characters who perform their distinctive "African" cultural identities for the reader. The theme shared by all of these dioramas is the breakup of the African nuclear family unit as perpetrated by the system of slavery.[3] The rest of the tales contained within the novels refer back to these traumatic scenes of African life in some way.

In the United States, experience museums such as the controversial Abraham Lincoln Presidential Museum in Illinois make the connection between the past of slavery and the threat that oppressive labor system posed to the nuclear family unit through the use of the diorama. This museum and presidential library celebrates the authenticity of its historical artifacts even as it touts its use of a professional production company to enhance its "storytelling technologies." The exhibit entitled The Journey, Part 1: The Pre-Presidential Years features a diorama entitled *The Slave Auction*, whose connection to Abraham Lincoln is entirely speculative. Its online summary in the museum's official Web site reads as follows: "The horrors of a family at auction being torn from one another by slavery and sold in separate directions are presented. This was a common tragedy in America at that time. Did Lincoln encounter such a scene during his trip down the Mississippi when he worked as a ferryman?"[4] The diorama is made up of life-size mannequins of a slave woman whose fully dressed son is pulling at her long skirts while his father, dressed only in a pair of sackcloth pants and wearing shackles around his ankles, is being led away. A white auctioneer stands behind the family with his arm raised up in the air.

Covering the controversial museum's opening, the reporters Christi Parsons and Ray Long mention that: "Curators say many visitors have been moved to tears by a lifelike diorama of a black family being separated at a slave auction."[5] Three-dimensional representations of select cultural or historical scenes like these elicit a visceral response from visitors by confronting them with the spatial reality of events they usually think of through the curricular framework of history lessons. The only justification for including this melodramatic diorama as a "scene" from the young future president's life seems to be the fact that Lincoln effectively ended such scenes of family trauma through his presidential leadership, demonstrated by the Emancipation Proclamation and his unwavering commitment to bringing the Confederate States back under Union control.

An example of a more historically grounded use of the diorama as a visual narrative tool to convey information about the experience of slavery can be found in the International Museum of Slavery, located in Liverpool, England. In 2007, this museum replaced what had been a permanent gallery with an exhibit titled Transatlantic Slavery: Against Human Dignity. According to Anthony Tibbles's entry on the museum's Web site, the exhibit was organized around two central dioramas: the first, "a diorama of the trading process in action and a display of typical trade goods," was meant to illustrate European involvement in Africa, while the second was "a diorama of a slave auction in Brazil."[6] Of the two, the diorama set in Brazil represents the site at which most families became separated: the auction block.

Since then, the museum has also added an online feature called "Slaves' Stories," which uses fiction as a medium through which to make their diorama displays more interactive. Featuring four representative African characters, "Slaves' Stories" allows users to click on each of their icons to learn more about their stories of what constituted typical African life for four different ethnic groups before their capture. It also includes first-person accounts of what the slaves experienced during their transport in the Middle Passage, and of life in bondage in a new place. Of the four Africans depicted, two are children who are torn apart from their parents and villages by capture: Okechukwu, an Igbo, and Kofi, a Fanti.[7] This museum's use of the interactivity of the World Wide Web and the powerful evocative medium of first-person narration conveys a sense that mere images are not enough to communicate the stories that curators, historians, and other museum professionals hope their visitors learn about during their actual, or virtual, engagement with the collections.

The same is true of the literary techniques D'Aguiar, Condé, and Phillips use to achieve dioramic effects within their novels. Always already texts about the past, dioramas are organized from the vantage point of what is meaningful to present-day audiences. Both literary and visual dioramas represent the curator's/writer's interpretation of a particular point in (a past) time; therefore, they in no way convey an immediate "authentic" reality but, at most, offer only a mediated version of past events through the prism of what the present finds important. Their very lack of geographic specificity renders dioramas hyperreal—more representative than images of any one location because their aggregate qualities surpass those of an individual site. To this end, their formal composed quality and the effort to represent the typical create an impossibly consistent and coherent collection of meaningful and significant objects that only comes into focus through the a temporal ethnographic gaze. Neither mere aesthetic objects nor primary documents in and of themselves, dioramas are useful interpretive constructs that display general historical facts freely adapted to apply to a collective Everyman and, therefore, to no one in particular.

In his meditation about anthropological museums and their relationship to the cultures they represent, James Clifford invokes Mary Louise Pratt's work when he suggests that we view museums as "contact zones":

"'museums' increasingly work the borderlands between different worlds, histories, and cosmologies. . . . [O]bjects currently in the great museums are travelers, crossers—some strongly 'diasporic' with powerful, still very meaningful, ties elsewhere."[8] By placing the term "museums" inside quotation marks, Clifford opens up the concept beyond its traditional association with physical, bricks-and-mortar institutions that act as repositories for, and venues for the display of, artifacts collected long ago and far away. Clifford's invitation to consider how objects themselves may be "diasporic" through their out-of-context presence in a Western institution whose mission is both to educate and entertain presents a fruitful way for us to read the African and American literary dioramas present in all these postmodern novels as reflective of the Caribbean writers' own views about diaspora.

Barbara Kirshenblatt-Gimblett offers another alternative when she explains that "ethnographic artifacts are objects of ethnography. They are artifacts created by ethnographers. Objects become ethnographic by virtue of being defined, segmented, detached, and carried away by ethnographers."[9] Ethnographic museums display objects belonging to an individual culture, but taken away from their original contexts. Kirshenblatt-Gimblett draws a distinction between academic ethnographic displays and the physical reenactment of history and/or culture carried out by professional performers in front of a live audience in public settings: "It is one thing, however, when ethnography is inscribed in books or displayed behind glass, at a remove in space, time, and language from the site described. It is quite another when people themselves are the medium of ethnographic representation, when they perform themselves, whether at home to tourists or at world's fairs, homeland entertainments, or folklife festivals—when they become living signs of themselves."[10] Ethnographic museums often construct life-size dioramas as hyperreal representations of how people "perform themselves." The interactive dioramas included within the Streets of Old Milwaukee exhibition in the Milwaukee Public Museum are a demonstration of the first category of ethnographic representation. I describe this exhibition in more detail later in the chapter, but here I identify it simply as display that uses three-dimensional house- and storefronts with windows that provide a view into the interiors decorated with period objects to recreate different aspects of local culture in situ. By placing each type of ethnic household or business in close proximity to one from a different ethnicity, the exhibition represents the ethnic and cultural diversity present in Milwaukee in the 1880s.

The literary dioramas I discuss in *Segu*, *Higher Ground*, and *Crossing the River* fall into the second category of ethnographic representation Kirshenblatt-Gimblett names because they constitute instances in which characters become "living signs," so to speak, of their own ethnic or national identities. The descriptions of "traditional" African family life in these novels function as normative domestic scenes from which specific characters are suddenly, and irrevocably, separated through the transatlantic slave trade. The literary dioramas within each of these texts portray African tribal life as more culturally authentic than the kind of makeshift domesticity enslaved characters devise for themselves once they arrive upon the shores of the New World and enter into the harsh realities of plantation life.

Like the paintings and engravings discussed in the previous chapter, the literary dioramas that these postmodern novels create present a historically significant projection of iconic scenes from the past. This allows the reader/visitor to witness firsthand the cadences and routines of the "traditional" life from which the enslaved characters are cut off. On a literal level, Phillips's *Higher Ground* and *Crossing the River*, Condé's *Segu*, and D'Aguiar's *The Longest Memory* thematize the harrowing separation of parents from their children. The scenes of domestic tranquility in Africa prior to the capture and enslavement of the focal character serve as the ersatz painted backgrounds against which readers view the enslaved character as a featured literary object within these narrative dioramas. Because they so convincingly create a sense of these enslaved character's childhood home as the place where they rightfully belong, these literary dioramas cast a long shadow, which has the effect of making these characters seem eternally out of place in the locales where they end up.

These texts also invoke the trauma of familial separation as a metaphor for the forced dispersal of African peoples away from their continent of origin. The Caribbean region does not figure within this dynamic of separation because of its geographical insularity. The inter-island trade in slaves was relatively small compared to both the triangular trade routes linking Europe, Africa, and the Americas and the domestic North American slave route along the Mississippi River. The textual dioramas featured in each novel highlight the family unit's role as the most basic (and, presumably, most authentic) representation of the social structure of the African and American civilizations affected by the slave trade. To balance out the scenes of rupture or destruction of the family unit in the literary dioramas, *Segu*, *Higher Ground*, and *Crossing the River* posit the existence of alternative communities that provide emotional support or comfort to the enslaved person disconsolate over his or her separation from the family.

Dioramas of African Family Life

Maryse Condé's family saga *Segu* and Caryl Phillips's *Higher Ground* and *Crossing the River* feature set pieces that take place in sub-Saharan Africa.[11] These novels' shared Afrocentric outlook refuses to essentialize the continent as merely the helpless victim of European imperialism; in their respective tales, Phillips and Condé emphasize the diversity of lived experience within tribal society, as well as the internal conflicts that led to African participation in the transatlantic slave trade.[12] Each text's description of an "authentic" African family in its own "native" setting constitutes the literary diorama, though the texts themselves quickly problematize these absolutist terms. Despite their shared Afrocentrism, *Higher Ground*, *Crossing the River*, and *Segu* reject the idea of a return to Africa as the solution to mend the broken ties of traditional kinship structures. Instead, these three novels promote a newly reconfigured model of nonhierarchical kinship structures that extends beyond the barriers of space and time to maintain an ongoing, vibrant, and transnational familial identity that includes a diasporic element.

Condé's and Phillips's novels portray their own versions of a "traditional" tribal African family defined as a patriarchal, polygamous kinship structure, where one man fathers children by multiple wives and the entire extended family lives together in an enclosed compound. Neither Phillips's nor Condé's portrayals of African kinship systems are any more historically accurate than the other. Condé finds the continuity of African family structures comforting; she reads this refusal to change as a measure of resistance to the cultural imperialism of religious and commercial outsiders. Phillips condemns the rigidity of native customs that refuse to change with the times and therefore inflict as much emotional damage on the life of the affected ethnic groups as the Europeans mete out physical torture.

Each novelistic interpretation bears the curatorial stamp of its respective writer's view of the African diaspora as either isolated and culturally distinct groups of people with little in common besides race (Phillips), or else as a large, dynamic network of distantly related societies and cultures orbiting around a mother continent (Condé).[13] Their contradictory opinions regarding the African diaspora notwithstanding, both writers' decision to set part of their slavery tales in Africa suggest not only their strict adherence to historical sources but, more importantly, their continued emotional investment and interest in creating in their novels what Arjun Appadurai has called "diasporic public spheres." Appadurai defines these networks as follows: "Diasporic public spheres, diverse among themselves, are the crucibles of a postnational political order. The engines of their discourse are mass media (both interactive and expressive) and the movement of refugees, activists, students, and laborers."[14] Within their widely available, interactive, and expressive historical novels, Condé and Phillips portray African histories and cultures as part of the postnational heritage shared by Afro-diasporic populations. The absence of the Caribbean from these texts reinforces the idea that the interpersonal and transnational connections matter more in shaping a diasporic identity than do emotional ties of loyalty to any one nation-state or locale.

The literary dioramas about African life featured in *Segu, Higher Ground*, and *Crossing the River* are the objects that convey a sense of authenticity by emphasizing the exotic otherness of the culture even as this message is transmitted through the familiar medium of the novel acting as a virtual ethnographic museum. In his chapter on museums, Clifford analyzes two American exhibits featuring African art in communication with European art, and concludes: "Africa and Europe have been thrown together by destructive and creative histories of empire, commerce, and travel; each uses the other's traditions to remake its own."[15] In this context, I would like to consider briefly how two permanent exhibitions in museums in Milwaukee, Wisconsin—the European Village exhibit of the Milwaukee Public Museum and the African Village exhibit of America's Black Holocaust Museum—can shed some light on Condé's use of an extended literary diorama in her novels.

A unified visual text, the African Village exhibit consists of one panoramic mural that illustrates various aspects of life in a West African setting. Rather than depicting the village and its inhabitants through an ethnographic lens, by emphasizing its particular customs and traditions, this generic depiction of a "typical" village is cast ideologically as the innocent victim of ruthless European imperialism and mercantilism. The museum's Web site promises that the exhibit will deliver "a view into the rarely shown images of a great culture and people."[16] In the larger context of the museum in which it appears, the mural immediately precedes the three-dimensional diorama of a slave ship for the Middle Passage: A Voyage to Slavery exhibit, which is a fifteen-foot reproduction of a slaving vessel "from the vantage point of Africans enslaved in a cargo hold," as the Web site proclaims. Together, these two iconic scenes, one of typical family life before the chaos and disruption caused by the transatlantic slave trade, and the other an imaginary firsthand perspective of the trauma of enslavement and displacement of the Middle Passage voyage itself, are the sum total of the museum's view of the origins of the African diaspora.

The European Village exhibit in the Milwaukee Public Museum showcases various re-creations of typical domestic scenes in the several European countries from which people immigrated to Wisconsin. Both installations present their featured peoples as the viewing public's revered ancestors; the different histories of immigration that brought them to the American continent are likewise intertwined on some level. The interactive, three-dimensional installation in the Milwaukee museum effaces geographic national boundaries to present a somewhat uniform picture of the European continent as the home of predominantly "white" immigrants to the New World, figured here specifically as the state of Wisconsin. Spectators walk in and around the "streets" of a simulacrum of Old Milwaukee and look in the windows of each domicile or business to see scenes of "authentic" cultural performance, often related to the consumption or preparation of meals.

Despite sharing a similar emphasis on these two emblematic representations of African life, Condé's portrayal of this same historical time period in her novel expands upon and complicates the ideological assumptions that underlie the two African-themed dioramas in the Black Holocaust Museum. Rather than blaming only European imperialism for the disorder and disruption that arose from the development of the transatlantic slave trade, Condé grounds her depiction of tribal life in Africa in an understanding of the African slave trade as a longstanding means of dealing with one's enemies and subjugating weaker ethnic groups. She also discusses the phenomenon of Islamic expansion throughout Africa, the conversion of formerly pagan individuals, and the Muslim participation in the slave trade.

The family compound–centered dioramas of *Segu* deemphasize the cyclical nature of time by conflating key set pieces surrounding recurring events like births, deaths, and journeys within the animist, Muslim, and Christian branches of the Traore family.[17] Much as Condé anchors her African literary dioramas with plotlines tracing the dispersal of the family unit in both of her novels, the European Village exhibition features a similar emphasis on the dispersal of various European peoples from their countries of origin, as the Milwaukee Public Museum Web site reveals: "The Village provides a picture of daily life, skills and traditions that were characteristic of many Europeans who came to the United States at the time. This setting has been created to promote a better understanding of some of the diverse European heritages in the United States." These "white" immigration dioramas emphasize those groups' ties to the Old World and the persistence of the cultural traditions they brought with them in modern-day Milwaukee. European immigration to the New World colonies was a volitional act on the part of autonomous subjects seeking greater freedom of opportunity and religion, unlike the forced repatriation and subsequent sale of millions of African slaves who were brought in chains, against their wills, to be treated like chattel at auction houses. Whereas the Streets of Old Milwaukee exhibit portrays images of family togetherness, Condé's historical novel thematizes the rupture of the extended family unit and/or the idealized village society. The latter is disrupted, corrupted, and destroyed from without by incursions by white Europeans and their African collaborators.

While the Milwaukee display explicitly avoids discussing the sociopolitical conflicts and prejudices that may have existed between the various European countries from which immigrants to the state hailed, *Segu* imagines Africa as a continent full of diverse groups of people who come into conflict with one another over religion, commerce, and land. *Segu* is the first volume of Maryse Condé's two-volume epic novel about the Bambara Empire in Mali; it takes place during the centuries when the transatlantic slave trade flourished. The novel conveys Condé's version of the traditional African kinship system and celebrates its dedication to preserving family traditions, language, and cultural values. *Segu* traces the fortunes of the Traore family and those who live within its compound. They survive attacks by slave traders, Islamic militants, and neighboring tribes. Together, the two novels read like an enormous panoramic mural depicting a modern re-creation of what life may have been like in the past. The scholar Chinosole has argued that, "Like the traditional African epic, *Segu* is performative, addressing an audience in the here and now with historical insights on the 18th and 19th centuries."[18] Chinosole attributes this text's performative quality to the griot role Condé plays as the storyteller in the African oral storytelling narrative tradition. I, on the contrary, locate the novel's performative dimension in the literary dioramas it creates through long and detailed descriptions of life within the African family compound. The scenes of functional and orderly family and village life contrast with the sense of loss that follows the breakup of a family unit through kidnapping, desertion, suicide, murder, or war.

More than any other text discussed in this chapter, Condé's epic family drama *Segu* showcases different aspects of slavery both from an transatlantic perspective—by including characters who find themselves in bondage in Brazil, in the Caribbean islands, as well as in the African slave ports—as well as from the perspective of the internal African slave trade, in which captured warriors were enslaved by rival tribes after losing a battle, long before the arrival of European colonialists. In its mixed didactic and dramatic tone, the novel shows, rather than tells, its audience how painful and confusing the loss of personal freedom can be. Set against the background of the vast Bambara Empire, the opening chapter in *Segu* emphasizes the family's wealth and high status within this society: "Dousika was a nobleman or *yerewolo*, a member of the royal council, a personal friend of the king and the father of ten legitimate sons, ruling as *fa* or patriarch over five families, his own and those of his younger brothers. His compound reflected his standing in Segu society. Its tall façade overlooking the street was ornamented with sculptures as well as triangular patterns carved into the clay, and surmounted by turrets of varying height and pleasing effects. Within were a number of flat-roofed huts, also of mud, connected by a series of courtyards."[19] The novel portrays the futures of this family and of Segu as intertwined, much like physical dioramas in museums offer up a representative family unit that stands in for the whole of a given society.

Already from this first view of life in Africa, slavery is at the heart of the Traore family's prosperity, both as an inherited system, the "house slaves," and as a method of punishment for disgrace in the field of battle. Thus, it comes as no surprise that several of the Traore kin eventually become slaves themselves who end up transported to foreign lands. While the extended family unit suffers loss and separation, the novel's overall tone is celebratory—the elders look upon the abduction, dispersal, and conversion of various family members as minor footnotes in the larger story of how the family adapts to changes to ensure its continued survival within the empire. The Traore family line endures all and remains in its village.

To Caribbean readers, the African settings of this two-part epic novel seem "foreign." The Traore compound dioramas are "diasporic" in Clifford's sense of "diasporic objects" because their Africanness conveys different things depending on the context and the audience that regards them. The perspectives of the characters vary. For the unlucky Traore family members who find themselves far from home, the memory of these domestic scenes allows them to develop a diasporic, rather than an African, consciousness of themselves. They mourn for the loss of their traditional way of life in the home of their ancestors and thereby experience both grief over their forced separation from kin, and nostalgia for an idealized memory of the compound and its comforting routine.

The character of Eucharistus, a Traore man formerly known as Babatunde, proves an interesting case study in this context. Born in Africa, he was baptized a Christian and receives his religious education in England, where he quickly climbs the ranks of the church hierarchy. From there, Eucharistus is sent to Jamaica, where he is to find a wife, and he then prepares himself to follow his orders and go spread the Good News in the interior of the African continent. Eucharistus actively mourns for the death of his African self-identity, bristling against the thought of having to convert fellow Africans into an English faith and way of life. Because the pagan religion Babatunde/ Eucharistus rejected when he embraced Christianity is organized around ancestor worship, his conversion entails yet another break with the African family unit of his youth. Even as he establishes his own, Westernized nuclear family unit through marriage, Babatunde/Eucharistus finds himself in the unlikely situation of having to act as the agent of further disruption to African families.

Condé gives her readers a visual supplement to her fictive narrative through the paratextual elements included in the novel's front matter, such as various maps of the region and the Traore family tree. As a Western document reflecting the current interest in the African American and Afro-Caribbean community in finding out about their African ancestors, the family tree diagrams function as a virtual visitor's map to the dioramic mural that is the plot of the novel.[20] The many marriages, births, and deaths noted within the family tree constitute key aspects of the overall dioramic mural Condé sets up for her readers within the novel, but the genealogical texts themselves are not available to the characters except as part and parcel of their ancestor worship. Those members of the Traore extended family who remain in the land of their birth go on with their daily lives; they change and adapt their ways according to the passing of historical epochs or shifting political alliances without letting these variances define them. For them, the domestic scenes are mere touchstones in the family lore, parts of their heritage that help explain why the family's socioeconomic status and political alliances have shifted through the generations. They rarely learn about the fate of their relatives who have been forcibly taken away. The juxtaposition of the supplementary materials with the fictive narrative implicitly contrasts the internal changes sweeping through the African continent—such as the spread of Islam—to the external changes that happen to African-born characters as they struggle to assimilate within their new societies in the Caribbean, Brazil, and elsewhere in the New World. In Condé's historical diorama, the one constant that spans across time and space is the characters' identity as members of the Traore family. The nature of the family structure has been affected by historical change, but the bond of kinship remains intact, however far the bloodlines stray from their home of origin.

Unlike Condé, Caryl Phillips does not rely upon self-referential, ex-tratextual diagrams to convey to readers his critique of African society, but employs the diorama within the novel itself as his most frequent stylistic organizing principle.

Whereas the two volumes of *Segu* constitute one coherent family saga spanning several generations, Phillips's historical novels are comprised of discrete narrative units whose topics and settings vary across time, space, and genre without providing much explanation as to why or how they belong together to form an overarching storyline. Phillips's depiction of African complicity with the slave trade as a constant theme in his novels can be read as a diasporic expression of Afrocentrism, albeit more indicting than Condé's. After all, without the large-scale importation of Africans to serve as unpaid agricultural labor, the story of New World slavery would only cover the Spanish Crown's *encomienda* system, which awarded both tracts of land and their native Amerindian inhabitants to selected Spanish colonists.

Caryl Phillips takes a more sinister view of the African extended family than does Maryse Condé; while both novelists suggest that the preservation of the larger African kinship unit comes at the expense of the sacrifice of disposable individuals, Condé depicts this as the unfortunate effect of interaction with colonizing outside forces—be they African, Arab, or European—while Phillips places the blame squarely upon the inflexibility of "native" African patriarchal structures. Both novelists emphasize the continent's historically diverse experience of internal and external enslavement, but where Condé strives to create a positive vision of African cultural richness unmitigated by its various brushes with Eastern and Western colonizers in her texts, Phillips's *Crossing the River* and *Higher Ground* emphasize the betrayal and displacement members of the African diaspora feel even to this day. Condé's museum-novels look backwards to the past, while Phillips's museum-novels project the ongoing relationship of the history they contain into our understanding and construction of the present through the shared experience of oppression.

Of the three distinct episodes or chapters in *Higher Ground*, "Heartland" is the only one that directly addresses African complicity in the slave trade. At the microlevel, "Heartland" depicts the separation of an actual family unit by slave traders to illustrate how the institution of slavery affected rural African villages. At the macrolevel, the slave fort itself symbolizes the metaphorical separation of African "offspring," whatever their age or circumstance, from their continental "motherland" through the Middle Passage voyage. Then "Heartland" can be read as a literary diorama that highlights the intersection of oppression from without (the British) and within (intertribal warfare and betrayal) with disastrous effects upon the most basic structure of social formation: the family unit.

The first-person narrator of "Heartland" is an African working as a translator for the British at a slave fort like those in Elmina Castle in Ghana. When speaking to the fort's newly arrived British governor, the African narrator briefly recalls his own traumatic separation from his nuclear family ("I tell him about my village, about the woman I called wife, about the child I called son")[21] so as to put a human face on the concept of bondage for the neophyte administrator, who is unfamiliar with the distasteful details of slaving. The first-person narrator reports this conversation rather than depicting it, thereby denying readers of the tale direct access to his private emotions regarding this separation from his family. By mining events from his own past, the narrator acts as both a native informant to an uninitiated outsider (the governor) and collaborator with the colonial exploiters of his people (the British). The repeated use of the past tense, "I called," implies that this pattern of claiming kinship existed at one time but is now in the past. Since he is physically separated from his native village and the life he once led there, the narrator no longer feels connected to the family to which he once belonged. Given the context of the setting, readers can assume that the narrator's wife and child could be dead or that they could have been taken far away across the seas already.

When he is eventually transported to the New World, the narrator evokes the memory of his previous life as he stands on the auction block in an unspecified port, but it brings him no comfort: "Neither my long-forgotten wife, nor my disregarded son, discovered a way to minister to my cold heart."[22] Rhetorically, the narrator blames his wife and son for failing to leave an emotional impression upon him that would sustain the narrator during his time of trouble. This formulation allows the narrator to absolve himself for having "forgotten" and "disregarded" his family. While these two isolated allusions to the past would appear to be the key scenes of family separation occasioned by slavery in "Heartland," the traumatic break they describe takes place extradiegetically, before the start of events in the narrative.

What the novel showcases instead is an irreparable break within the African family structure explicitly caused by contact with a European slave dealer and the native translator/collaborator. Rather than portraying this destruction of the social order solely as an act of imperial exploitation of the native Other, however, "Heartland" suggests that the rigidity of native customs is as much to blame for the negative impact on the African kinship system as are the abuses and excesses of outsiders. The "Heartland" episode of Caryl Phillips's *Higher Ground* examines a rural village's cruel response to the rape and torture of the chief's daughter at the hands of a white British officer. Abandoned by her attacker and shunned by her family, the young woman finds temporary solace when she is rescued by the African narrator, who works in the British slave fort and collaborates with the European occupiers by acting as a translator.

The first-person narrator is complicit in this particular attack upon the social fabric of African families because his British commanding officer demands the use of his services as a translator as he travels to a village near the fort. As he conveys the officer's demands for a "young girl" upon which to satisfy his lust, assuring the Head man that she will not be sent across the sea like the other slaves, the narrator acts as both a translator and a pimp. He succeeds in the latter capacity, by securing a native young woman for his master, but fails in the former role, because he cannot make either the British soldier or the African chief realize the extent of the cultural divides attendant upon the transaction they are conducting. In "Heartland," the narrator's willed amnesia about his earlier life as a native enables him to endure the constant betrayal of his fellow Africans demanded by his position as a translator collaborating with the foreign occupier. As long as he acts as a go-between, he loses his integrity but maintains a level of personal autonomy that comes to resemble freedom.

Although there is no evidence in the text that he would have cared about the ultimate fate of his victim, the British officer's feeble assurances to the tribal leader attest to his utter ignorance about the villagers' different cultural values. The British man considers sexual degradation a better fate for his young victim than the permanent exile and hard physical labor of slaves shipped to the American colonies in the Middle Passage. The villagers, in contrast, regard the prospect of life in chains in a foreign shore as a positive alternative to the shame of submitting to the European's lust. When the officer returns the girl to the village, her tribe formally banishes her; she is expected to live alone and completely fend for herself.

In a gesture of atonement, the narrator returns to the village to find the girl, who tells him about the cruelty of the village's strict family custom: "As soon as the man chose me I was tainted. My father had to disown me.'"[23] This encounter with the shunned daughter makes the translator realize his capacity for forming bonds of love and, potentially, of kinship, an ability he had assumed was stunted within him by the constant betrayal he commits to earn his keep. However, his illicit relationship with the girl, whom he keeps hidden in his room at the fort, does not reawaken the feelings he claims to have felt for the nuclear family from whom he is separated. The translator neither mourns nor remembers the life he had before. He lives in the suspended nontime of the empty fort as it awaits its next cargo.

The novel frames this literary diorama as the meeting of two worlds: it presents the narrator's interaction with the girl as an ethnographic discussion between a cultural outsider and an inside informer, despite the fact that both the subjects hail from similar backgrounds. The narrator's contact with the British slave traders and his prolonged collaboration with their enterprise have apparently turned him into a colonial mimic, unable to recall his cultural roots. Thus, in telling him of her village's customs for dealing with women defiled by Westerners, the Head man's daughter teaches the narrator and, through him, the novel's readers learn about the emotional separation that can break up a family unit despite the physical proximity of all its members. Unlike the dioramic mural of Condé's *Segu*, which emphasizes the preservation of the extended family unit's integrity despite the dispersal of some of its branches, the African family diorama in "Heartland" depicts a set of contradictions: a village preserved through personal sacrifice and a divided family residing within the same territory. Ironically, the novel resolves the paradox by contradicting the British officer's assurances to the Head man: upon their discovery, both the narrator/translator and the village girl are sent on the Middle Passage voyage to be sold at auction on a foreign shore.

As a literary diorama, this moment of cultural exchange between the native African woman and her Europeanized African oppressor/rescuer brings to light the continent's conflicted history with regard to the slave trade. As Kwame Anthony Appiah points out in a recent essay in the *New York Times Magazine*: "The rise of settled states in West Africa, as in much of the New World, seems often to have depended on the rise of plantation agriculture, and plantation agriculture depended on involuntary labor. Just as in the New World, moreover, the legacy of slavery has proved curiously durable."[24] Despite its staying power, Appiah emphasizes the concomitant social silence regarding how internal and international slavery shaped dynamics of the African family unit. Just as the unnamed tribe hoped to expiate its brief and involuntary association with the British slaver by banishing the young woman he victimized, so, too, in the Ghana of Appiah's childhood, the family's refusal to acknowledge the inherited power dynamics that originally gave rise to current familial relationships means that the shame associated with the condition of both bondage and slave ownership is not easily shed by modern-day descendants of masters and slaves. In articulating this intertwined history of oppression and betrayal through this literary diorama, *Higher Ground* lifts the veil, so to speak, shrouding Africa's self-reflexive consideration of its own legacy of participation in the slave trade to reveal a continent that was not only the weak victim of the Western imperial powers, but also a ruthless exploiter of its most valuable natural resources: people.

While *Higher Ground* presents Atlantic slavery as one in a series of monumental human rights abuses around the world, in *Crossing the River*, Phillips writes what amounts to historical reenactments of specific aspects of the experience of slavery and its legacy in England, the United States, Liberia, and the waters of the Atlantic Ocean. Much like From Slavery to Freedom, the permanent core exhibit in the National Underground Railroad Freedom Center in Cincinnati, Ohio, which is organized into distinct areas representing demarcated temporal and geographic boundaries ("The Arrival," "The Atlantic Slave Trade," "The Middle Passage," "The Plantation Generations," "The Revolutionary Period," etc.), Phillips's novel is divided into an untitled frame narrative and five discrete vignettes, of which three are directly related to slavery: "The Pagan Coast," "West," and "Crossing the River." The families in question all feature at least one member who was born in the African continent.

Like the slave fort diorama in "Heartland," the first of the two literary dioramas featuring scenes of African lives in *Crossing the River* also depicts a primal scene of paternal betrayal: during a time of famine, an African father sells his children into bondage in exchange for unspecified goods. This act is narrated within the pages of the untitled preface to the novel. The guilty father confesses his transgression: "A desperate foolishness. The crops failed. I sold my children,"[25] thus introducing the idea that people are salable commodities. These three sentences, which open and close the vignette, constitute the leitmotif that runs throughout the novel and each of the dioramas: the dispersed family. They also suggest the idea of Africa's ongoing regret for those "foolish" actions, thereby setting the stage for future reconciliation and a coming together of the peoples of the diaspora, figured in this novel primarily as African American slaves and their descendants.[26] The unnamed father figure speaks again in the end, and proclaims his unending vigilance over his dispersed children, each of whom is featured in the titled chapters that constitute the novel. However much he feels connected to his diasporic offspring, among whom he lists a white English woman, however, neither he nor the novel entertains the possibility of undoing the temporal and geographic break that now separates African peoples.

The second diorama in *Crossing the River* occurs in "The Pagan Coast." This vignette portrays Edward Williams, a southern white plantation owner who travels to Liberia in search of his favorite ex-slave, Nash Williams, whom he had earlier set free and sent to live with his wife and children in Liberia. One of the three children supposedly sold by the unnamed African father in the novel's preface, Nash grows up on the Williams plantation in Virginia. He addresses his letters to Edward by calling him "My Dear Father," thus highlighting the double betrayal (by white Americans, by Africans) he has suffered at the hands of both of his father figures.

Several years after being forcibly repatriated, Nash disappears and Edward undertakes a reverse Middle Passage journey, of sorts, to discover his whereabouts. In Liberia, Edward hires Madison, another of his manumitted slaves whom he had sent to live in Liberia, to act as his guide and "native" informant. This episode culminates in Edward's discovery of Nash's death and his visit to the almost abandoned African compound thought to be Nash Williams's final dwelling. There, Edward finds the only trace Nash left behind of his time in Liberia, and this scene constitutes the literary diorama: "There, spread before him, he could now see the litter of brown cones that constituted the final Nash Williams settlement. Madison took the lead and ushered Edward forward and into the unkempt filth of the place. Everywhere he turned,

Edward's eyes were assaulted by natives who squatted idly, their bodies resting awkwardly on their foundations, like their infantile shacks."[27] Nash's attempt at living an African life is as much a simulacrum as his previous life as a college-educated slave in Virginia. Edward's tutelage has meant that Nash cannot claim to be either authentically American or authentically African, but only an ill-defined mixture of the two. By emphasizing the filth and disorder of Nash Williams's family compound, *Crossing the River* implicitly echoes the lonely fate to which the villagers had relegated the "tainted" Head man's daughter in *Higher Ground*. Both vignettes contain an implicit criticism of African tribal society's exclusivity. The implication here is that the lines demarcating cultural insider and outsider are so rigidly defined that there is no flexibility for those who do not fall neatly into either category.

Nash's domestic simulacrum can be read as the complete opposite of Condé's authentically African Traore compound. While "natives" abound in both dioramas, they clearly participate in the established family order in both volumes of *Segu*, while they seem out of place in Nash's empty set of houses ("shacks"), and their primary narrative function is to witness Edward Williams's mental decline as he tries to sing a hymn without producing any sound.

Nash Williams's American-born wife and child, who were also repatriated by the master, die soon after their arrival in Liberia. This crisis, and the lack of correspondence with his master, eventually leads Nash to give up his missionary aspirations. Despite being abandoned by Edward and rejected by both African "natives" and his fellow expatriates, Nash eventually "goes native" and fashions a sort of African life in the territory in which he finds himself. Because it was built in isolation and without the cooperation or know-how from the locals, the neo-tribal abode Nash manages to erect never becomes more than an imitation of authentic African kinship structures in a country that itself is both a simulacrum of Western-style democracy and of African multiculturalism. Unlike the smoothly functioning Traore compound, which carried on its daily routine without the presence of those family members lost to the slave trade, Nash Williams's improvised homestead falls apart upon his death, thereby displacing his African-born descendants who survive him.

Phillips's provocative evocation of slavery in these two novels challenges his audience's preconceived ideas about everything from the deep tribal and sectarian divisions separating the peoples of the entire African continent that resulted in one group selling members of another to

European slave traders, to what the pioneers in the Old West looked like and, finally, to the effectiveness of the American Colonization Society's schemes to send African American missionaries to places like Liberia and Sierra Leone.[28] The overall theme of Phillips's slavery fiction seizes on "ancestral" Africa's betrayal of its diasporic "offspring" as the reason why no slave family units can successfully stay together thereafter either in Africa or in the United States. By reading the assorted dioramas embedded within his fictions, Phillips's audiences can mourn for the protagonists' actual deaths without developing the impression that the life they had left behind in Africa was an Edenic past of familial bliss.

Unlike Phillips's and Condé's novels, which prominently feature their respective African-born father figures and have long scenes that take place in specific parts of the continent, Fred D'Aguiar's *The Longest Memory* is set entirely on a Virginia plantation. Readers find out only indirectly that the old house servant Whitechapel was born in Africa. The various chapters in the novel are told from the points of view of different characters, so it is not until Whitechapel's adult great-granddaughter speaks in her own chapter that readers find out about her ancestor's African lineage. While the bulk of the novel could be read as a literary diorama for life on a Virginia plantation, the great-granddaughter's chapter constitutes the only literary diorama about life in Africa.

Speaking out of an unspecified sense of frustration with her beloved relative for withholding important family information, the great-granddaughter recalls a taciturn man more worried about his progeny's wellbeing than preoccupied by his own past: "He never talked about Africa. It was his view, I found out later, that such talk promoted day dreams and insolence on the plantation. He said Africa was his past and not ours. If anyone had the right to dream about it, he did and he chose not to, so why should anyone else."[29] Whitechapel's reticence about the continent of his birth resulted from two traumas. The first was his own violent separation from the family into which he had been born: "No one lifted a finger to help a ten-year-old boy. Women and men were like children in the hands of those who held them captive."[30] In Africa, Whitechapel suffers alone, though surrounded by countless helpless others like himself. On the Virginia plantation, however, Whitechapel is a bondsman but assumes positions of responsibility in his own and his master's households. He reaches the elevated rank of trusted servant and lives a stable life unmarked by change. Whitechapel fathers twelve daughters with his first wife, and a son with his second wife. As an Uncle Tom figure, Whitechapel experiences relative success in the plantation due to the loyalty he feels toward both the family who owns him and his descendants, as well as to the well-defined parameters of the plantation itself, which constitute the whole of the world for him. His blind loyalty and his unstated fear of journeys into the unknown, probably borne out of his traumatic experience of the Middle Passage, cost the old slave his son.

The prevalence of African father figures guilty of breaking up their own families in these five novels signals how angry contemporary museum visitors and readers of postmodern novels are apt to feel toward a "parent continent" they feel has fully abandoned them in their exile. The physical break with the African family symbolized through the literary diorama in *The Longest Memory* has as much to do with the violent disruption of a patriarchal system based on primogeniture that does not value the love of daughters as much as that of sons, as it does with the raw wound left by America's political independence from England. Set two years before the War of 1812, *The Longest Memory* anticipates another bloody conflict with the "mother" country to cement the separation between them. By creating an emotionally intense scene that both readers and characters themselves are compelled to revisit over and over again, the literary diorama in *The Longest Memory* manages to educate as well as it entertains, thus fulfilling the two primary goals of a museum exhibition.

Phillips's and Condé's novels spread the moral blame widely, but they also propose that as long as characters maintain strong ties of kinship and ethnic identification with their African legacy, the sacrifices of those ancestors who endured life in bondage will not have been for naught. D'Aguiar's text, in contrast, suggest that people of both European and African descent currently living in territories that were formerly British Crown colonies, such as the West Indies and the United States, have more history and life experience in common with each other than they do with either modern-day or ancestral residents of their long-lost motherland in either Africa or Europe.

4 Between Plantation and Living History Museum

WHEREAS BOTH the ethnographic museum and literary dioramas of the African villages discussed in the previous chapter maintain a sense of the historical divide separating visitors/readers from the scenes depicted by emphasizing their subjects' exotic otherness, plantation and living history museums try to do the reverse: they emphasize the historical authenticity of their location in order to integrate their visitors into the intimate settings of everyday life to make history come alive for them. Unlike auction blocks or slaving vessels, which are archaic artifacts fairly unique to the administration of the institution of slavery and therefore not part of a museum visitor's personal realm of experience, historic homes and entire villages that re-create an earlier way of life seem familiar to visitors, even as their lack of modern conveniences and their period decorations clearly mark them as belonging to a different era.

The major difference between how ethnographic museums depict life elsewhere and how plantation or living history museums portray life at an earlier time is the amount of mediation each establishment provides between the visitor and the exhibitions. As institutions with a scientific mission, ethnographic museums see their displays as metonymic examples of the individual cultures under investigation, and therefore they try to mediate a visitor's reaction to any one object through long explanatory labels accompanying each display. As is the case in other bricks-and-mortar museums, different parts of the ethnographic institution's permanent collection are displayed in specific galleries or exhibition spaces, divided according to some larger order—by geographic area and/or time period, for example. The main categories and order of the venues never change, although the specific items displayed may vary from time to time. However, despite the curatorial desire to fix a meaning upon the objects on display, unless a visitor explicitly requests a museum tour, s/ he is free to ignore the labels altogether and simply wander around looking at whatever piques his or her interest.

Living history and plantation museums explicitly appeal to their prospective visitors' interests instead of trying to advance the progress of science. More narrowly focused than ethnographic museums, these cultural institutions are not constrained by a scientific mission. Instead, they are more firmly entrenched within the tourist economy than any other type of museum except for the World Heritage Sites that I discuss in the next chapter. As such, their greatest competition for visitors comes from amusement parks and other similar entertainment venues. Thus, plantation and living history museums face a lot of pressure to showcase their collections in such a way as to satisfy their visitors' desire for a pleasurable and enriching engagement with the past.

Plantation museums are former, or reconstructed, dwellings that historically belonged to a recognized plantation in a specific location where the institution of slavery was practiced. Whereas plantation museums in the U.S. South developed as a way of paying homage to the Confederate way of life that declined after the Civil War, the development of plantation museums in the Caribbean is a more recent phenomenon, spurred by the tourist industry, which took an active role in its promotion. As Polly Pattullo argues in her history of Caribbean tourism, *Last Resorts*: "The new trends in heritage tourism have not only turned plantation houses into museums, but have also transformed them into hotels (such as the up-market examples on Nevis), while parts of the capital of Aruba, Oranjestad, have even been rebuilt in colonial style."[1] The colonial past and the legacy of slavery held no inherent romance or mystery for local inhabitants, especially since small islands like St. Kitts and Nevis have only recently stopped producing sugar commercially.[2] These islands have now turned to tourism as their largest source of revenue and thus have begun paying attention to colonial architecture, historic landmarks, and other elements from their past that might appeal to the kind of traveler interested in what the region has to offer beyond sandy beaches and fruity drinks. Heritage tourists can now find information online to help them plan ahead and include stops to local museums in their itineraries. Travelers to the United States Virgin Islands who want to visit actual plantation houses and slave quarters can stop by the Cinnamon Bay Plantation in St. John, which dates to 1717, and/or the Whim Museum, in St. Croix, home of a very prestigious plantation house in operation from the seventeenth to the nineteenth century.[3] Both of these plantation museums are administered by the United States National Park Service. For its part, Trinidad claims to have the only "haunted" plantation house in the region: the long-dead owner of the cacao plantation at the Lopinot plantation reportedly has been seen to walk around the house and its environs.[4]

As a genre, plantation museums both in the Caribbean and in the United States have been criticized for the Euro-centric bias evident in their tendency to celebrate the glamorous elements of plantation life while ignoring or downplaying the significance of the slave economy that made such luxury possible. Pattullo mentions the Sunbury Plantation Museum in Barbados in *Last Resorts*, as an instance in which the symbols of the British colonial plantation economy have been exoticized for an audience of outsiders, thereby privileging the house's distinctive architecture and the family's elegant possessions. The museum does not include any discussions of slaves within the plantation household, nor does it allude to the family's role as slave owners who controlled the sugar economy. She points to Jamaica as an example of an island that has expanded the plantation museum model into a larger project of commemorating its national heritage. Pattullo's comment signals her cautious optimism about the potential for heritage tourism to demand a more Afrocentric discussion of plantation history within the Caribbean.

In their coedited volume *Slavery, Contested Heritage and Thanatourism*, Graham M. S. Dann and A. V. Seaton also cite Jamaica as an example of more racially balanced portrayals of plantation history: "In the Caribbean itself, the link between tourism and slavery is far more pronounced. In Jamaica, for instance, Great House tours are on offer, along with a visit to a maroon village."[5] Dann and Seaton's reference to Jamaican plantation museums does not mention whether or not the Great House tours address their respective plantations' resident slave populations but, rather, contrasts the plantation house to the runaway slave settlements, or maroon villages. This view locates each domestic scene at opposite ends of the freedom spectrum. Dann and Seaton's remarks come in the context of their larger critique of tourism as a monopolizing industry primed to become its own kind of economic colonialism: "Possibly the greatest paradox and problem of all, though, is that tourism, particularly in those former colonies which have experienced the plantation system, is seen not as its polar opposite, but as its natural successor."[6] Since there are fewer lucrative job opportunities for workers in the Caribbean than there are in the United States, for instance, there is a real possibility that museum and tourism employees will end up portraying some aspect of their colonial past for paying audiences not because they enjoy engaging with their national history, but because they have few other options.

Plantation museums in the United States are also tied in to the tourist economy. The development of the interstate highway system in the United States after World War II made long-distance travel by car both affordable and safe, which, in turn, allowed Americans from a broad range of socioeconomic backgrounds to travel together with their families. This infrastructure helped make museums attractive destinations for internal tourism, and thus visitors to the plantation museums are as likely to have descended from the slaves that once toiled in the grounds as they are to be related to the influential leaders within the plantocracy. Caribbean tourism, in contrast, is primarily external because it depends on airline and cruise ship travel to bring foreign visitors to the islands. These modes of transportation are more costly than driving, so the various islands compete with one another for the limited number of tourists who have enough disposable income to enjoy the same level of luxury today that only plantation owners could experience in the past.

In the United States, plantation museums are tied into a somewhat different notion of heritage than are their Caribbean counterparts. While they are undoubtedly a part of the national heritage, American plantation museums have a stronger regional identity as icons of a lost birthright, especially for people who are interested in tracing their own genealogy. Visitors to these places, then, are in search of a more meaningful connection to their own and their family's past than they are eager to visit a historic landmark, for example. Regardless of the nuanced differences in their interpretation of heritage, both American and Caribbean plantation museums share a propensity toward creating racially unbalanced portrayals of plantation life.

In their study of plantation museums in the American South, *Representations of Slavery*, Jennifer L. Eichstedt and Stephen Small call this a "white-centric" bias and outline four different representational strategies museums use to discuss slavery. Among these, I find their third category, "segregation and marginalization of knowledge," to be the most pertinent to this discussion because it applies to both the Jamaican example mentioned previously as well as to Colonial Williamsburg, the most famous example of the museum genre I will discuss shortly, the living history museum: "found at sites that include information about enslaved people but present it largely through separate tours and displays that visitors can choose to see or ignore, depending on their desire."[7] Whereas most plantation house tours are mediated through an individual tour guide's official narrative and explanations of what visitors are seeing, one plantation can offer various different tour packages from which the visitor may choose. Thus, it is possible to tailor the plantation museum experience to suit individual tastes much in the same way that visitors to ethnographic museums can circumvent the itinerary suggested by the curators in favor of their own idiosyncratic routes.

Richard Handler and Eric Gable, anthropologists who studied Colonial Williamsburg, describe how these two types of performances function within their chosen field site in *The New History in an Old Museum*: "'Historic interpreters' led groups of visitors through particular buildings or on outdoor walking tours focused thematically. . . . 'Character interpreters' were 'living history' performers who spoke to the public in the 'first person.'"[8] Handler and Gable's descriptions apply to white performers at Williamsburg; they add that African American museum interpreters combined "character" and "historic" interpretation when teaching the black history of colonial Williamsburg.

Living history museums afford their visitors even more freedom to make their own way through history because they are "open-air museums," or institutions that exhibit their collections outdoors. These museums set out to re-create an entire community's way of life and employ the technique of "historic interpretation" as a tool through which guides dressed in period costumes perform tasks typical of a particular time period and explain what they are doing to the general public that comes to view this spectacle. The performances included within these types of museums can range from demonstrations of a given trade, like agriculture or carpentry, or craft, such as weaving or quilting.

Historical interpretations at living history museums typically include a question-and-answer period in which the visitors can ask for more information after watching the performance of the trade, craft, or life story. Depending on the locale and the preference of the individual interpreter, these exchanges take place either wholly in character or in real time, with the performer identifying him- or herself as a museum professional and explaining the history behind the action or speech, or answering questions about the museum's mission or collections.

Conner Prairie Living History Museum in Fishers, Indiana, is another such open-air museum that makes use of "historic" and "character interpretation" to entertain and educate its visitors. People can even choose to participate in a hyperreal museum experience by signing up for a "simulation of the Underground Railroad Experience."[9] Paying visitors reenact the role of runaway slaves by running in the dark while being pursued by museum patrollers. More intimate performances include biographical sketches, through which individual "interpreters" perform dramatic monologues in order to convey their character's personal stories to the assembled crowds.

Although both Colonial Williamsburg and Conner Prairie are large living history museums rather than private plantation museums, their programming closely corresponds to the "segregation and marginalization of knowledge" representational strategies outlined by Eichstedt and Small because they are primarily "white-centric" in their approach to history. Both institutions have created slavery-related heritage tours that are different from their main historically centered attractions. This segregation implies that African American history is not a part of the larger American story of progress and success. So, while it is possible to learn about the domestic life of blacks and whites during the eighteenth and nineteenth centuries, doing so will cost extra and take more time.

While they share with ethnographic museums a desire to educate the public about the cultural meaning of their collections, living history museums rely on the dynamic medium of live performance, rather than the static display of select representative artifacts, to convey the type of information they want their visitors to know. Through their forays into dramatic monologues, the museum professionals whose job it is to "interpret" the historical facts affirm the value of fiction as a teaching tool to disseminate information and promote a specific emotional connection to events and people from long ago. Traditional historical novels have long used this technique to both entertain and instruct their reading audiences about the past. Examples of American traditional historical novels set in the time of slavery include Margaret Mitchell's expansive Civil War historical romance *Gone with the Wind*, which uses the plantation as its central metaphor for the entire South. While the convoluted plot of Mitchell's epic novel includes a few black slave characters, they are exaggerated caricatures based on racial stereotypes. This "white-centric" view of life in a southern plantation portrays the antebellum period as a time of maximum glamour and sophistication; Mitchell's novel and its subsequent adaptation into film have popularized the concept of the plantation museum beyond the local southern audiences who might be able to trace their family tree to some grand old plantation of their own. The huge economic success of both the book and movie versions of

Scarlett O'Hara's life and loves have catapulted *Gone with the Wind* to a global stage; it continues to appeal to new generations of fans.

African American family epics published after *Gone with the Wind*, like Margaret Walker's *Jubilee* or Alex Haley's *Roots*, use the slave cabin, rather than the plantation house, as their dominant paradigm for domesticity. Walker's and Haley's tales are narrated exclusively from an Afrocentric perspective, and the few white characters who appear within these texts do so to represent their historic roles as masters, overseers, and patrollers. Whereas it is easy to see how the grand architecture, luxurious decor, and ornamental landscape of the big house appeals to modern aesthetic tastes, it is harder to quantify the draw of slave huts on a purely aesthetic level. As Pattullo points out in her study, "most slave accommodation, built of wood or wattle and daub, has disappeared or has been destroyed."[10] Their architectural design was subordinate to their function as a mere shelter against the elements. Comfort and luxury played no part in the construction or dwelling within slave huts. However, the critic bell hooks points to how African American women recuperated these ramshackle structures from the abject by imbuing them with positive cultural associations.

In "Homeplace: A Site of Resistance," bell hooks celebrates black women's transformation of the domestic sphere, however humble, into a site of both self-affirmation and resistance to oppression. hooks argues that: "Historically, African-American people believed that the construction of a homeplace, however fragile and tenuous (the slave hut, the wooden shack), had a radical political dimension. . . . This task of making homeplace was not simply a matter for black women providing service; it was about the construction of a safe place where black people could affirm one another and by so doing heal many of the wounds inflicted by racist domination."[11] By establishing a "homeplace," African American women developed a particular domestic culture that celebrated the home as a communal safe haven from the troubles and indignities of the day. For hooks, making a "homeplace" was not a regional phenomenon peculiar to African American women. Instead, she claims that "this task of making a homeplace, of making home a community of resistance, has been shared by black women globally."[12] The house demarcates the boundary between public and private spheres, between women's social function and their personal memories.

Caribbean novels have often portrayed the plantation house in a negative light, as the site for women's madness. Two well-known examples include Jean Rhys's *Wide Sargasso Sea*, a retelling of Brontë's *Jane Eyre* from a Caribbean perspective, and *La mulâtresse Solitude*, a novel jointly attributed to André and Simone Schwarz-Bart, which tells the story of a Guadeloupian slave who rose up to resist the French reimposition of slavery in that island in 1802. However, both novels take place after slaves have been emancipated (if only temporarily) in their respective islands. African-descended characters play strong roles in both texts, but the Caribbean plantation gradually fades from view as the action moves away to the forest or to the English countryside, as the case may be. Thus, neither can be said to constitute a virtual "plantation museum" in the same way that I will argue other Caribbean texts can.

These traditional historical novels about slavery, *La mulatrêsse Solitude*, *Roots*, *Jubilee*, and *Gone with the Wind*, rely on third-person narration to describe general aspects of plantation life and, thus, they function at a remove from the action, in a similar style to how "historical performers" from the living history museum use third-person narration to explain the significance of the buildings and activities visitors see taking place around them. Most of these novels also fall within the representational category of "segregation and marginalization of knowledge" outlined by Eichstedt and Small because although they portray black and white experiences of slavery within one primary plotline, the white and black characters' awareness of the other's way of life never affects their own understanding of their respective places within the social hierarchy. Scarlett O'Hara may find herself forced to fashion a dress out of her window treatments, but her poverty does not lead her to treat her former slaves any more kindly than she did when she was the belle of the ball. In contrast, Antoinette Mason's family falls victim to their former slaves' pent-up rage, and after their plantation house burns, the young girl becomes the object of her African descended playmate's scorn.

Wide Sargasso Sea illustrates that not all Caribbean postmodern historical novels that include scenes of plantation life within their pages function like plantation museums. Reinaldo Arenas's *Graveyard of the Angels* is another case in point. It portrays both the urban and the agricultural dwellings of its Cuban slave-owning family, but the third-person omniscient narrator describes the household dynamic in each setting as absurd, relying on exaggeration to convey his sympathy for the household slaves who have to meet the family's unbearable demands on a regular basis. Slaves live within the family compound in Havana, but in the country they are housed in separate quarters, or "straw huts."[13] Despite shedding some light on the urban living arrangements in which wealthy, slave-owning families in Havana participated, and which are not frequently depicted in historical fiction about slavery, *Graveyard of the Angels*'s frenetic pace and minimalist narrative give its readers but a glimpse of what the daily lives of both domestic slaves and their masters might have been like. Likewise, *I, Tituba*, *L'esclave vieil homme et le molosse*, *Crossing the River*, and *Feeding the Ghosts* all feature rural plantation life in the background, but this aspect of the plot is not discussed in much detail. References to Caribbean and/or American plantations function as shorthand to ground the characters and their tales within a particular type of plantation economy that provides the setting against which the novels stage different kinds of museum effects, as I have argued earlier.

Postmodern historical novels that specifically focus on plantation life as their primary topic differ from traditional historical novels' depictions by portraying only moments of crisis or unusual domestic arrangements that are atypical of how most plantations were actually run. American examples of this genre include: Toni Morrison's *Beloved*, which features the ironically named Sweet Home Plantation, where the Schoolteacher has free reign to conduct his unorthodox "experiments" to determine whether or not slaves are human; Sherley Anne Williams's *Dessa Rose*, where a white widow cooperates with the band of runaway slaves who gather in her house and helps them escape bondage by pretending to be their mistress; and Edward P. Jones's *The Known World*, which features a working plantation in the South run by a family of manumitted slaves. While their portrayals of domestic arrangements within southern plantation households are unusual, these novels' narrative structures are relatively linear and proceed along conventional lines, maintaining the same narrative perspective throughout. The notable exception here is the Middle Passage scene in *Beloved*.

Caribbean examples of this genre differ from their American counterparts through their use of pastiche to juxtapose different kinds of discourses about slavery within one larger narrative frame. Caryl Phillips's *Cambridge* (1991) and Fred D'Aguiar's *The Longest Memory* (1995) contain both the slaves' and the plantation owners' narratives about specific traumatic events within the plantation economy, such as the whipping of Chapel, the young runaway in *The Longest Memory*, or the eponymous character's murder of the plantation overseer in *Cambridge*. These novels mimic or parody different styles of writing— from newspaper articles and editorials, to private diaries, slave narratives, heroic couplets, and free-style verse—in an effort to create as rich a narrative tapestry about plantation life through fiction as can be done in historiography, by drawing from different types of primary sources. Despite this penchant for intertextuality, neither novel aims for verisimilitude. Whereas Hayden White tells us in *Metahistory: The Historical Imagination in Nineteenth-Century Europe* that historiographers use literary techniques like "emplotment" to guide them as they piece the various bits of information they glean through archival research into a cohesive narrative that creates a historical context that explains the significance of past events, these postmodern novels refuse to assign narrative closure to the events they portray, because they equate filling in the gaps between these distinct narrative units through the prism of a constructed cohesion with suppressing these different voices. Ironically, although postmodernist novels generally do not value realist description or verisimilitude, this mimetic reproduction of distinct genres with no explicit connection or reference to one another more closely parallels the way in which modern people gather information on a day-to-day basis than do the linear narrative structures of both traditional historical fiction and historiographic nonfiction. Living in the moment, without the benefit of hindsight, people can only guess what aspects of the news they hear today will matter to future historians.

Novels as Plantation Museum

Among the primary documents that make up the narrative fragments of Caryl Phillips's *Cambridge* are the confession, or slave narrative, supposedly penned by the title character, and the diary kept by the absentee plantation owner's daughter, Emily Cartwright. Although this division may suggest that *Cambridge* engages in the discursive strategy of "segregation and marginalization of knowledge" explained earlier, this is not the case. The two characters live in the same plantation but rarely speak to one another, much less exchange the particulars of their life stories. However, both Emily in her diary and Cambridge in his confession wonder about what it would be like to live the life of the other. Through the juxtaposition of their individual texts, the reader soon finds out that they have more in common than either character would guess: both Cambridge and Emily are immigrants who have arrived on the island from England, a land to which neither will return; both are literate, although Cambridge seems to be better read than Emily; both of their claims to an independent identity are subjected to the approval of powerful white men of means, like Emily's father or Cambridge's benefactor;

both end up losing their only children at birth; and the domestic tranquility they had each enjoyed was disrupted by the overseer, Mr. Brown.

Cambridge kills Mr. Brown to avenge the wrongs done to his wife, Christiana, and to the woman who owns him, Emily. Mr. Brown abandons Miss Cartwright, the plantation owner's daughter, shortly after she arrived to claim her place within Caribbean plantation society and became pregnant with his illegitimate child, just as he had previously cast off his former paramour, Christiana. Cambridge's wife goes mad with grief because of this rejection, and the concomitant loss of the "homeplace" she had established within the big house.

As Jenny Sharpe has persuasively argued, the real battle between the two female characters is over the title of "mistress,"[14] instead of over one man's affections. This is the context in which *Cambridge* functions as a plantation house museum. When Emily Cartwright first sits down to dinner within her father's big house, she is astounded to see that Christiana had taken her customary seat at the opposite side of the table from her. The discussion that ensues reveals each woman's expectations of how the plantation household should be run. Emily initially orders Christiana to get up from the table and "put on a serving gown and take up a role among my attendants, male and female, who properly circled the table to wait upon their mistress" working from the logic that "on a property belonging to Christian owners, this was her rightful place."[15] Christiana replies by explaining that her behavior is in keeping with what has been the norm in the Cartwright plantation: "'Massa say I can eat at table. Why missy not like me?"[16] While Christiana's intransigence frustrates Emily, it also demonstrates that as a newcomer she has yet to establish her domestic authority within the household she runs in name only. Failing to make the servant bow to her will, the English heiress has to appeal to the overseer's greater familiarity with the slave system so as to bar Christiana from the table. Each woman scores her own victory: Christiana wins the initial shouting match, but Emily succeeds in banning the slave from the Great House altogether.

These two characters' discussion about who should sit where during dinnertime "interprets" the social (and sexual) hierarchy at work within the plantation domestic culture for the novel's readers. Although Emily's plotline is undoubtedly "white-centric," the plantation part of her Caribbean experience is only half the story. Eventually, she has to leave the plantation household in disgrace because of the shame her out-of-wedlock pregnancy has brought upon her father's name and reputation. Emily takes up shelter in an abandoned cottage in the woods once she becomes a social outcast and depends upon the charity of her former body slave for her sustenance and care. Thus, while Cartwright is still technically being cared for by black slaves, she occupies a lower place in the social hierarchy than they do because of her moral transgression. From the heights of luxury and entitlement, Emily has sunk to the depths of poverty and depravity.

Cambridge's murder of Mr. Brown ushers in the third type of narrative document contained within the novel: the newspaper account of the murder, Cambridge's trial, and his execution. Cambridge's violent action removes him from within the relative safety of his Caribbean domestic life as much as Emily's social infraction exiles her from the Great House. Through his imprisonment, he is separated from both the plantation itself, as well as from his slave quarters. However, the crime also gives him the occasion for speaking, and he writes the confession, which functions like a slave narrative, as he sits at home, awaiting arrest.

Because Phillips does not formally link together the various narratives contained within his novel, it is impossible to determine whether anyone other than the reader ever has access to Cambridge's text. He addresses himself to an audience made up of "those of my dear England, Africans of my own complexion, and *creoles* of both aspects."[17] Despite finding himself in bondage in the Caribbean, Cambridge anachronistically proclaims his cultural identity to be a "Black Englishman"[18] and recalls his days of freedom when he lived as one of the growing numbers of black Britons in London. This is yet another way through which *Cambridge* serves as a plantation museum: by contrasting the slave's experience of exploitation and abuse as a house slave within a Creole plantation Great House to his more pleasant memories of employment within a respectably middle-class British household in England proper. Emily, too, comes to understand the Great House she has inherited through the lens of her experience running a British household. This is an unusual frame of reference through which to discuss Caribbean plantation houses within the Anglophone Caribbean islands because the British masters were often absentee landowners.

Museum as Postmodern Novel

Caribbean plantation museums, like the ones mentioned at the beginning of the chapter, operate as isolated examples of a larger geographic trend; they refer to themselves as epitomes of the plantation architecture and sources of local history. Because this novel so fully incorporates the black and white experiences of the domestic plantation economy, it also carries that dynamic into its discussion of England as a land of opportunity for manumitted slaves. Early in her narrative, Emily refuses to speculate whether she will bring her personal slave, Stella, with her if she ever returns to England, but Cambridge benefitted from just such a journey, as he describes in his confession. *Cambridge*'s portrayal of the burgeoning black population in London mentions that some freed slaves have trouble assimilating into British society, while still others face intense prejudice even in light of their conversion to Christianity. Thus, the novel extends the idea of the plantation house beyond the Caribbean, and uses it as a metaphor to evaluate how the treatment slaves received during their years in bondage would prepare them to live alongside their European former owners.

Museums productively blur the line between historical fact and fictionalized reconstructions of the past within their exhibits to successfully educate and entertain their paying visitors. One history museum that uses the idea of the plantation as a metaphor for describing the successful integration of ex-slaves into the fabric of a free American domestic community is the Milwaukee Public Museum, which in the 1990s added the "Watson Family Home" display to its popular The Streets of Old Milwaukee. Unlike the Eurocentric cultural pastiche of the European Village exhibit I discuss in chapter 3, which was meant to highlight the ethnic diversity of the city's white population, this particular display is geographically situated within a real historical and architectural landscape—the city of Milwaukee. Like the discussion of black Englishmen in London in *Cambridge*, this exhibition portrays manumitted slaves living within a predominantly white, urban setting, and establishing a household of their own choosing.

Billed as "a tribute to one of Milwaukee's first prominent African American families" on the exhibit's Web site, the "Watson Family Home" display is one of two households depicted in the three-dimensional re-creation. Like the plantation museums in both the Caribbean and the United States, the scale version of the Watson home features a collection of household goods, photographs, and other heirlooms owned by the family of freed slaves from Virginia who settled in the city before the Civil War. Unlike other displays in the same exhibition, the Watson home is accompanied by what the museum curator Al Muchka calls in an interview, a "didactic, teaching level case" to provide historical context for the visual material.[19] This narrative element of the display is significant since it addresses a segment of urban history, the lives of the free people of color and manumitted slaves residing in Milwaukee, about which not much was recorded until the close of the twentieth century. Thus, this display acts as a supplement and corrective to the historical effacement of the cultural contribution African Americans made to white urban communities in the Midwest.

The "Watson Family Home" display of The Streets of Old Milwaukee exhibit adopts the interpretive function of living history museums like Conner Prairie and Colonial Williamsburg through the projected reconstruction of Sully Watson's life story, available in the teacher's resources portion of the Milwaukee Public Museum Web site. This downloadable document includes front matter similar to the paratextual material that frames Condé's *Segu*, such as maps and a family tree that traces the Watson family back to West Africa. The accompanying narrative includes an account of how Sully Watson gained his freedom and met his future wife, as well as a description of the Watsons' subsequent travels north to Ohio and then west toward Wisconsin. This teaching case makes use of primary documents, such as family photographs, and secondary sources, like existing state laws at the time, to come up with a fictionalized projection into the family's possible motives for moving and settling where they did. Thus, this display provides interesting insight into the ways in which technology allows museums to function like postmodern novels as much as novels incorporate museum and curatorial techniques into their narrative structures.

Another history museum in the United States that appropriates the generic conventions of the plantation museum is the National Underground Railroad Freedom Center in Cincinnati, Ohio. This museum incorporated a part of plantation life within its design and architecture through the inclusion of an actual slave pen that was relocated from Germantown, Kentucky, and later reassembled inside the museum as part of its permanent exhibitions.[20] The reconstructed edifice features small, open-air windows and space for a wide chimney that has been reconstructed out of steel beams so visitors can not only see, but walk through it. This steel cage both represents an absence—that of the heat and bricks of the chimney—while it also provides modern-day visitors more access to light and to space than the enslaved inmates of this pen would have had.

Outside the door of the slave pen visitors can read a facsimile of the 1834 probate inventory of the slave pen owner's property, which lists several bondsmen by name, thereby preserving some aspect of their individuality. In his museum review of the National Underground Railroad Freedom Center, Edward Rothstein, a *New York Times* critic-at-large, reads both the names and their surrounding artifacts as examples of how "slavery's evil becomes palpable": "Next to the pen is a list of its former owner's possessions, which included 32 slaves, like 'one Negro child, Matilda' (value: $200), along with a kitchen cupboard and a copper kettle."[21] Rothstein's reference to the presence of the cooking items and the display's own silence regarding their probable provenance present another suggestive juxtaposition that blurs the boundaries between authenticity and poetic license, between fact and fiction. That kind of full disclosure of information is exactly what is necessary for the logic of the exhibit to be transparent to visitors, who might otherwise read about the cupboard and kettle and reasonably assume these were at some point part of the pen itself. If so, their absence from the display changes the visitors' perception of how harsh the living conditions inside this building would have been. Access to cooking tools, while hardly providing the comforts of "homeplace," would have at least facilitated some semblance of domestic order, to say nothing of much-needed sustenance. If, on the contrary, these objects were never included within the slave pen, then their presence on the probate inventory highlights how matter-of-factly the dehumanizing discourse of slavery equates living beings and inanimate objects as different examples of property.

The Freedom Center's visitor's guide urges patrons to "touch the walls in this authentic wooden structure that was used to warehouse slaves being sold down the Ohio River to points south and west from northern Kentucky," as if through tactile sensation visitors might glean some small aspect of the hardships suffered in these cramped quarters. This gesture toward establishing tactile understanding not only has a physical appeal, but it also works as a descriptive trope in fiction, as I demonstrate in my reading of Patrick Chamoiseau's *L'esclave* as a mourning museum in chapter 6. Therein lies another fundamental problem with the exhibit's repeated claims of authenticity: it implies that patrons can gain unmediated understanding about the experience or reality of slavery through mimesis, by repeating or imitating the very act of touching the walls as the slaves themselves must have done upon first entering the pen, rather than through the more abstract process of learning by doing research and reading documents and academic accounts of the past. Unlike the steel cage of the chimney, the directive to "touch the walls" does not undo the walls' status as historical artifacts belonging to a building that once held captive slaves but, rather, shifts the emphasis away from historical slaves and resituates it on the modern-day visitors. This change privileges the immediacy of imitation or impersonation, acting or feeling "how" or "as" abstract, imaginary slaves may once have done, above the more gradual process of edification that only becomes possible through reading, listening to, or viewing primary documents and art of the time to learn what life was like for both slave owners and those people they regarded as mere property.

The third aspect of the slave pen exhibit that attracted my attention precisely because of its banal appearance was the surprising, to me at least, presence of two narrow, weather-beaten benches inside the old building. Since there was no plaque around to explain either their historical role or significance, I asked one of the official guides whether these benches were a new addition or if they had indeed been part of the original structure. According to the guide, one beam was left over after the pen was reassembled and someone decided to keep the beam together with its fellows by transforming it into the benches. This account is somewhat at odds with the assurances of the online text accompanying the description of the slave pen's history on the Freedom Center's Web site, which emphasizes the authenticity of the reconstructed building by attesting to the involvement of unspecified "preservationists" who took the building down and reassembled it: "The Pen was donated to the Freedom Center after being remarkably preserved, carefully dismantled by preservationists and then rebuilt for this exhibit." It would appear the "preservationists" were not so careful after all!

I find the benches themselves problematic for two reasons: first, no one is allowed to sit on them, and second, like the references to the "cupboard" and "kettle" in the display area mentioned above, the benches' presence inside the pen gives visitors a false impression of comfort that was historically unavailable to the itinerant occupants of such a structure. The anachronistic benches are the element that most clearly undercuts the exhibit's claim of authenticity by highlighting its status as a simulacrum, a fictive re-creation of a historical building rather than a historically accurate duplicate of the same. For masters to have provided benches for their slaves to sit upon would have entailed some small recognition of the slaves' humanity and propensity to experience discomfort, a consideration that was absent from the original design and maintenance of this building as both a holding pen and a temporary shelter from the elements. Thus, the benches constitute a modern projection of an amenity enjoyed neither by the slaves who were housed in the pen nor, ironically, by contemporary visitors.

The disconnect between the wood of the benches, which gains historical significance by having been part of the "original" slave pen building as it stood in Kentucky, and the absolute lack of utility of the same wood

once it has been transformed into the ersatz benches, renders them a frivolous addition to what is supposed to be "the central exhibit" (Rothstein)
of the Freedom Center. This suggests that historical verisimilitude is not,
after all, the goal of this display. Susan A. Crane would call these benches an example of historical "distortion," since she observes: "Museums
are not supposed to lie to us; this act seems a breach of faith. Assuming
that our own memories are fallible, we rely on museums as well as on
historians to get the past 'right' for us. Even if we don't remember every
museum experience, we know that that 'straight' version of the past is
available to remedy our 'queered or distorted memories.'"[22]

As simulacra, the slave pen's benches merely have symbolic value, but
what is it they actually represent? As apocryphal, nonfunctioning artifacts, the benches are not as anchored in the discourses of slavery, abolition, or even lived experience as is the see-through, steel-cage chimney.
More than anything else, the benches are a postmodern projection into
the past of slavery that has the effect of displacing the fear, suffering,
and uncertainty enslaved peoples must have felt while occupying the
premises from any degree of empathy that twenty-first-century museum
visitors could muster. While the visitor's guide urges patrons to imagine the past of slavery by "touching" it through the walls, the sight of
furniture made from a superfluous bit of the same walls brings visitors
back to their contemporary reality, where the comfort of having a seat
is something they take for granted. Yet, within the recognition of the
benches as banal, everyday luxuries lies the first moment of real empathy
museum visitors can experience—the presence of the benches within the
historically reconstructed cabin highlights their very absence (along with
that of any other creature comforts) within the slave pen when actual
people were held there. Thus, the visitors' familiarity with the benches
heightens their understanding of the slaves' deprivation of such small
relief, thus viscerally conveying a sense of their discomfort.

Finally, the benches mirror common gallery design practices in art
museums, where visitors are invited to sit down and contemplate the
works of art and fully take in the ambience of the particular exhibition
room. This structural element of design points to the fact that museums encourage patrons to take a contemplative and tranquil approach
to appreciating the materials presented for their judgment and reflection.
This sort of repose and the freedom to take it all in is exactly what the
pressure of being trapped in the slave pen denies to its prisoners through
its poor ventilation, lack of light, and the inescapable smell of human
misery and duress. The slaves who were being shipped down the river to

the Deep South probably agonized over being ripped from their "home-place" and the uncertainties of the future.

While I view the presence of the benches within an "authentic" slave pen as remarkably ahistorical, visitors who do not ask about them do not necessarily experience this temporal incongruity. The silence and darkness of the reconstructed slave pen attempt to communicate something about the experience of confinement and terror that often punctuated life in bondage; the compromises that the curators of this exhibit had to make with modern conventions and norms, such as fire code and easy access and egress, paradoxically point to the nearly impossible task of attempting to simulate both history and the representational status of a different kind of museum. As a visual and physical representation of a liminal space of uncertainty located somewhere between the tedium of plantation toil and the humiliating terror of the auction block, the slave pen building itself represents slavery as through a thoroughly modern lens, calling it "un-freedom," without revealing any of the actual secrets of what went on within its walls.

As a temporary domicile, the slave pen is closer to the slave fort, discussed in more detail in the next chapter, than it is to either the plantation's big house or even the slave quarters. Whereas the latter abodes represent the two extremes of domestic living, they do embody within them some measure of predictable routine dictated by the regular schedule of tasks that need to be performed in order to keep the household and the fields running in their proper order. The flip side of these small comforts of domestic life is the unstable living arrangement and unpredictable nature of waiting to be taken toward an unknown future experienced by those housed within the confines of the slave pen.

Whereas the Underground Railroad Freedom Center's slave pen lost some of its historical specificity when it was transplanted to its new location in Cincinnati, Ohio, perhaps it gained greater symbolic value as an icon of oppression. Historically, the slave pen served as a temporary shelter and holding facility for slaves about to be sold or shipped "down the river" along the internal slave trade route that culminated in the auction block in the Deep South. The allusion to this small-scale Middle Passage movement of slaves stands in stark contrast to the northerly course of the Underground Railroad, whose ultimate destination lay in the free North; however, this juxtaposition of northern and southern slave journeys serves as a powerful reminder of one potential fate that could befall those runaway slaves who looked to the North Star for guidance as they tried to flee the cruelty of the plantation.

The Freedom Center's child-centered exhibit on the Underground Railroad features a short film about the emotional toll a young man's sudden decision to run away takes on his enslaved family. Entitled *Midnight Decisions*, this film is primarily designed to celebrate the successes of the Underground Railroad, rather than to commemorate the sacrifices of slaves who sought freedom but were recaptured. This movie presents the slave family's fear and worry without scaring its core audience too much. In *The Longest Memory*, Fred D'Aguiar relies on self-reflexive postmodern pastiche that overtly resembles a museum exhibition in order to achieve a similar feat: to convey the senseless murder of a recaptured runaway slave at the hands of the overseer without turning off its core audience.

Like Phillips's *Cambridge*, D'Aguiar's *The Longest Memory* features an intertextual jumble of fictitious newspaper editorials, poetry, diary entries, and first-person accounts of events from various perspectives. Both texts also feature the violent death of an enslaved African-descended male: one hung for avenging the rape of his wife, and the other whipped to death before his father's eyes in the aftermath of a journey north gone wrong. However, each text functions as a different kind of museum. *Cambridge*'s focus on the domestic makes it closer to a plantation house museum, while the novel's emphasis on the drama that takes out of doors makes *The Longest Memory* function more like a living history museum, with each character serving as a different kind of "historic interpreter."

Novel as Living History Museum

The Longest Memory takes place almost entirely within the Great House and the slave quarters of the Virginia plantation. Whitechapel's life is defined primarily by being the most trustworthy and reasonable slave within the plantation. He achieves that status through an act of willful forgetting of the African homeland from which he was abducted, as discussed in chapter 3. Whitechapel becomes an ideal personal servant to the master, and, in exchange, he is allowed the privilege of raising his family within the confines of his own "homeplace" in relative peace until the day his son decides to run away and join his beloved white mistress in the North.

The Longest Memory functions as a living history museum when it describes the everyday tasks and routines that make the Great House and its agricultural fields function smoothly. Whitechapel's second wife describes the overlapping roles she plays within these two households by using food as a metaphor: "All my life two pots are never empty. One is in the master's kitchen. The other is my own. I sometimes take from one to fill the other. Or after the sight of the first one all day, I can hardly face the second. . . . My master's pot is full of the best things my hands will touch but my belly won't see. Yet my pot is sweeter to me. Sweet because I take from it and fill two plates for the people I love, my husband and son."[23] Cook assumes a maternal relationship toward her master's family as well as her own in this passage. D'Aguiar's portrayal of this contented cook suggests that her peace of mind comes from her unique ability to nourish her family with the skills she has developed by working in the Great House. In this way, she could be seen as having successfully created "homeplace" within two different domestic realms that she alone controls: her own, and that of the kitchen in the planter's house.

D'Aguiar's positive overall portrayal of the planter class in this novel falls under the "trivialization and deflection" representational strategy in Eichstedt and Small's catalogue. They define it as: "Narratives and pictorial images that serve to demonstrate the benevolence of plantation owners and the affection of 'faithful slaves' for these owners."[24] Only Whitechapel really exemplifies the stereotype of the "faithful slave," and his private narration reveals that this is not his natural tendency but, instead, a response he conditioned himself to make in order to live as long as possible. When he tries to pass on that wisdom down to his grandchildren, they ignore him, but the master listens to him and treats him with respect.

Whitechapel's (adopted) son, Chapel, represents the opposite response to the condition of slavery; his rebellious spirit stems from his desire to prove himself and establish his manhood outside of the context of slavery. However, by depicting Chapel as a young man in love with his master's daughter, *The Longest Memory* suggests that both the impulse to stay and serve and the one to flee the plantation are mediated by what level of intimacy and trust each slave feels he has developed toward his master. In this regard, the novel's depiction of the likely emotional involvement between individuals living in such intimate conditions affirms both the slaves' and the masters' common humanity in a more concrete way than any of the other novels mentioned in this chapter.

Although *The Longest Memory* functions as a living history museum and *Cambridge* works like a plantation house museum, both refuse to assign narrative closure to the events they portray because they equate filling in the gaps between these distinct narrative units through the prism of a constructed cohesion with suppressing these different voices.

By openly incorporating narrative elements into their displays and didactic performances, plantation and living history museums can reach their audience's emotions more powerfully. Perhaps by developing a strong, personal connection like that, more people will be inspired to come back and see what is new at the museum again.

5 World Heritage Sites

The Fortress

THE ISLANDS circumscribed by the Caribbean basin bear the ruins left behind by violent encounters between transnational antagonists too numerous to tally. Architectural and geographic landmarks situated throughout the islands silently attest to the physical and temporal reality of these bloody episodes in the region's history. Military forts scattered throughout the Caribbean archipelago that were once sites of unspeakable carnage and devastation now have become part of the heritage tourism circuit. As primary sources for historical investigation, landscape and architecture pose an inherent challenge to the way the museum has developed into a cultural and historical institution that houses objects outside of their cultural context.

As we saw in chapter 4, historic homes and plantation estates in the Caribbean have either been kept up or eventually restored so as to attract visitors from the cultural tourism circuit. Military forts pose a different challenge because of their larger scale and contested history of ownership. Simply put, since they belong to the entire nation instead of to an individual family, the task of defining their cultural and historic significance must be carried out by consensus among a number of different interest groups.

Polly Pattullo points to the parallel development of the cultural tourism industry in the Caribbean and a renewed interest in the islands in developing a museum culture that preserves a sense of their history. Whereas in the early part of the twentieth century, national museum displays in islands such as Barbados or Puerto Rico focused on documents that recorded the European achievements in the Caribbean and on archaeological artifacts that documented an Amerindian heritage that could be reconstructed, any objects related to the African-descended experience of slavery and emancipation received little notice, as I argue in chapter 1, specifically in the context of Puerto Rico.

Also initially excluded from the discourse of what constitutes cultural "heritage" or a national patrimony were local buildings whose distinctive architectural history was ignored. Pattullo argues that as the islands turned more toward a tourist economy, old buildings were viewed as outdated and razed by both local and foreign hotel chains in favor of the type of institutional architecture pleasure seekers would recognize as "resort" style: "The idea that tourists could be interested in a built environment beyond a beach is not restricted to Cuba. Slowly the rest of the region has awakened to the attractions of its own architecture. Yet for decades, with a disregard for its own architectural traditions, the Caribbean tore down its old buildings to promote other people's."[1] Pattullo notes that this trend toward homogenization has been on the wane of late. Now, "there is more attention paid to vernacular architecture (paralleling the developments in museums), if sometimes only in a post-modernist mode."[2] Heritage tourism in the Caribbean supplements or enhances the travel experience for visitors seeking to enjoy the islands' tropical charms. By promoting their historic landmarks, these islands celebrate their own heritage and culture as well as their natural resources. Since people already come there for the fun in the sun, the task is not so much to attract a new slew of visitors as to get the ones who do arrive to venture beyond the shore and to the interior.

In chapter 4, we saw how certain examples of historically significant architecture, such as the slave pen in the National Underground Railroad Freedom Center, can indeed be transferred from their original locations to the museum halls. However, scale and materials were factors here because the structure in question was made of wood, and relatively small in size. It was possible to incorporate this slave pen as a museum exhibit because that the Freedom Center was still in the planning stages so its architecture could be modified to accommodate the display. Speaking from a European context, André Malraux, a French novelist and minister of culture under President Charles de Gaulle, notes how the limited physical space occupied by any one museum makes it difficult to include samples of architecture within its permanent collections. In *The Voices of Silence*, Malraux remarks that "our knowledge covers a wider field than our museums," and specifically points to the inherent rootedness of architecture as one reason why this art form is not duly represented within European art museum collections. He wryly points out that "all Napoleon's victories did not enable him to bring the Sistine to the Louvre."[3] Malraux argues that due to limitations of both space and money, the museum as an institution can only be a repository of portable artifacts, be they works of art or sociocultural artifacts of historical significance; items such as tapestries, large sculptures, and fixed objects like stained glass windows, to say nothing of architecture, are not represented within most museums' collections.

Pointing to the increased commodification of art and the proliferation of images in what Benjamin termed "the age of mechanical reproduction," Malraux suggests that art books, with their color reproductions and juxtaposition of great masterpieces from multiple collections across the world, constitute a kind of "museum without walls" that provides a more complete and comprehensive picture of works of art as objects that exist simultaneously within both aesthetic and cultural contexts than a visit to any one museum, with its necessarily incomplete collections and displays of art, could do.

As portable and affordable goods, books can reach a much wider audience than bricks-and-mortar museums because many more books are printed than there are people able or willing to travel to museums. With the distribution networks of libraries and booksellers, even those people who go to the museum can purchase a book-as-museum to keep at home and re-create some aspect of their visit. Current technological advances have even rendered art books unnecessary, if not obsolete. Nowadays, most museums have official Web sites that showcase parts of their permanent collections and provide supplemental informational material such as study guides for use in the classroom, provenance information, archived descriptions of previous traveling exhibitions that had been shown at that museum, and links to other resources available through the World Wide Web. These new technologies have even made it possible for the UNESCO World Heritage Sites project to function as its own type of virtual museum, highlighting images and curatorial information about the places, and structures, included within its vast archives.

Well before the advent of the personal computer and the development of the Internet, postmodern historical novels such as the ones under discussion in this study already functioned as their own kind of "museum without walls." Unlike physical museums, postmodern historical novels are not limited by the constraints of space, and, therefore, they can spend as much time as they please displaying and curating architectural landmarks for their readers. They can include historically accurate information within their stories so as to enhance verisimilitude, or they can introduce apocryphal historical events and anachronistic details to remind the reader that the story s/he is reading did not actually take place. Postmodern historical novels set in real-world locales like slave forts during the time of slavery can engage in the same type of imaginative reconstruction of history as do ethnographic, plantation house, or living history museums such as Colonial Williamsburg in Virginia and Conner Prairie in Fishers, Indiana. As works of art themselves, postmodern historical novels also contribute to the world's artistic heritage through their aesthetic contributions to the literary genre.

While Malraux holds that art books outdo art museums by bringing together reproductions of the world's masterpieces in any medium between their two covers, postmodern historical fiction manipulates perspective, point of view, the laws of time and physics, or the official historical record to imbue otherwise "real" historical facts with a fresh breath of imagination that allows them to maintain their historical authenticity while being overtly and self-consciously fictitious. Postmodern historical fiction challenges the official version of "history" contained in textbooks by asking its reading audience to regard the novels themselves as mini-museums, interactive repositories of information that may or may not be true. By depicting Caribbean architecture or landmarks of historic significance as valuable to humanity's shared heritage without restricting the possibilities for interpretation available to their readers, postmodern historical novels also function as "museums without walls."

Caryl Phillips's novel *Higher Ground* is one such literary virtual museum that features three distinct exhibitions within it: "Heartland" showcases an African slave fort; "The Cargo Rap" is an exhibition of African American males within the criminal justice system in the 1960s; and "Higher Ground" chronicles a little-known chapter of the history of the Holocaust as it portrays a survivor's descent into madness after being liberated from one of the death camps. All three of the novel's parts share a concern with physical and psychological imprisonment. In chapter 3, I explore how "Heartland" contains within it a diorama depicting the trauma that slavery had upon "traditional" tribal life by separating family units. In this chapter, however, I consider how the inclusion of the white British governor and colonial soldiers as central characters in "Heartland" adds an important perspective to our historical understanding of the significance that cultural agencies like UNESCO assign to the various slave forts included within its listing of World Heritage Sites.

Set in a British slave fort in an unspecified part of Africa that probably is intended to represent Cape Coast Castle in Ghana, "Heartland"

is narrated by the resident African translator, who tells the British soldiers about any sign of impending trouble, such as plots to rebel, developing within the dungeons. To a lesser extent, the translator explains
how things work to the newly captured prisoners brought to await their
Middle Passage. As the intermediary between the "native" locals and the
"foreign" colonizers, the translator serves as the reader's guide through
the maze of the slave fort.

The novel's description of everyday life within the slave fort emphasizes how much more time the European soldiers and administrators
spent at the garrison than their captives, as well as how comfortable their
accommodations were compared to the dungeons where their human
cargo was kept. Like its historic counterpart, the fort in "Heartland"
houses the governor, his private staff, and the army officers in the upper
floors. The enlisted men are assigned to the barracks, and sentries stood
guard around the perimeter of the structure. The African translator has
his own room in some remote part of the fort, which affords him not
only privacy, but the comfort of being away from direct sunlight. There
is a courtyard where soldiers gather and practice their military drills.
The slaves are kept underground in the dungeons, which have little ventilation and make no allowances for personal hygiene.

Phillips's initial description of the dungeons takes place when the fort
is empty of its human cargo, as it is now. The recently arrived governor
takes a tour of the facilities, much in the same way that heritage tourists who visit former slave forts in Elmina Castle, Ghana, Gorée Island,
Senegal, or Ouidah, Benin, can tour the sites. As he recalls the initial
tour of the dungeons that he gave to the governor, the African translator reconstructs their conversation: "He points: 'And these markings?'
I follow the line of his finger. 'Those with small pox, when they move
they leave behind skin and blood. Then, of course, many have dysentery.
Such stains are common.'"[4] Both modern-day visitor and nineteenth-
century civil servant notice how the human misery enclosed within this
small space has permanently changed it. African guides "interpret" the
empty spaces of the slave holds for their visitors; they mention historical events, such as recorded outbreaks of dysentery and malaria, not
by means of statistics, but through an appeal to the physical evidence
they left behind. Whereas the labels surrounding the slave pen in the
Underground Railroad Freedom Center urged visitors to "touch the
walls" of the structure as a sign of emotional solidarity with its past occupants, these inmates left few telltale signs of their individual presence.
The indelible mark of illness and decay that remain to this day on the

walls of slave forts throughout Africa is a physical reminder of the pain, sorrow, and hardship that enslaved Africans endured even before they entered the miserable holds of the slave ships that would take them to unknown lands.

While contemporary tourists can leave the fort after seeing the infamous "door of no return" through which slaves were loaded onto the ships that would transport them to the New World, the governor in Phillips's novel had to stay and live with the knowledge that he commanded the entire slaving operation. He falls gravely ill, and the military routine is disrupted such that order is severely compromised. Eventually, a new coffle arrives at the citadel, and the fort begins to fulfill its primary function: storing human cargo awaiting its final destination. By providing his readers some insight into the entirety of the colonial, commercial, and military undertaking in a given European slave fort on African shores, Phillips presents a more historically accurate (though nonetheless melodramatic) picture of the African slave forts as both military and cultural strongholds.

African Slave Forts

In the powerful memoir *Lose Your Mother*, the American writer Saidiya Hartman discusses her experience of visiting Elmina Castle and following the slave trade routes in Ghana as both a heritage tourist and an academic researcher. She explains the economic impetus driving Ghana's move to commodify its past of slavery and market it to African Americans as an act of understandable desperation: "Few of the tour operators, docents, and guides put any stock in the potted histories of the 'white man's barbarism' and the 'crimes against humanity' that they marketed to black tourists or believed the Atlantic slave trade had anything to do with them. They only hoped that slavery would help make them prosperous."[5] Hartman resents the patronizing attitude that is at the heart of this tourist economy, which places her into the ready-made categories of *obruni*, or stranger, or else claims an excessive amount of intimacy by referring to her as "Sister." Primarily, though, Hartman bristles at the thought that the packaging of transatlantic slavery for African American heritage tourists effaces any discussion of the internal slave trade within African societies. Like Phillips does in *Higher Ground*, Hartman uses her memoir to call for a greater accounting on the part of African countries to recognize their own complicity in the triangular slave trade and the toll that this cooperation exacted from their communities' future development.

Elmina's brazen marketing of its slave past also irritated Phillips, who, years earlier, had written *The Atlantic Sound*, his own account of retracing the triangular trade journey through travel. In part 2, "Homeward Bound," Phillips interweaves the interviews he conducted with both Ghanaian politicians and prominent African American settlers in Ghana about local attitudes toward the slave forts and the influx of heritage tourists from the diaspora, with his own impressions of participating in the cultural tourism economy. Phillips attended the Panafest Historical Theater Festival held within the grounds of Elmina Castle accompanied by a local Ghanaian tour guide, Mansur, whom he had met while the latter was an illegal immigrant residing in England. Phillips retraces the history of both Elmina and Cape Coast Castles from their European foundations to their twentieth-century makeovers into tourist attractions. As Phillips portrays it, the sheer artificiality and derivative nature of the various "rituals" and performances meant to simultaneously celebrate the diasporan travelers' arrival back at a "home" their ancestors never lived to see again, mark Panafest as a profoundly self-referential event, where little new is learned and African-descended people from all around the world come to feel good about themselves. What Phillips objects to most during this performance of diasporan solidarity is not the content of any of the featured events but their poor overall execution. Nothing starts on time, and the performers are often inebriated by the time they take the stage. He considers this event a poor memorial to the victims of slavery, and an embarrassment for both the participants and the organizers.

By reducing the historical importance of the slave forts to their role within the transatlantic slave trade, and not addressing their significance as the most concrete tools of European empire building within the African continent, Panafest and other similar cultural events pander to tourists' sentimental desire to engage with their own history in isolation. This limits the slave forts' significance to the cultural heritage of the world only as symbols of unthinkable oppression or bastions of cruelty. Including a fuller discussion of the slave fort's negative impact on the native trade structure and some reference to how the forts were put to use after the end of the slave trade would do more to reclaim these cultural resources in a broad historical context than simply mentioning one defining aspect of their overall history.

Although Elmina Castle and the other forts I have already mentioned are located in Africa, they are the product of European design and coerced local labor. Likewise, the design for military fortresses in the Caribbean was primarily European, but it quickly became creolized through both the materials and slave laborers who helped build these structures, as well as by the additions and revisions to the original design necessitated by the constant attacks upon the islands by buccaneers and hostile armed forces. Just as Phillips's vignette "Heartland" recovers a history of European presence at the African forts, Alejo Carpentier's *The Kingdom of This World* and Edgardo Rodríguez Juliá's *The Renunciation* and *La noche oscura* inform their contemporary readers about the different ways in which Caribbean military fortresses supported, or were made possible by, transatlantic slavery. These novels have a broader worldview than did "Heartland" because their discussion of these fortresses happens in the larger context of the Haitian Revolution, an event they view as the most idealistic and iconic version of Caribbean self-determination. By overlapping the intimidating presence of the military fortress on their respective island, San Felipe del Morro or the Laferrière Citadel, with more mundane scenes of utter political failure, *The Kingdom of This World*, *The Renunciation*, and *La noche oscura* imply that no amount of fighting, whether international or domestic, can ensure the emergence of a stable and independent island government.

Laferrière Citadel and *The Kingdom of This World*

The Laferrière Citadel in Milot, Haiti, was commissioned by Henri Christophe, the self-styled first king of the island, in the years immediately after the end of the Haitian Revolution (1791–1804). The Citadel is an impressive fortress. The compound encompassing the fortress and royal residence has been designated a "National History Park" within the island, and its image features prominently in the country's international tourism campaign. The Citadel's primary purpose was to protect the young country against a potential French assault, but it never fulfilled the role for which it had been built. In 1820, a sickly Christophe, fearing a coup, committed suicide and was buried within the fortress so his body would not be mutilated. The royal suicide and burial within the Citadel further transformed the building's function; what had started out as a fortification now became, effectively, a mausoleum, as I explain in the next chapter. By having his remains immured within the grounds of the Laferrière Citadel, King Christophe I imbued both the fortress and his royal person with military and historical significance that endures to this day.

The Citadel and Christophe's official residence, the Palace of Sans Souci, suffered major structural damage during an earthquake in 1842.

In 1982, both were officially added to UNESCO's list of World Heritage Sites, a project that identifies places that contribute to humanity's connection to the legacy of the past. In an effort to overcome the barriers of geography and distance, UNESCO chose places whose historical significance is such that "they belong to all the peoples of the world, irrespective of the territory on which they are located."[6] Information and pictures of all the sites are now available online, and constitute a virtual heritage "museum without walls." As a corporate entity, UNESCO has curated these buildings for public consumption through the official summaries that accompany the images. According to the official UNESCO online entry: "The Palace of Sans Souci, the buildings at Ramiers and, in particular, the Citadel serve as universal symbols of liberty, being the first monuments to be constructed by black slaves who had gained their freedom."[7] This brief descriptive summary of the building, then, tries to read the "fragment" of Christophe's fortifications, the ruins of the Citadel and Sans Souci, only in the context of the Haitian Revolution, which predated their construction. The text in the Web site proclaims that the value to humanity of the Laferrière Citadel and the Sans Souci compound consists entirely of their association with the legacy of slavery on the island. In this light, the buildings gain universal cultural significance not because of the elegance of their design, or even due to their massive scale but, rather, because the laborers who worked to build them had once been considered chattel. This interpretation downplays the buildings' strategic value as military installations made to withstand the assault of well-equipped European forces. Where they could have been appraised as architecturally innovative defensive structures, Sans Souci and the Citadel have been reinterpreted only as emblems of freedom in this internet museum.

The word choice employed in UNESCO's official interpretation of the buildings' value to humanity is flawed in several important ways. First, it implies that the ex-slaves' labor on this project was both voluntary and celebratory, instead of coerced by force. Second, it conflates the architectural soundness of the buildings with the political and moral achievements of the Haitian Revolution, which had ended several years prior to their construction. Third, it fails to recognize that at the time the two colossal structures were under construction, Haiti was a young nation torn by civil war, and that ex-slaves were as likely to support Christophe's political rival, Alexandre Pétion, as they were to rush out to build a military monument to "freedom" for the self-proclaimed king. In fact, Henri I compelled his workers to toil under extremely oppressive conditions, as the anthropologist Michel-Rolph Trouillot points out: "Hundreds of Haitians died building his favorite residence, its surrounding town, and the neighboring Citadel Henry, either because of the harsh labor conditions or because they faced the firing squad for a minor breach of discipline."[8] As was the case in other French New World territories, where slavery was officially abolished in 1794, only to be reimposed by force in 1802, so, too, in Haiti a parallel system of exploitative forced labor resurfaced throughout the country in the aftermath of the successful slave insurrections that culminated in the birth of the country.

According to C. L. R. James, Toussaint L'Ouverture forced people back into abandoned plantations and made them cultivate land so as to provide food to support fighters.[9] L'Ouverture insisted they be compensated for their labor, but the conditions under which they toiled were harsh. During Christophe's reign, erstwhile free people were also pressed into forced labor but only in order to carry out his grandiose architectural schemes. By glossing over these human rights abuses in Haiti's history merely because their perpetrator had once been a slave himself, UNESCO tacitly endorses the view that black-on-black state-sponsored violence is not as serious a matter as was the European colonizers' exploitation of their African-descended subordinates. Clearly, the short narrative summary accompanying this display that functions as a de facto curatorial statement ought to be updated to celebrate the remarkable architectural achievement the structures of both the Palace of Sans Souci and the Citadel represent despite the huge cost in human lives and freedom attendant on their construction. Although Sans Souci and the Citadel never repulsed European invasion, they stand as testaments to the Haitian people's collective resolve to deter further efforts on the part of the French to reimpose colonial dominion and the plantation system of slavery. They are the products of a Haitian Creole national identity that knowingly borrows from its colonial past in order to better prevent a threat to its autonomous future.

Haitians have wanted to capitalize on the visibility that UNESCO's "World Heritage Site" designation has brought to their country's historic architectural landmarks but have experienced financial and political setbacks. In 1995, Trouillot expressed doubts that even a thorough renovation of the Citadel would be enough to restore what he feels is its lost aura of historical authenticity. He argues: "In spite of the devotion of two Haitian architects, its restoration lags behind schedule, in part for lack of funds. Further, even a reconstructed Milot will not have the same claims to history as a regularly maintained historical monument, such as the palace at Potsdam. The surrounding town of Milot, in turn, has lost historical significance."[10] Trouillot's pessimism should be tempered by remembering Pattullo's observation that this tendency to let old colonial structures decay is a Caribbean-wide phenomenon so, in that regard, the Citadel's current state of disrepair and its renovation, whenever it happens, is in keeping with the history of the region as a whole. Thus, if anything, the Citadel gains greater historical significance as a sign of the times as well as a product of forced labor, both of which attest to coercive forces frequently at work in the process of nation building. Whether or not it turns out to have been a quixotic quest, the Haitian government continues its commitment to promoting both local and international tourism to the Citadel precisely because of its historic significance as a landmark of architectural import and as a concrete document of the high level of military sophistication reached during Christophe's reign.

The official Web site of the Haitian embassy to the United States (Haiti.org) features a tab labeled "The Secretary of State for Tourism" that gives visitors the option of choosing among three Web sites to find out more about what places to visit in Haiti. Of the three sites, the only one to feature the Citadel is Lonelyplanet.com, which warns potential tourists that the political situation in the country is still unstable, but nonetheless offers a description of the fortress that takes into account Christophe's tyranny: "The fortress was completed in 1820, having employed up to 20,000 people, many of whom died during the arduous task."[11] This sentence acknowledges the sacrifice of the countless workers whose backbreaking toil crafted this huge, imposing stronghold, without directly blaming Christophe and his cruelty for their suffering. It also does not situate its description of the slave fortress in relation to anything else on the island. More balanced and historically accurate than the paragraph posted by UNESCO, this blurb nonetheless is written from an outsider's point of view, and thus is of only limited value to gauge popular reaction to this fortress.

A different Web site not affiliated with the Haitian government but that promotes international travel to the island, *Discoverhaiti.com*, is written entirely from a Haitian perspective and, thus, can serve as a means of documenting how local people in the tourism industry portray this important landmark to outsiders. In its "Let's Visit Cap-Haitien" page, this Web site addresses itself to international heritage tourists planning to travel to the island and mentions both Laferrière Citadel and Sans Souci as ideal destinations that offer spectacular views and insight into historic periods in the country's fight for independence and autonomy. The paragraph that describes the Laferrière Citadel presents a more balanced view of the human cost of building the fortress than does UNESCO's enthusiastic blurb: "In the days after the independence, preparing against a retour en force of the French was in everyone's minds. Jean-Jacques Dessalines had asked all the regional leaders to build forts across the country in preparation. The Laferriere [*sic*] Citadel was built by King Henri Christophe between 1805 and 1820. It covers 10,000 square meters with walls up to 40 meters high. It is said that 20,000 people were pressed into its construction."[12] This brief statement acknowledges the sacrifice and horrible work conditions that those who were compelled to work endured in order to transform Christophe's fortress from a dream to a reality, while acknowledging that these extraordinarily oppressive measures occurred during a time of national crisis, disorder, and imminent danger.

Having contextualized the fortress's grandiose scale through a reminder of the blood that made such an architectural feat possible, this description implies that what makes the fortress so remarkable is how much it is the fruit of the Haitian national imagination and ingenuity. By claiming the Citadel as a particularly Haitian attraction, instead of decrying the Western influence of its overall design, the Web site grants it a certain level of legitimacy as an expression of national aesthetics.

Discoverhaiti.com next highlights the specific appeal such a building holds for potential visitors, who will have to endure "a steep 5 kilometers hike up to the fortress" in order to see Christophe's fortress up close. Ranking high among the attractions are the views, as the next paragraph explains: "The views offered by La Citadel are very impressive and breathtaking. Cuba can be spotted on a clear day." The reference to Cuba indirectly contrasts the open and welcoming nature of Haitian society with the oppressive dictatorship style of the Castro brothers, who rule their own country with an iron fist. This approach is particularly effective for United States visitors to the site, for most of whom travel to the Communist country is unthinkable, given the U.S. government's ban on spending American currency on the island. The section on the Citadel concludes by pointing out that the structure has recently undergone a large-scale renovation that the locals consider highly successful: "The two-century-old fortress has been under restorations [*sic*] for years and a beautiful job was done." Thus, the site promotes the historical value of this locale as a key landmark in Haiti's history of nation building, as well as the way in which the architectural landmark works in harmony with the island's natural beauty.

However, this assessment may be a bit optimistic as a representation of national sentiment. In an article dated August 9, 2007, and published on the newspaper *Le Nouvelliste*, Jean Gardy Gauthier decries the state of disrepair into which the fortress has been allowed to fall, by describing Sans Souci, Ramiers, and the Citadel as being "in a pitiful state."[13] Gauthier reports that President René Préval wants to see the area renovated so it can once more attract tourists to the region. The costs for the renovation are estimated to be around $2 million (U.S.). The same news organization published a story on February 14, 2008, that announced the new plan unveiled by Patrick Délatour, the Haitian minister of tourism, to finish renovating several prominent tourist destinations in the island, le Parc Historique du Nord first among them.[14] Mr. Délatour signaled that the Ministry of Tourism has already received pledges of economic support from local industries.

Whether or not accounts of the remodeling of the Citadel Laferrière have been exaggerated, the Haitian nation seems to be united in its desire to market its historic architecture to capitalize on the cultural tourism UNESCO is trying to promote in relation to slavery. In 1993, Haiti took the lead in asking the General Conference of UNESCO to approve a resolution instituting the "Slave Route" project, which works to create greater awareness of the history and legacy of the transatlantic slave trade.[15] This newer effort overlaps with the World Heritage Sites, but is designed to stimulate research and scholarship that considers the transatlantic slave trade from a global perspective rather than through the more limited lens of nationalism. Writing about the World Heritage Sites, Barbara Kirshenblatt-Gimblett explains what activities or plans UNESCO includes under that category: "cultural tourism, including the development of museums and exhibitions, restoration of sites, and creation of tourist routes."[16] Thus, the proposed renovation of the Laferrière Citadel would fall within the purview of UNESCO's projected "Slave Route" project, which is intended to increase a global tourism trade focused on the consumption of cultural, as well as environmental, goods on the island. By creating these suggested itineraries, UNESCO may be redefining its own mandate, and filling the void left by the disappearance of travel agencies as viable business enterprises in this increasingly computerized and wireless world. The "Slave Route" project may, in fact, appeal to the would-be heritage tourists' sense of historic irony by placing so much focus on the two fortresses as getaway destinations, when they were built expressly to keep intruders away.

Like the criticism both Caryl Phillips and Saidiya Hartman levy against the commercialism of Elmina Castle in Ghana, Kirshenblatt-Gimblett argues that receiving a "World Heritage Site" designation from UNESCO may hinder a country's internal efforts to establish its own independent and nonmarketed identity: "Designation as world heritage [*sic*] has local political effects that can run counter to UNESCO's professed goals and produce not only resistance to normative heritage interventions but also alternatives to those interventions. Moreover equality in the world heritage space can produce inequity on the ground."[17] At least in the popular imagination, Haiti's historic fortress and palace already have suffered from the "inequity on the ground" since the overarching plans for this region have not yet been internationally vetted and only sporadically funded from within.

The Laferrière Citadel is a highly interactive site, where tourists listen to the locals. Despite its status as a national historic park, the official guides who take tourists around are not park employees, as they would be in an equivalent attraction in the United States but, instead, work for nearby hotels in the region. This situation lends further support to viewing the Laferrière Citadel as a "museum without walls." The historical information visitors learn during their private expedition differs from the objective distance that official curators strive to maintain in more conventional museum settings. People who choose to drive to Le Cap on their own tend to end up hiring a local guide not affiliated with a specific tourist agency. *Discoverhaiti.com* encourages its visitors to do likewise, with the added warning that they should, "agree on a price in advance." The local color that these freelance guides provide carries a different form of authority, which the Web site explicitly promotes. It lists the benefits tourists will reap from such an interaction: "Be ready for some of the most fascinating history," which will likely include "a touch of the typical exaggeration of the facts."[18] This description plays up the entertainment factor of the local guides' propensity to indulge in hyperbole while at the same time suggesting that such tall tales are the only information that should be considered "authentic" because they are the creation of local residents who live with this fortress day in and day out instead of an academic interpretation of facts from a curator who may or may not specialize in the theme of an exhibit.

The Laferrière Citadel is simultaneously a military fortress and the burial place of Henri Christophe, the first king of Haiti, as I explore in more detail in the next chapter. In the personal narrative part of his historical and anthropological analysis of what he terms the three faces of San Souci—the Haitian royal residence; its European double, Sans Souci Palace in Potsdam, Germany; and the historical person named Sans Souci—Michel-Rolph Trouillot shares with the reader the stories his Haitian family would tell each other in the United States about Henri I. Later, Trouillot recounts his first visit to the Citadel: "I saw the grave at once, an indifferent piece of cement lying in the middle of the open courtyard. Crossing the Place d'Armes, I imagined the royal cavalry, black-skinned men and women one and all on their black horses, swearing to fight until the death rather than to let go of this fort and return it to slavery. . . . I did not need to read the inscription to know the man who was lying under the concrete. This was his fort, his kingdom, the most daring of his buildings—The Citadel, his legacy of stone and arrogance."[19] Trouillot's family regularly criticized Christophe, but his father and uncle also had a favorable view of this deeply flawed leader. He explains, "They were often critical, for reasons I did not always understand, but they were also proud of him."[20] The young Trouillot's family felt a personal connection to their country's history by declaring their intellectual investment in evaluating Christophe's legacy as a leader of men and as a shaper of memory. While the older men mourned the dead king's memory by talking about him, Michel-Rolph Trouillot's journey to the fortress allows him to see it in a larger context of European architectural history and other personal stories.

The Cuban novelist Alejo Carpentier opens the prologue to *The Kingdom of This World* with a reference to his own visit to the monuments Henri Christophe had erected during his reign. Conveying both his wonder at what he saw there and his sense of history as he surveys the scene before him, Carpentier writes: "Toward the end of 1943, I had the good fortune to be able to visit the kingdom of Henri Christophe—the poetic ruins of Sans-Souci, the massive citadel of La Ferrière [*sic*], impressively intact despite lightning bolts and earthquakes."[21] The implication here is that Carpentier not only traveled to a different country in order to reach his destination, but that he in some ways also traveled back in time to when the buildings he saw belonged not to the country of Haiti as configured in 1943, but to Christophe's mythical sovereignty as it stood at the height of its glory. This visit prompts the Cuban novelist to consider how the landscape that surrounds him and that characterizes the islands of the Caribbean basin gives rise to a different sense of reality, and dictates what kinds of phenomena the inhabitants of the region are willing to include in their own definition of "normal." As readers, then, our first encounter with the novelist is through his self-portrayal as a visitor inside the "museum without walls" that is Haiti's most famous military fortress.

The prologue is the document in which Carpentier first sketches the outlines of what would become his theory of the marvelous real (*lo real maravilloso*), and though subsequent versions of the novel have been published without this text, it nonetheless continues to serve as an autobiographical lens through which to interpret Carpentier's depiction of Haiti and its history.[22] Carpentier does not mention whether or not he had a local guide when he went to the Citadel. However, the next reference he makes to walking around the grounds demonstrates that although he tries to understand the majesty of the structures he observes on their own terms, he ultimately resorts to his personal knowledge of European art history for some basis of comparison: "I entered the La Ferrière citadel, a structure without architectonic antecedents, portended only in Piranesi's *Imaginary Prisons*. I breathed the atmosphere created by Henri Christophe, monarch of incredible undertakings, much more surprising than all the cruel kings invented by the surrealists, who are very fond of imaginary, though never suffered, tyrannies."[23] Even his recall of Haitian history, figured here through the allusion to Christophe's unmatched cruelty, is mediated by Carpentier's investment in the tradition of European art as represented by the labyrinthine structures imagined by the eighteenth-century Italian artist and architect Giovanni Battista Piranesi, and by the fantastic artistic and literary images of the twentieth-century surrealists. So, while Carpentier appears to move about freely in the Citadel, his experience of this fortress is always already mediated by his familiarity with countless other museums or European works of art. Never an innocent bystander, Carpentier relies on his internalized art historian to make sense of what he sees as he explains the experience to others.

By virtue of being preceded by this groundbreaking prologue, *The Kingdom of This World* could be read as the novelist's test of the very principles he outlines. I choose to read it somewhat anachronistically, however, less as an experiment and more as an especially artistic end product of one person's interactive engagement with a military fortress as a site of both Caribbean, and world, heritage. The novel faithfully incorporates the overall historical sequence of events of the Haitian Revolution, from the influence of Mackandal's Rebellion in 1758,[24] to the successful insurrection against the white planters and battles against mulattoes and various European powers, led by Toussaint L'Ouverture,

Henri Christophe, Jean-Jacques Dessalines, and André Rigaud. The novel also depicts the subsequent leadership struggles between Toussaint's
successors and weaves these into a whimsical narrative that celebrates
the "natural" magic inherent in the Caribbean landscape and recognized
in vodun rites.

Narrated from the point of view of Ti-Noel, an enslaved Everyman figure that interacts with various historic personages, *The Kingdom of This
World* depicts several moments in which political power changed hands
fairly dramatically in Haiti.[25] The building of the Laferrière Citadel occupies a prominent place in the novel because the king's dramatic suicide
and his subsequent immurement provide a permanent place to visit his remains and contemplate his legacy. Carpentier's third-person, omniscient
narrator explicitly compares Henri Christophe's domestic forced labor
program in the northern part of Haiti to the European-imposed colonial
system of chattel slavery and concludes: "in other days, the colonists—
except when they had lost their heads—had been careful not to kill their
slaves, for dead slaves were money out of their pockets. Whereas here the
death of a slave was no drain on public funds."[26] Despite being an old
man who spent his life laboring hard in the cane fields, Ti-Noel is forced
to carry bricks up the mountain to help build the fortress. This passage
critiques Haitian human rights abuses of their fellows more strongly
than of those perpetrated by European slave masters, thereby reflecting
a late twentieth-century awareness of the ongoing political corruption
that characterized the aftermath of the Haitian Revolution. It does not
absolve Europeans of the morally reprehensible past of slave ownership,
but the novel puts this flaw in the context of a global, capitalist market
economy where concerns of profit and loss prompted somewhat conser-
vative attitudes toward punishment.

The Citadel episode comes toward the end of *The Kingdom of This
World*. In its juxtaposition of the two distinct events, the slave uprisings
of the Haitian Revolution and the building of the Citadel, Carpentier's
text ironically anticipates UNESCO's benign description of the fortress
on its Web site as a monument to freedom, and casts the latter undertaking in the glorious shadow of the revolution's success in breaking the
double chains of slavery and colonialism. The novel conflates the history
of the Haitian Revolution with the construction of the Citadel, portraying them as inextricably linked. It playfully compresses events into a
chain of cause-and-effect occurrences that cloaks some of the horror
of the building's construction in the glory of the struggle for liberation.
This text's attitude toward narrative history becomes most evident in its

discussion of the kind of textiles that might actually be seen in a physical museum's display about Christophe's reign in Haiti: uniforms.

The first uniform in question is not one Christophe wore while leading troops in battle but, instead, is an example of the type of royal regalia he donned to display the wealth and royal bearing he claimed as his due once the battles against the European enemies had ceased. Ti-Noel discovers and reclaims the garment when he raids the Palace of Sans Souci after Christophe's death: "the pride of the old man's heart was a dress coat that had belonged to Henri Christophe, of green silk, with cuffs of salmon-colored lace."[27] While the coat in question is laden with historic significance because it once belonged to the king, its power within the narrative is merely symbolic. By wearing the coat, Ti-Noel feels empowered to rule and command imaginary subjects, much like Christophe himself had hoped to become a king by dressing the part. In contrast to this frivolous article of clothing, the novel's narrator describes the gradual decay of the second uniform, an actual military garment worn in battle. An old man exhibits the uniform during the social gatherings that take place at Ti-Noel's house, both to awaken old memories and to commemorate the sacrifices of those who died fighting for freedom: "an old veteran, one of those who had fought against Rochambeau at Vertières, who brought out for special occasions his campaign uniform of faded blue and red that had turned strawberry from the rain that leaked into his house."[28] Though worn and tattered, the uniform exudes its own significance; the veteran does not need to put it on for others to recognize and admire what it represents. Carpentier's juxtaposition of the two uniforms, an official and an unofficial one, is a bold curatorial statement that implies a critique of Christophe's abandonment of his military credentials in favor of a life of luxury divorced from the most basic needs of the people whose freedom he helped to secure.[29] Since both people who wear the uniforms are old men, they represent history and the passage of time.

By depicting the Citadel as the work of manumitted slaves who were pressed back into forced labor, *The Kingdom of This World* critiques the enduring legacy of inefficient Caribbean self-government even as it educates its readers about Haiti's postcolonial transition into a nation of its own.[30] In contrast, the Puerto Rican novelist Edgardo Rodríguez Juliá crafts a version of history as it never was on the island by incorporating willful misreading of the history of colonial projects like the fortress of San Felipe del Morro that vaguely corresponds to the events of the Haitian Revolution.

San Felipe del Morro Castle and *The Renunciation* and *La noche oscura del Niño Avilés*

Edgardo Rodríguez Juliá's two apocryphal historical novels, *The Renunciation* and *La noche oscura*, try to pass themselves off as history texts by including numerous footnotes and quoting excerpts from both actual and fictitious sources. Each work actually takes liberties with Puerto Rico's official historical record about slavery by describing imaginary slave rebellions that, had they actually occurred, would have predated and anticipated the scale and horror of those that comprised Haitian Revolution.[31] Read together with *The Kingdom of This World*, *La noche oscura* and *The Renunciation* add a layer of complexity to our understanding of the significance of the Haitian Revolution.

La noche oscura and *The Renunciation* manipulate the scale of the conflict depicted, the time frame in which it supposedly unfolded, and the geographical specificity of the battles themselves. These two novels function as supplements to, not substitutes for, both the historiographic accounts of the Haitian Revolution and Carpentier's canon of novels about the conflict, which would constitute the "original" texts since they were published decades earlier.[32] *The Renunciation* and *La noche oscura* simulate a Caribbean past that the country in which they are set never shared; the novels' portrayal of "false" slave revolts emphasizes this lack of a tradition of resistance in the island. Rodríguez Juliá juxtaposes his fictive appropriation of the slave rebellions in Haiti with a self-critical examination of nationalist identity politics to suggest that Puerto Rico's current neocolonial relationship with the United States is due, in part, to the historical absence of a successful local tradition of large-scale resistance to both slavery and colonial rule.

While the sociopolitical upheavals of Rodríguez Juliá's two novels parallel the events of the Haitian Revolution, neither the author nor any of his narrators make an explicit connection between the fictional slave revolts in *The Renunciation* and *La noche oscura* and the lot of slaves elsewhere in the Caribbean. In their influential study *The Puerto Ricans: A Documentary History*, the historian Olga Jiménez de Wagenheim and journalist Kal Wagenheim point out that "there is no record of a large slave insurrection in Puerto Rico. The presence of a Spanish military garrison was one deterrent as was the fact that free men easily outnumbered slaves. In fact, many slave conspiracies were betrayed by slaves, who confessed to their masters, in exchange for their freedom."[33] The Wagenheims' reference to San Felipe del Morro Castle as "a Spanish military garrison" implies that the fortress repelled slave rebellion from within, as well as foreign attack from without. This is a provocative thesis, but the Wagenheims do not go on to explain exactly how they substantiated this claim. Perhaps the large numbers of military troops stationed within easy reach of local plantations made the threat of swift and immediate punishment seem more real to the slaves. There were no large-scale local plantations on the island until *after* the collapse of the Haitian sugar plantation system brought about by the revolution.

The prevalence of betrayal among the slave conspirators suggests either that slaves in Puerto Rico valued their lives more than they desired personal freedom, or that they felt greater fear of authority, or maybe even more loyalty toward their masters than to each other. However, this is mere historical speculation; it is impossible to establish how familiar slaves were with El Morro or how large the military threat loomed in their imagination. The atypical makeup of Puerto Rico's agricultural workforce, with its large population of free and indentured laborers, and the absence of the plantation model for cultivation until the end of the eighteenth century promoted individual advancement rather than communal bonding among the slave classes.

San Felipe del Morro fortress in Puerto Rico became another Caribbean addition to UNESCO's World Heritage Sites when it was added to the registry in 1983, one year after the Citadel's inclusion. Unlike the paean to freedom found in the entry of the Citadel in Haiti, the curatorial description of the military structure at San Felipe del Morro and its surrounding compounds places them in their proper context as buildings with a strategic defensive military value to the Spanish Crown: "Between the 15th and 19th centuries, a series of defensive structures was built at this strategic point in the Caribbean Sea to protect the city and the Bay of San Juan. They represent a fine display of European military architecture adapted to harbour sites on the American continent."[34] So many centuries after the island has ceased to be of interest for buccaneers and invading European naval fleets, the contribution these Puerto Rican buildings seem to make to humanity's heritage is primarily aesthetic, not military.

Given the early date of El Morro's construction, begun less than fifty years after Columbus first set foot on the island in 1493, the fort's architectural integrity is ascribed to European ingenuity, not to native or Creole vision as was the Citadel. The Web site's narrative summary emphasizes the compatibility of the European design of the fortress and the surrounding Caribbean landscape without minimizing El Morro's strategic value as a key military outpost. Nothing is said about the relative freedom, or lack thereof, of the nameless laborers who carried out the massive undertaking of constructing the fortress and its massive seawalls for over three centuries. In this curatorial interpretation, El Morro and its surrounding structures represent a benign, and successful, syncretism of European style and Caribbean function whose overall goal was to protect the status quo by preventing other European powers from challenging Spain's claim on the island colony. Today, El Morro's location within UNESCO's directory reflects the island's continued colonial status; instead of being listed under the heading of "Puerto Rico," the entry for San Felipe del Morro can only be found under the caption for the United States.

Because of El Morro's association with a recognized European architectural tradition and military technology, it is now preserved by the U.S. National Park Service as a museum of military and colonial history. As a colonial building, El Morro was designed, authorized, and built by Spanish colonizers who undoubtedly employed both African slaves and European indentured laborers, unlike Christophe's Citadel, which was designed and built by people of African descent after Haiti became an independent country. In another marked departure from the case of the Citadel, El Morro saw its share of combat as it regularly repelled assaults by foreign and domestic pirates and European sailors, whereas the canons at the Citadel never had occasion to fire the many cannonballs still stockpiled all around to this day. The El Morro fortress has been continually fortified and renovated since its original construction in 1539, whereas the Citadel has only recently been renovated on a large scale, or may be about to undergo such renovation, depending on whom one talks to.

Both the Citadel and El Morro feature prominently in their respective island's tourism industry, regularly attracting domestic and international visitors.[35] Although El Morro is one of the island's largest tourist attractions, local families come to fly kites and have picnics on its grounds during the weekend all year round. The fort is open to the public, who are free to explore it on their own, thus proving that El Morro can be considered a "museum without walls" as imagined by Malraux. However, Park Service rangers also act as guides to the fortress, leading countless groups of schoolchildren and tourists on guided tours down to the dungeons and around the cannons and *garitas*, or sentry boxes, every year. Puerto Rico's Tourism Company has adopted the *garita* as the official visual icon that represents Puerto Rico, thus conveying the island's embrace of this military installation as a central part of its own national mythology. Its official Web site touts the UNESCO designation, as well as several other official titles heaped upon the fortress: "El Morro is both a UNESCO World Heritage Site and a National Historic Site in the U.S. National Park Service. Fort San Felipe del Morro is part of San Juan National Historic Site, a unit of the U.S. National Park Service and a UNESCO World Heritage Site."[36] Even the Mexican American boxer Oscar de la Hoya, who is married to a Puerto Rican woman, had himself filmed jogging every morning on the lawns of El Morro, framed by the panoramic vistas of the sea crashing against the eighteen-foot walls during his HBO reality television series that led up to his fight with Floyd Mayweather in May 2007. While this decision may have been a blatant attempt to link his arduous training regimen to the fortress's invulnerability and effectiveness in repelling foreign attack, de la Hoya nonetheless lost the boxing match. This may be a case in point where El Morro has directly impacted popular culture, but the fortress's most immediate value to humanity may be more easily quantified in terms of the money it contributes to the local economy as a tourist attraction, rather than as an intangible asset to the world's collection of aesthetically pleasing edifices.

Part of El Morro's and the Citadel's ongoing appeal to tourists and local visitors is their very tangibility; they are physical reminders of distinct moments in history that people can not only touch, but also walk upon. This conflation of their roles as attractions and exhibits is a winning formula because it conveys an unassailable sense of authenticity. At the same time, in order to serve their strategic purpose, these fortresses had to be built on easily defensible outcrops that dominate the landscape around them. In their transformation into tourist destinations, these heritage-cum-architecture-museums now offer their visitors panoramic vistas. From these superior vantages, the viewer can look over the surrounding country and coast from the perspective once reserved for the islands' rulers. El Morro and the Citadel openly celebrate their iconic status as symbols for their respective countries' present position as destinations for cultural tourism and as representations of the legacy of their shared colonial past, so these buildings' value as historic and cultural landmarks remains untarnished, despite their explicit association with commerce. In fact, these tourist-friendly open-air museums may appear as less elitist than more traditional museums because of their easy accessibility to potential visitors, a perception that translates into a higher visitor volume and that, ultimately, means more people are exposed to the popular version of Caribbean history the Citadel and El Morro portray and embody.

Although a great deal of emphasis is placed on attracting international tourists, there are undoubtedly many attractions for local visitors, not least of which is that going in and out of these fortresses allows them to exercise a freedom of access and movement that they may not have enjoyed in years past when these military installations were still garrisoned. As historic landmarks, El Morro and the Citadel derive their significance precisely from their geographic and temporal specificity; both Caribbean military installations date back several centuries and have been involved in civil and military combat. They not only outwardly embody an all-encompassing abstract version of "History" for contemporary visitors, but these two fortresses have played a defining role in traumatic events that, through the passage of time and the intervention of historiography, have been incorporated into the official record of their islands' histories.

Antonio Benítez-Rojo dedicates an entire chapter of his landmark study *The Repeating Island: The Caribbean and the Postmodern Perspective* to *La noche oscura*. He acknowledges that the island's regional history does not accord with the pattern he himself has outlined for other Caribbean nations, but insists on reading this difference from the norm as further proof for both his theory and the novel's greatness: "The pan-Caribbean strength of *La noche oscura* comes from the fact that in Puerto Rico, it seems there was no runaway slave settlement of any importance. Thus the novel becomes an echo (or fiction, as it were) of a generalized Caribbean phenomenon although the latter never occurred in Puerto Rico."[37] By glossing over this absence in Puerto Rico's historical record in his reading of *La noche oscura*, Antonio Benítez-Rojo suggests that Rodríguez Juliá's use of the phenomenon of large-scale slave insurrections authentically represents the history of the region as a whole. While his fiction appropriates the pan-Caribbean model of plantation economy Antonio Benítez-Rojo describes, Edgardo Rodríguez Juliá spends absolutely no time describing what daily life would have been like for slaves in these apocryphal sugar plantations because *La noche oscura* begins in medias res, after the supposed large-scale insurrection has begun.

Unlike the Afrocentric narrative perspective of *The Kingdom of This World*, both Puerto Rican novels are written largely from the perspective of white men in power—a Puerto Rican history professor in *The Renunciation*, and various Spanish agents working for the bishops in *La noche oscura.* No slave characters do any actual work within the pages of the novels because they strategically lie in wait. The insurrection has either already started or is about to start so neither *The Renunciation* nor *La noche oscura* provides a clear structural framework against which the slave characters can legitimately rebel.[38] It becomes almost impossible for either the slaves or the novels to articulate what kind of alternate future they could or should imagine for themselves after they take up arms.

By not including an achievable vision of freedom within their pseudo-historical narratives, these novels accurately reflect the situation of slaves in Puerto Rico, who, after all, were not emancipated until 1873 by the Spanish Crown. The revolutionary impulse in Rodríguez Juliá's novels is neither fully utopian nor completely dystopian because it is borrowed, rather than autochthonous. The fictional uprisings depicted in both *The Renunciation* and *La noche oscura* result in the slaves' utter defeat, thus upholding the course of events reported in "official" history books. Whereas the Haitian Revolution ended both chattel slavery and French colonial rule, the slave characters' failure to win their freedom in either of these novels parallels Puerto Rico's inability to proclaim its independence from its own colonial masters: Spain and the United States. In this way, order is restored, and after a momentary break in the balance of power, the events in the novels ultimately support (although they do not exactly correspond with) the actual historical record.

Rodríguez Juliá's novels try to fill what he perceives as a gap in Puerto Rico's historical development: the island colony did not experience its first slave uprising until after the beginning of the Haitian Revolution.[39] Discussing *La noche oscura,* Rodríguez Juliá claims: "I also conceived of this novel as a pan-Caribbean nightmare, where different images of the Caribbean, such as the maroon community, large slave insurrections, etc., converge."[40] Where the Haiti-specific content of *The Kingdom of This World* marks the novel as a "museum without walls" of regional history, the explicitly ahistorical nature of *La noche oscura* and *The Renunciation* designates these texts primarily as museums of pan-Caribbean military history. Together, all three texts vividly portray the historical context of the plantation economy, or "machine," as Benítez Rojo calls it, and slaves' reactions against it in the larger Antilles. Carpentier's novel educates its readers by reproducing an authentic account that accords with the official history of the Haitian Revolution, while Edgardo Rodríguez Juliá's novels present such an outlandish version of history that readers are not content to accept it as the truth; they immediately want to know what actually took place.

In their roles as museums of pan-Caribbean military architecture, these two texts present not what actually took place within the islands but, rather, composites of what could have been. They also attest to how strongly the Haitian Revolution continues to influence artistic production in the Caribbean. The alternative version of history that *The Renunciation* and *La noche oscura* explore is one in which Spanish prelates, rather than appointed government officials, control internal political affairs within Puerto Rico. Both novels begin in medias res, with a slave insurrection already on the way or anticipated by the island's religious authorities. Contrary to expectations, both *The Renunciation* and *La noche oscura* portray the slave rebellions as static, not dynamic, events. The slave masses in both novels desire repatriation, not freedom, but they have no idea how to bring this about. Despair sets in, and all progress is lost. This is not the typical depiction of slaves as heroic martyrs that has characterized other Caribbean and novels about slavery like César Leantes's *Los gurerilleros negros* or Schwartz-Barts's *La mulatrêsse Solitude*.

Edgardo Rodríguez Juliá insists on writing El Morro into the history of slavery in Puerto Rico despite the fort's long history as a defensive military outpost, rather than as a slave port. *La noche oscura* uses the Spanish fortress to lend an air of historical authenticity to the fictitious events it describes. The novel follows the rise and fall of a maroon community that set up camp on the outskirts of San Juan, Puerto Rico, after carrying out a large-scale slave insurrection. Because they have no idea what to do after breaking free of the chains of slavery that bound them, the rebel slaves start to fight among themselves.

Two African-born figures, Obatal and Mitume, emerge as the leaders of different slave factions, and eventually the men prepare to face each other at El Morro in a battle not unlike the struggle for power that took place in Haiti between Dessalines and Christophe after Toussaint L'Ouverture's death. Like Christophe, Obatal also liked to commemorate his achievements through architecture by constructing strange or fantastic buildings that resemble beehives. His demise also echoes that of the doomed monarch: Obatal commits suicide by shooting himself in the fields next to El Morro castle before his rival, Mitume, reaches his camp. A disappointed Mitume and his followers then desecrate their enemy's body (a fate Christophe escaped thanks to his loyal subject's decision to bury him inside the Citadel compound). Eventually, Mitume leads his troops in a doomed fight against the colonial Spanish army.[41]

Since none of El Morro's specific qualities as a military fortress in any way affect the outcome of the battles described in the novel, readers are left in suspense about its larger significance within the tale. Thus, through its brief allusion to the colonial fort, *La noche oscura* prompts its readers to carry out their own supplementary research into El Morro's past. The novel's challenge is not only to function as a "museum without walls" in and of itself, but to encourage individual readers to become wall-less museums themselves, walking repositories of facts, dates, and images.

Written twelve years earlier than *La noche oscura*, *The Renunciation* also bears the trace of the Haitian Revolution in its plot. However, the comparisons it suggests between San Felipe del Morro Castle in Puerto Rico and the Citadel in Haiti are much clearer and more complex than in *La noche oscura*. Baltasar Montañez, the novel's protagonist (discussed in chapter 1), has suddenly become a leader of the slaves, but, like Obatal in *La noche oscura*, he has no clear expectations of what to do with the freedom that has been suddenly bestowed upon him after his high-profile interracial marriage and promotion to the position of secretary of state. As a pawn in the bishop's plans to stifle a slave insurrection that was brewing, Baltasar Montañez initially cooperates with the Spanish authorities but eventually rebels against both priests and bondsmen. Midway through the novel, he is supposedly imprisoned in the fortress of El Morro in a sort of internal exile during 1768. When this detention leads to violence and political chaos, the bishop attempts to bring Montañez back into public life. The latter chooses to remain in the El Morro rather than act as the bishop's pawn. Thus, through this renunciation of power, Montañez symbolically immures himself within the military fortress in life as much as Christophe was interred within the Citadel upon his death.[42]

Though he was elevated to a position of authority by the bishop with the expectation that he would be easy to manipulate, Baltasar Montañez proves to be his own man. He refuses to play along as the bishop's pawn or as the slaves' representative. Instead, Montañez dedicates himself almost exclusively to the contemplation of how architecture can help him solve all manner of political and personal problems. Montañez rebels against his forced marriage by hiring an architect who specializes in designing indoor spaces with good acoustics, Juan Espinosa, and charges him with the task of designing and building his house so as to continually torture his white wife by constantly subjecting her to the sounds of his infidelity. Not content to merely act as a patron of architecture and the persecutor of colonial womanhood, Baltasar Montañez worries about possible foreign attacks upon his island. Like Haiti's King Christophe I, Montañez designs a formidable military defense system whose construction supposedly began in 1766.[43] The design comes to Montañez in a vision; with no formal training at all, he draws up plans for an architectural innovation to boost El Morro Castle's already strong defenses. The result, "A Chronicle of a Most Ingenious Plan for a Military Architecture Consisting of the Disposition of Nature in a Mortal Language,"[44] is a sort of evil landscape design not unlike Christophe's master plan for his own fortifications in Milot. According to the fictional Montañez's blueprints, this living garden (which never actually existed) would protect the fort and, by extension, the island from either foreign or internal attack: "And it was this dream which brought me to lay out a Garden of Afflictions which will protect our precious realm. It shall be planted as a military defense on the tableland of El Morro Castle, and shall consist of soothing and tranquil glades and grottoes sheltering the most terrible traps: pits which flood with water, nests of poisonous or stinging creatures, and all manner of horrible fell death. This Garden shall be a part of the system of defensive walls even now being constructed, and such a combination of defenses shall be impregnable even for the most formidable of enemy."[45]

Although the result of a disturbed imagination, this mad scheme represents a way to creolize or domesticate the colonial fortress of El Morro. Not only does a man of African descent devise these modifications to the Spanish colonial fortress, but his vision for the project as a whole and the blueprints he writes out in particular are inherently Creole creations. They are not the result of direct influence of the Western aesthetic but, instead, they manipulate the paradisiacal nature of native resources, the local flora and fauna, to increase the fortification's strategic advantage over intruders. The plans work so well when they are carried out that the builders of the Garden of Afflictions soon become its first victims, much as the people who were compelled to construct Haiti's Citadel often fell prey to exhaustion, punishment, or accidents. The Catholic Church excommunicates Baltasar and moves him down to the dungeon in El Morro, away from his luxurious cell.

Rodríguez Juliá's two novels actively undermine the notion of a single, overarching grand narrative through which the past can be reconstructed or understood authentically. Instead, like Phillps's *Cambridge*,

Rodríguez Juliá's *The Renunciation* and *La noche oscura* cite a myriad of source materials or textual "documents," some real and some made up, to support the various claims they make. The reader feels such uncertainty around the historical events mentioned within the novels that he/she has no recourse but to turn to history textbooks and other academic publications to distinguish between actual historical facts and imaginary source material. In contrast, Carpentier's *The Kingdom of This World* fictionalizes the historical events surrounding the Haitian Revolution by presenting them through the unified prism of Ti-Noel's point of view and personal experience. Readers who find this protagonist sympathetic may want to find out more about the plight of historical figures like him, who suffered oppression under both the European and Haitian political systems.

The three texts' insistence on exhibiting a military fortress within their narratives demands a final reconsideration of what a heritage museum or display tries to achieve per se, besides the overall goal of making readers/visitors better acquainted with each country's official monuments to history. Whether in book form, on the World Wide Web, or housed within a bricks-and-mortar building, museums contribute to an ongoing, interdisciplinary debate about the role of memory and purpose in shaping our current perceptions of the legacy of the past and its continued relevance to our lives. As long as a text or a museum display is self-aware of how its contemporary circumstances affect the way it constructs and displays the historical past for the consumption of others, it can claim historical authenticity, regardless of whether its influence extends to the entire world.

6 Mourning Museums

Diasporic Practices

THERE ARE PUBLIC memorials erected in memory of important historical figures that rose up against the plantation system of slavery and gained fame and prominence in their fight for liberty throughout the islands of the Caribbean. These monuments not only commemorate the heroic actions of brave individuals who usually lost their lives in the struggle for freedom, but also serve as public indictments of the racist ideologies that attempted to deny these people their humanity and label their resistance as "unlawful" and "barbaric." As structures specifically created to mark the end of a person's life, monuments, sculptures, and mausoleums all belong to the larger category of museums of mourning because they represent a specific moment in time in which a group of people thought that there needed to be a concrete way to physically attest to the fact of a given person's existence. Statues, monuments, shrines, and tombs allow the living to pass on their sense of what the present saw fit to salvage from the past and preserve for the future as a source of inspiration and edification for generations to come.

A case in point is the monument erected in Claude Stuart Park, Port Maria, Jamaica, which commemorates Tacky, fearless leader of the large-scale 1760 Slave Revolt.[1] He led hundreds of slaves as they killed their masters in bed on Easter morning and then stole guns and ammunition. Militia men overpowered the group, killed Tacky, and publicly displayed his severed head to warn others against plotting future attacks. Today, Tacky's monument has recuperated the slain fighter's image as a source of national pride. No longer is his head a sign of repulsion and fear; now, a statue bearing the likeness of Tacky's entire body has been erected by the Jamaica National Heritage Trust. It does not stand alone, but is surrounded by monuments to other national heroes, such as members of Parliament and the Jamaican casualties of the two world wars. Rather than catering to foreign tourists, the memorial is directed primarily to a local audience. As a part of the island government's project of reclaiming its own heritage, the words on the plaque describing Tacky's actions celebrate his humanity and idealism, thereby rhetorically undoing the armed forces' desecration of his body. While ostensibly paying homage or lending respect and dignity to the deceased, memorials and mausoleums primarily serve to soothe the living in their grief.

In contrast, cemeteries and mausoleums are big tourist attractions in Haiti, the first independent republic in the Caribbean. Mausoleums may be tombs themselves or larger buildings containing graves or otherwise housing human remains, as is the case with the Laferrière Citadel in Milot, Haiti, where Henri Christophe is buried. Unlike mere cemeteries, which contain many private shrines bearing little relation to one another, mausoleums are destinations in and of themselves; they not only attract bereaved family members, but are also public sites of tranquility and reflection for people who may not be personally acquainted with the deceased. By creating a formal space for the living to confront the reality of death, mausoleums facilitate the work of mourning; through their architectural design, they allow for myriad emotional responses to the fact of the death, from grief or pity, to awe or reverence. A mausoleum may be either somber or celebratory, depending on who erects it and on its interpretation of the meaning of the life or death it memorializes. The remains of the country's first president, Jean-Jacques Dessalines, rest within a mausoleum in Port au Prince.[2] As mentioned in the previous chapter, Haiti's first self-declared king, Henri Christophe, is buried within his great fortress, the Laferrière Citadel in Milot.[3] Graves and mausoleums are structures erected to honor the memory and legacy of specific individuals who have died, but whose influence on the living continues in the present.

Political instability, natural disasters, and periods of foreign occupation have all befallen Haiti during the two centuries since it declared itself an independent nation. These circumstances tend to intensify the Haitian public's need to celebrate whatever symbols of national accomplishment are available. More recently, Haiti has returned its attention to its historic past in hopes that foreign interest in the island's symbolic status as a beacon of freedom will translate into tourist income to fund its infrastructure and stabilize its economy.

Unlike his peers, the great leader of the Haitian Revolution, Toussaint L'Ouverture, died in captivity in Europe, far from the island he helped liberate. Toussaint's name and likeness have acquired a political and cultural value worldwide that attest to his idealism as much as or more than they are associated with his political and military successes. Ironically, though, as I mentioned in chapter 1, plays, novels, biographies, and history books continue to be written about Toussaint L'Ouverture well into the twenty-first century even as the country he fought so hard to establish, Haiti, has yet to fulfill the promise of its inception. The great leader's remains are buried in the Panthéon in Paris, the national mausoleum for great European thinkers. In death, L'Ouverture has inspired countless liberation movements around the world, beginning with the abolitionists during the nineteenth century, and on into the mid-twentieth century during the decades of decolonization and the struggle for civil rights. To this day, Toussaint L'Ouverture's tomb continues to be one of the more popular stops for travelers who enjoy visiting famous people's final resting places.[4]

In 1996, A. V. Seaton proposed the term "thanatourism," to describe the kind of travel industry fueled by a desire to visit sites associated in some way with death or dying. The term is intentionally broad to encompass a large variety of motivations for these journeys. While before that date this trend in the travel industry had not been formally recognized, afterward scholars have expanded the general concept and tried to fit it within an even larger rubric of either "grief tourism" or "dark tourism," depending on the travelers' stated reasons for seeking out death-centric destinations. Those who experience a fascination with gruesome killings or crime sites clearly fall within the "dark tourism" category, whereas visitors to the Holocaust death camps or to the Vietnam Memorial go there to pay their respects to victims of geopolitical conflict. Battlefields and cemeteries attract a varying mix of thanatourists whose emotional connections to a nation's history place them firmly within the umbrella of the heritage industry.

Collaborating with Graham M. S. Dann, A. V. Seaton has added yet another category to this identifiable network of travel practices. He calls it as "slavery tourism" and defines it thus: "From an academic standpoint, slavery tourism may be considered as forming a sub-set of, sharing characteristics with, and raising similar problems to a wider tourism heritage field that has already begun to attract attention, one which has been variously labelled as 'thanatourism.'"[5] I would qualify Dann and Seaton's statement somewhat because not all aspects of slavery-related heritage travel involve contemplations of death. The discussion of plantation museums in chapter 4 illustrates their tendency to whitewash the more morbid details of slave history in favor of faithful re-creations of scenes of domestic life in all their luxury and glamour. However, visits to slave cemeteries or burial grounds, and even to museums that feature Middle Passage–themed exhibits or dioramas clearly fall within Dann and Seaton's definition of "slavery tourism," as I explain shortly.

Whereas the monuments and mausoleums I mentioned at the beginning of the chapter were all dedicated to preserving the memory of a particular individual who achieved distinction through leadership, Caribbean islands recently have begun commissioning statues or other artwork to commemorate those anonymous Africans who lost their lives while being transported to their shores during the Middle Passage. One such monument is the Mèmorial de l'Anse Caffard, a set of fifteen statues by Laurent Valère erected in Martinique in 1998 at the site where a slaving vessel broke apart during a storm in 1830, killing all the crew and its human cargo.[6] This group of statues visually represents the collective mourning that the people of Martinique can imagine feeling toward the long-dead slaves who never made it to shore. The statues' sad faces and droopy shoulders convey an expression of inconsolable grief. Catherine A. Reinhardt describes the monument as "perhaps one of the most remarkable memorials erected in memory of slavery and the slave trade during the past ten years in the French West Indies."[7] All three of these public artworks exist in isolation, each apart from the other two; thus there is no cumulative power of their exposition unless one visits all three places, looks all of them up online, or reads a book about Caribbean slavery monuments that functions as a "museum without walls."

One such compelling volume is Reinhardt's *Claims to Memory: Beyond Slavery and Emancipation in the French Caribbean* (2006), which suggests the as yet unrealized potential of these sites as stops within a historic slavery pilgrimage circuit. The establishment of such a network of artistic and historic places could promote a more socially engaged type of tourism as well as spark renewed interisland conversations about the legacy of this cruel period of history.

In contrast, both slavery museums and historical novels bring together more than one historical referent against which to understand the horror and tragedy of death in bondage. Readers and museum visitors can revisit these "sites" of memory often, and incorporate the official written or oral narratives within which objects featured in books or exhibits exist into their own sense of history. Many of the novels discussed in this study follow the same routes that such an imaginary pilgrimage would take, pausing at significant historical junctures and entrepôts on the network of transatlantic slavery. While these geographic spaces are fast becoming marked by commemorative plaques, monuments, and museums for cultural tourism, the literature about them dramatizes the events in its effort to map the New World African diasporic experience into its historical coordinates.

Some Caribbean postmodern historical novels about slavery exhibit public and private mourning rituals within their pages as they establish an interactive dialogue between the present of their international reading public, and the past, as embodied by their transported African protagonists as well as their displaced descendents. Offering the illusion of an eternal afterlife through the trope of ghostly or zombie slave narrators, Caribbean postmodern historical novels allay their readers' subconscious fears by implying that the death of the body does not entail the absolute end of a human being's consciousness and individual identity but merely diffuses it. *I, Tituba, L'esclave, Feeding the Ghosts, Crossing the River*, and the HBO film *Middle Passage* feature both living characters that mourn for their deceased fellow slaves, as well as dead characters who do not trust the living to remember them and thus speak out for themselves from the great beyond.[8] These constructions of the afterlife owe something to the model of West African animist belief systems, but they are inherently creolized hybrid conceptions that also draw on the spiritual beliefs of European Christianity and the literary conventions of ghost stories and related genres.

Playing the role of museum educators, zombie narrators like Condé's Tituba, the eponymous old man from Chamoiseau's novel; Mintah in D'Aguiar's text; and the nameless African ancestors in Phillips's novel and Deslauriers's film instruct their respective audiences about the proper rituals of mourning and commemoration practiced during their (fictional) lifetimes, clearly noting whether these observances are improvisational in nature or belong to older traditions. While death is a central subject in these novels and this film, they all focus primarily on the living. Their function as museums of mourning is to record and explain customs for slave funerals in context. Their emphasis on the coping mechanisms of the living allow *I, Tituba, L'esclave vieil homme, Feeding the Ghosts, Crossing the River*, and *Middle Passage* to achieve a feat few physical museums exclusively dedicated to commemorating slavery manage successfully—to imbue their discussions of bondage with a clear undercurrent of optimism, implying that the lives of the past should continue to matter to contemporary audiences, who can pay their respects through the very act of reading the novels themselves or visiting the museum exhibitions.[9]

In both their physical and textual incarnations, mourning museums or museums of funeral history and/or customs are secular institutions that highlight the importance of grieving rituals in cementing social and communal bonds. Instead of celebrating the illustrious achievements of deceased individuals, mourning museums take a more anthropological approach, by documenting the gradual changes in bereavement rituals and practices among the living in specific times and places. Often located within cemeteries or mausoleums, museums of mourning draw their audiences from among both the bereaved, those who only wish to pay their respects, and those who are simply curious.

The Freedmen's Village slave cemetery within Arlington National Cemetery in Virginia is a slavery-related example of this genre of museum.[10] The Freedman's Bureau had set up a village for slaves who ran away from Confederate troops during the Civil War. Although it was initially conceived as a temporary arrangement, the village existed for more than thirty years, and those of its inhabitants who died are buried in land that now belongs to the Arlington National Cemetery. Other examples of this type of museum include the Museum of Funeral Customs in Illinois, which documents the history of the funeral profession and also multicultural mourning practices; the National Museum of Funeral History in Houston, Texas, which promotes awareness about the funeral industry; the Museum of Mourning Arts in Pennsylvania, which is dedicated entirely to George Washington's funeral and the national period of mourning that followed his passing; and the Mourning Museum in Virginia, which addresses nineteenth- and twentieth-century mourning practices in the United States.[11]

As Karla F. C. Holloway points out in the opening pages of her study about African American ways of mourning, there has been a recent increase in public interest in matters of death and dying: "As the twentieth century came to a close, matters of death and dying were the subject of vital public discussion, invading radio and newspaper stories, launching best-selling books about the funeral industry, producing documentaries about the ethics of death and dying, and sustaining debates about how to die well, whether to die at all, and who should assist."[12] To this catalogue, I would add films and novels celebrating the noble sacrifice of the slaves who perished trying to bring about emancipation for all, such as *Glory*, *Amistad*, *Beloved*, and the PBS documentary *Slaves in America*.

It is only natural that the curious public would turn its attention to death-themed museum exhibits, especially those who commemorate the nameless dead who succumbed to the unspeakable oppression of the Middle Passage voyage and New World slavery.

Bricks-and-mortar mourning museums try to breach the temporal divide separating their visitors from the featured subject's particular experience of the past by relying on the curatorial function—by means of written tags that accompany displays of artifacts, as well as by making use of a wide range of multimedia outlets, like dioramas or archived audio or video clips, narrated tours, or even printed exhibition catalogues—to approximate the direct connection novels can easily establish with their readers through descriptive prose passages.[13] However, since they are bound by the constraints of historical authenticity, these institutions cannot escape the fact of their subjects' mortality in the same way that the novels can through the use of artifice.

Both mourning museums and postmodern historical novels that describe specific funeral ceremonies address themselves directly to their audiences to tell the stories behind their showcased social rituals for honoring the dead. By contextualizing these acts within a given time period, geographical location, and/or economic class, historical novels and museums create a sense of specificity about the death rituals. The novels have considerably more latitude in this regard, and their specificity is not synonymous with a claim to historical accuracy because the emphasis is more on process and on the spiritual investment in physical action than on historical accuracy.

Museum displays or novels' plots aim to tell their respective audiences a particular story about the inherent value of knowing something of the past. When the topic under consideration is the burial of slaves' remains, slavery museums and historical novels take two basic approaches: (1) emphasizing the huge numbers of African casualties that resulted from disease, mistreatment, and shipwreck during the Middle Passage journey from the African continent to the islands of the Caribbean or the American coasts;[14] and (2) celebrating the well-documented achievements of individual slaves whose identities are known so as to incorporate these personages into a new, more representative, revisionary history of life in the Caribbean and American colonies when African bondage was the law of the land. Both approaches carry the risk of completely subsuming what little we know of the lived experience of the silent multitudes of anonymous slaves under the rhetorical scaffolding of conflicting ideologies of twenty-first-century race relations.

Modern conceptions of liberty, dignity, and work encroach upon these portraits even as they try to affirm their status as historical sources documenting a past that significantly differs from the present in its civic institutions and laws, customs, material conditions, and worldview. The context of our allusions to transatlantic slavery reveals whether we see aspects of its legacy that can be recuperated in a positive light, or consider the same to be part of an undifferentiated and unmitigated evil that still permeates the fabric of our society. A comprehensive view of the burial practices and mourning practices carried out by and for slaves, whether the cause of death was accident, mistreatment, or old age, allows readers and museum visitors to consider the slave communities in their religious, emotional, and political dimensions across time and geography.

Mourning museums, either as buildings or as narrative structures within a novelistic text, demand that readers and visitors confront death and grieving as integral parts of the social life cycle, thereby affirming the strongest grounds for historical understanding by reaffirming the shared fact of mortality. In emphasizing death as the great equalizer, mourning museums and novelistic mourning museums focus on the one dimension of shared humanity that no system of unequal oppression or degradation can negate. Privilege and subjection mean nothing beyond the grave and in the act of producing suitable mourning sites, even the material differences inscribed in cultural memory can be bridged.

UNESCO's efforts to stimulate public interest in cultural tourism across the world, especially visible in its 2004 celebration of the "Slave Route" project mentioned in chapter 5, may be responsible for bringing a cultural awareness of the global scope of Atlantic slavery as a socially disruptive economic program. Readers of Middle Passage–themed historical fiction also seek out films and museum exhibits on this theme because of their interest in preserving civil rights and human equality among the races. Readers' and museum visitors' historical awareness of slavery is also informed in a very tangible way by their historical understanding of the Holocaust, a twentieth-century tragedy of genocide, torture, and exploitation that has also been publicly commemorated in film, literature, museum exhibitions, memorials, and cemeteries across Europe.

The historian and museum curator Faith Davis Ruffins points out what she calls the "museumizing" of slavery in the United States. While the historical trauma of mass killings and exploitation is parallel in both circumstances, no one shared cultural or religious context exists in which to mourn for the nameless dead Africans resting on the ocean floor as there is for the Jewish victims of German extermination. Ruffins argues that the Middle Passage has become the defining event through which popular media outlets like film, literature, and museum exhibits portray the experience of slavery to American audiences. She uses the term "death-centric" to refer to public representations of Atlantic slavery that portray it as part of a larger Black Holocaust, or systematized violence against people of African descent. Ruffins concludes that "the memorialization of the Middle Passage has now been performed in so many different African American museums and conferences that these public rituals have taken on formulaic qualities. Middle Passage events resemble traditional Black Protestant funerals in many ways."[15] While the structure and order of these events may be explicitly designed to correspond with African American styles of mourning, the audiences that participate in these proceedings are not at all racially homogeneous.

However closely the public performance of mourning in an American museum or gathering may approximate the behavior of the bereaved at an actual black Protestant funeral, a fundamental difference between the two situations remains: the victims of the Middle Passage are forever shrouded in anonymity, whereas attendees at a funeral usually know who the dead person(s) was/were.

Slave cemeteries are another public forum for the communal mourning of dead slaves. Some colonial cemeteries, like the slave cemetery in Belle Eau, Guadeloupe, have been preserved and renovated on a continuing basis, while archaeologists have only recently unearthed others in the Caribbean islands and elsewhere. In 1991, for example, the remains of a slave cemetery dating back to colonial New York were (re)discovered during the excavation of a field for the construction of a federal building. Contemporary civic, museum, and government leaders in New York faced the dilemma of how best to publicly commemorate the anonymous slaves whose graves had been disrupted.[16] The skeletons were moved from their original location in Manhattan to Howard University in Washington, D. C., since the tide of progress, or at least, of real estate development, could not be stemmed.[17] Once a new burial site was chosen and a suitable monument built, the now-anonymous slaves' remains were reinterred in 2003 following an (improvised or reconstructed) (pan) African protocol for the mass burial, a ceremony the African Burial Ground's official Web site calls "Rites of Ancestral Return."[18]

The reporter Junious Ricardo Stanton was present at the festivities and described the event as follows: "Each stop along the symbolic and ceremonial journey featured the pouring of libations, prayers, and songs as crowds turned out to pay homage to the remains of those unknown Africans."[19] Ironically, the identities of these slaves have only been erased by the passage of time and the burial accumulation of dirt and debris atop their tombs. At the time of their demise, at least their families, peers, and masters knew who they were.

Faith Davis Ruffins also attended the ceremonies and notes that "the New York African Burial Ground project generated an extraordinary amount of public attention to the enslaved dead, and has increasingly served as a model for slavery memorials and museums."[20] The event itself was celebratory rather than mournful, despite the fact that the memorial is basically nothing more than a cemetery and that the public ceremony of interment was an actual burial, albeit of a symbolic number of dead slaves who had already received funeral rites once. The stated purpose of the reinterment was to pay homage to the slaves' endurance and bravery in the face of inhumane treatment, as evidenced.

The National Parks Service plans to implement a formal interpretive strategy for the African Burial monument. which would achieve, among other things, a diasporic outlook through narrative: "Media and programming will connect stories to physical settings, such as the site of reinterment, the larger footprint of the burial ground, and the 'sites of life,' i.e., the African homelands, the Caribbean, and the New York homes and work sites of the early generations of Africans and African descendants."[21] Once this didactic dimension is added to the Burial Ground, it will become a museum of mourning and of burial practices, as well as the final resting place of the re/moved slaves whose claim to an African identity we can only assume.

Ruffins sees this move toward a new recognition and respect for the lives and deaths of slaves as an outward sign of an ideology of reconciliation, which tries to make peace with the past without forgetting what has happened. In contrast to the Afrocentric emphasis of the Black Holocaust view of transatlantic slavery through the prism of the Middle Passage, Ruffins points out that monuments and official gestures commemorating the lives of slaves in the territories to which they were brought grow out of "interracial frameworks and a predominantly non-Black political base."[22] There is worldwide interest in visiting the fields where slaves toiled to bring sugar back to the merchants' homes in England, France, Portugal, the Netherlands, Spain, and even Denmark.

Thus, despite the fact that instances of slaves dying during the Middle Passage are a key element in the plotlines of novels such as Condé's *I, Tituba*, D'Aguiar's *Feeding the Ghosts*, Phillips's *Crossing the River*,

Chamoiseau's *L'esclave*, and even Deslauriers's film *Middle Passage*, these texts do not traffic in pathos but instead depict bereavement didactically, almost ethnographically. The Middle Passage journey emerges from a joint reading of these texts, not as an immediate death sentence, but as a rite of passage for both sailors and their human cargo to overcome.

Rather than perpetuating a negative image of slaves as helpless victims of fate, these postmodern historical novels and film celebrate the depth of feeling and ingenuity exhibited both by surviving slaves and their Caribbean descendants as they devise impromptu ceremonies to honor those who perish while in bondage. Considered together, or read on their own, Delsaurier's film and the novels about slavery perform their Caribbeanness through their unapologetic celebration of hybrid burial ceremonies combining ritual and artistic modes of commemoration and mourning that expressly envision an intersection between the worlds of the living and the dead. Their portrayals of individuals in mourning examine how, within the African diaspora, the slaves' displacement from their respective countries of origin gives rise to improvised social practices to honor the dead, whether these ceremonies occur at the time of death or later. All these depictions attest to the fact that despite all the adversity that they faced on a daily basis, enslaved people were able to fulfill their familial and community obligations to the dead, even if in constrained and improvised forms.

Although they all feature similar creolized hybrid mourning practices performed by, or for, their slave protagonists, the texts themselves fall into one of two large categories: either they depict the Middle Passage as a central and formative part of the development of their enslaved characters' consciousness, or they depict the trauma of deterritorialization without mentioning the sea voyage at all. There are no heroic death scenes in any of these narratives. Instead, each text contends that both the living and the dead feel the need for some type of ceremony, icon, or other concrete means of acknowledging a given character's transition from life to death.

Despite the focus on the supernatural, the dramatization of mourning practices in these texts does not take place in an explicitly religious context; no character makes reference to any heavenly power or even articulates what expectations they have of life or existence after death as they dispatch the remains. Deslauriers's *Middle Passage*, Chamoiseau's *L'esclave*, D'Aguiar's *Feeding the Ghosts*, Condé's *I, Tituba*, and even Phillips's *Crossing the River* portray mourning as a strictly secular, social interaction temporarily linking two communities, the living and the dead, as they progress on their own migrations and transmigrations. In their function as museums of mourning, these novels and the film ask their readers to pause and consider their own emotional, communal, and historical investment as modern observers looking back upon these fictional reconstructions of social grieving practices. By highlighting their protagonists' ingenuity in finding their own unique way to bid farewell to their peers, friends, and loved ones, these texts prompt their audiences to question their own experiences of death and dying.

Burial at Sea: Guy Deslauriers's *Middle Passage* and Fred D'Aguiar's *Feeding the Ghosts*

Guy Deslauriers's film about the African slaves' traumatic transatlantic voyage, *Middle Passage*, premiered at the Toronto film festival in 2000, a full year before the Taubira law was passed in France. The film shares with the piece of legislation a similar sentiment that the slave trade and its victims ought to receive some measure of national recognition and collective mourning. Patrick Chamoiseau was the author of the original French text. After its Toronto debut, HBO films bought the distribution rights to the movie and asked the African American novelist Walter Mosley to adapt the film's poetic voice-over narration into English.[23] Thereafter, the network has aired this film in observance of African American history month in the United States. Thus, HBO itself performs or enacts the function of a national, though virtual, museum of slavery by showcasing the film *Middle Passage* alongside other thematic programming in February in order to entertain and educate its viewing audiences about African American history and culture.

Deslauriers's film is a curious text that primarily functions as a visual novel: it features absolutely no dialogue. The voice-over narration directly addresses the audience, alternating between first and second person. The narrator is a long-dead African slave contemplating the future and addressing a young African-descended boy from beyond the grave to reveal the horrors of the Middle Passage journey and point to the bones and chains still hidden beneath the sea. The visual images that accompany this narration are a series of tableaux vivants: the actors who play the roles of African slaves pose silently and unmoving before the camera. With its scattered references to the history of African enslavement and segregation in the United States, panhemispheric and black diasporic perspectives efface the specifically Caribbean origins of the film, producing a hybrid text with some odd incongruities. For example, the first-person African narrator tells the young African-descended child of the future not to consider slaves who committed suicide to be weak, since they paved the way for those who opposed Jim Crow.

In the biographies of the cast and crew found among the extra features in the HBO DVD of the film, Deslauriers acknowledges his Caribbean roots in Martinique and also criticizes the deficiencies in the school curriculum in that overseas department and, by implication, in France, which do not include any mention of the Middle Passage. By now, Maryse Condé's leadership of the French committee to commemorate slavery should have fixed this sin of omission. The comments included within his official biographical entry demonstrate that personally, Deslauriers subscribes to the Black Holocaust view of the Middle Passage discussed earlier: "While a schoolboy in Martinique, director Guy Deslauriers did not learn about the journey of slaves to the New World. 'The subject is still taboo in the Caribbean and Europe, but it is the biggest genocide in the world,' he explains."[24] The reference to genocide links the Middle Passage to the worldwide catastrophe of the Holocaust despite the structural differences between the two events. Whereas Jews throughout Europe were targeted for extermination by the Nazi Germans and their associates, the Africans who were captured and sold into bondage were expected to survive not only the harrowing journey, but also the harsh Caribbean climate and oppressive work conditions. Despite the director's personal outlook, the film, which functions as a visual novel, promotes a less death-centric view of both slavery and the Middle Passage. Its diasporic vision encourages all people of African descent to develop an idea of Africa as their originary "home."

This film's museum function is prescriptive; it tells contemporary viewers to actively mourn the slaves who died long ago, instead of suggesting suitable activities to be performed in honor of these victims. As such, it opens up the space for new, individualized hybrid and creolized forms of mourning for the past, such as the statues that comprise Martinique's Mèmorial de l'Anse Caffard, mentioned earlier. *Middle Passage* ostensibly sets out to celebrate the life made possible by "the survivors" of the slave trade who arrived upon New World shores. The dead African's spirit reaches out to the future generations, those African-descended inhabitants of the New World, and asks them to include people like him as part of their patrimony. Through the film's dedication to its intended (or ideal) audience, "To Africa, the crucified/To the slaves of yesterday/and their descendants today," *Middle Passage* highlights its own status as an object that can be symbolically given to various groups of people. In this way, it most clearly carries out its function as a mourning museum.

The single narrator claims to speak for a mass of undifferentiated "Africans" displaced from their homelands through transatlantic slavery whose complaints are voiced by a single, male voice.[25] This approach is problematic on many levels, most obviously in its assumption that there is now, or ever was, such a thing as a continental identity shared by and recognized among the various inhabitants of the distinct regions in Africa. This clearly ahistorical view underestimates the European slave traders' organized campaigns to disorient their prisoners by isolating them linguistically from their fellow passengers aboard the slaving vessels. Furthermore, this image of a timeless Africa denies that continent entry into modernity—if the eternal Africa is the continent victimized by the slave trade, none of its current political tragedies can match the scope or devastation of that historical "genocide." However problematic, it is from this vantage point of a timeless (or atemporal) united African continent that the film addresses itself to a contemporary child supposed to represent the future of the African diaspora. This depiction clearly infantilizes the diaspora, the "youngest buds" of the Middle Passage survivors, as young and inexperienced in relation to a wiser, and therefore more authentic, African culture located outside of time and space.

The disembodied narrator instructs his young listener to: "Take your child's hand and honor their [the slaves who died during the Middle Passage] memory. In doing this, you may help the lost souls of Africa find their way back to the shores of their long ago and forgotten ancestors."[26] The speaker does not explain *how* the child is supposed to use his hand to carry out this work of mourning, especially since the bones of the "lost souls of Africa" are resting at the bottom of the sea. Thus, while this call to action is amorphous, it also emphasizes the need for mourning practices to be embodied and leaves the actual nature of the ceremony up to the discretion and creativity of the childlike New World audience to figure out.

Fred D'Aguiar's Middle Passage novel *Feeding the Ghosts* also suggests that Creole art—both wood carvings and oral storytelling—can be fitting memorials through which to remember the dead. The novel's female protagonist, Mintah, is an English-speaking African woman who had been baptized a Christian by European missionaries earlier in her youth. Mintah survives being thrown overboard during the Middle Passage voyage from Africa to Jamaica by catching hold of a rope while she was underwater, and climbing back onboard the *Zong*.[27] The novel functions as a museum of specifically female mourning practices, borne out of Mintah's internalized memory of the trauma of being thrown into the sea. As such, the mourning rituals she devises for her fellow slaves who perished during the Middle Passage take place completely within the prelingual emotional space that Lacan calls the realm of the imaginary.

Mintah improvises two rituals for honoring the memory of her peers who plunged into the water with her, both of which involve reproduction on some level: the first is by planting one tree per victim on the property she buys in Jamaica after she purchases her own freedom. This act turns mourning into a celebration, by changing the landscape of the island in a tangible and positive way. This willed act of reforestation is also a small blow against the European-fostered ecological sabotage that turned the fertile islands of the Caribbean into large-scale, mono-crop agricultural "factories," or plantations, which, in turn, required the extensive physical labor that Africans were imported to provide.

The second, Creole way Mintah mourns her fellows is by carving wooden images to represent the dead, a skill she developed only after her traumatic voyage. The figures Mintah carves represent and commemorate both the actual lives that were lost during the *Zong* massacre, as well as the potential lives that never materialized, those of the children she never had. In this way, their commemorative function is similar to that of the Middle Passage sculpture monument in Martinique that I mentioned earlier, the Mèmorial de l'Anse Caffard. Mintah's carvings comfort her by giving her something to do after she finally purchases her freedom in the United States and moves to Jamaica to teach both young and old how to read. While her literacy-based community service helps Mintah contribute to the well-being of the future generations, her artwork connects her past and present lives. Like the wood (trees) she has herself planted, the funerary objects she creates are Creole works of art, born of the island and from the experience of slavery.

Since her trees and figures are available for all to see, Mintah's mourning is both public and private. She alone knows the fullness of their meaning. She perceives this project as her way of giving life to the dead and the unborn, thereby imbuing the entire mourning ritual with an inherent femininity. Her ritualized interaction with the figures extends beyond the phase of creation, and continues as part of her everyday life, like when she cleans: "Often they get dusted by me in a process that is more an examination of each. I turn them over in the light, weighing them up in my palms, and I rub the wood with a cloth as if massaging the grain."[28] This conflation of feminine duties—mourning and cleaning—renders the domestic sphere as the site of the sacred in the novel and parallels the modern American convention that assigns responsibility for tending graves to the surviving female members of a family. The novel never depicts what Mintah's life was like when she was a slave in Maryland. She only appears within a domestic space after the time when she has supposedly purchased her freedom. When Mintah finally dies, both her house and the statues she carved burn up with her in a great conflagration, thus symbolically uniting her with the spirit of those fellow Africans with whom she had been consigned to die on the day the *Zong*'s captain decided to dump his human cargo into the ocean. In this instance, fire acts to purge the taint of the drowning, and symbolic balance is restored between these two natural elements.

The very act of making art demonstrates a level of agency and choice that was denied to Mintah, first when she was thrown overboard, and later as she lived out her years in bondage in the United States. Her talent for carving gives rise to an interesting paradox: the figures she makes are so captivating that those who see them recognize only their aesthetic value instead of their symbolism as funerary objects. Mintah carves other functional pieces that she has no trouble selling, but she keeps the figures to herself because she regards them as spiritually charged: "If only they could see that what they are laying their hands on is a treasure, that it harbours the past, that it houses the souls of the dead and that the many secrets of the death are delivered up in it."[29] For Mintah, the figures she carves are as tangible a reminder of those people's time in the world as any other monument, public or private, that could be erected, so she displays the fruits of her labor throughout her house, where they keep her company. They also are the most tangible proof of her own freedom, since they are objects she can make and choose to keep or sell at will. In tending to them, she performs the sort of dutiful obligations that families have traditionally shown to their ancestors in cultures where family forms a spiritual community across time.

Mintah's impulse to honor her fellow passengers by carving their likeness is an improvised and Creole gesture of commemoration. As was the case in *Middle Passage*, where the dedication immediately preceded the film credits, the revelation of Mintah's private mourning ritual comes only at the end of D'Aguiar's *Feeding the Ghosts*. The novel's most obvious curatorial intervention comes in the epilogue, where a disembodied narrator who both is and is not Mintah strikes a note similar to the view of *Middle Passage* mentioned in the production notes. The narrator begins by proclaiming, "We were·all dead. The ship was full of ghosts."[30] However, the epilogue undoes the negative connotations of the image of "ghosts" when the narrator explains to her implied listener that the way to appease the anger of these souls for not receiving a proper burial is to mourn them by telling the stories of their lives over and over: "I'm not sure who is who, you or I. There is no fear, no shame in this piece of information. There is only the fact of the *Zong* and its unending voyage and those deaths that cannot be undone. Where death has begun but remains unfinished because it recurs. Where there is only the record of the sea. Those spirits are fled into wood. The ghosts feed on the story of themselves. The past is laid to rest when it is told."[31] Thus, the epilogue carves out a narrative space in which the novel itself can be interpreted as a funerary object like Mintah's wooden figures; by reading what is contained within its pages, people "tell" the story of the past, much like Mintah remembers and honors the lives of those who perished at sea each time she looks at or cleans the little statues she has carved in their honor. Thus, *Feeding the Ghosts* deploys a complex web of interrelationships through which the reader mourns even as s/he continues to read the story.

By depicting these improvised rituals to honor the dead near the conclusion of their respective texts, D'Aguiar and Deslauriers enact a circular ending to the tales they tell. This type of narrative structure demands that readers go back to the beginning and reread (or re-view) the book or film in order to fully appreciate the significance of the private ceremonies about which they have read. Readers embarking upon this second reading would be fully aware now that the slave characters featured in the narratives are dead. Although this circularity undoes the element of suspense to a large degree, it better simulates the experience of walking through a museum of mourning and viewing the different objects showcased through the predetermined prism of death as a fundamental part of life. Whereas museum visitors attending an exhibit for the first time have a fairly good idea of what kinds of objects they will see displayed, novel readers typically want to be surprised by the unfolding of the plot. By demanding a second reading/viewing, *Feeding the Ghosts* and *Middle Passage* ask to be considered as museums of funeral practices and mourning.

Slave Cemeteries

The Middle Passage serves only as historical background that informs the predominant plotlines of Fred D'Aguiar's *Feeding the Ghosts*, Maryse Condé's *I, Tituba* and Caryl Phillips's *Crossing the River* without dominating them. Thus, these texts represent a move toward reconciliation as the primary ideology through which to understand Phillips's, Condé's, and Chamoiseau's portrayals of death and mourning in the context of transatlantic bondage. Unlike the countless anonymous slaves who perished at sea during the Middle Passage journey, and whose remains were thrown overboard, the slave characters who die in *Feeding the Ghosts*, *I, Tituba*, and *Crossing the River* leave behind the earthly burden of their bodies for the living to dispose of. These three novels also affirm the communal nature of burial as a social function that affects the individual, the family unit, the community, and even concerned strangers.

Since the deaths portrayed within these three novels take place far from anywhere the characters consider home, they require that outside witnesses to their dying improvise a fitting ritual to honor their passing. This inclusion of outsiders within the novels' circle of mourners mimics the way in which contemporary readers and museum visitors fulfill the role of symbolic mourners for long-dead, anonymous slaves when they visit slave cemeteries or museums of mourning and/or funeral practices. In their recognition that people other than those directly connected to the dead can nonetheless honor their memory centuries later by grieving their loss, *L'esclave*, *Crossing the River*, and *I, Tituba* call for an interactive approach to the task of incorporating the lessons of the past into our contemporary lives.

As a group, these novels may be read as slave cemeteries because they fulfill a double social function of housing the dead and allowing the living either the opportunity to come and express their grief or to tour the grounds and learn about a place's history. Since readers can choose to approach these tales either as mourners or tourists, then *L'esclave*, *I, Tituba*, and parts of *Crossing the River* resemble the African Burial Ground in New York City or the slave cemetery in Guadeloupe, both of which also allow their visitors to choose either of these subject positions.

When it depicts the intersection between the worlds of the living and the dead, Patrick Chamoiseau's *L'esclave* functions as a reliquary, a container to hold the sacred remains of a sainted figure. As discussed in chapter 1, the narrator is also a protagonist within the story; he is a writer who claims to have written the novel *Texaco*, the text that earned Patrick Chamoiseau's international critical acclaim. During a walk in the forest in Martinique, the narrator chances upon a set of human remains lying on a boulder. Although he is initially unsure whether the remains belong to an African slave or a Carib native, the narrator feels their inherent power when he touches them. The novel's narrator becomes obsessed with the skeleton he finds; the unburied bones haunt his dreams, making him think of the maroons, runaway slaves who hid in the forests to escape the chains of bondage. The narrator feels that the spirit of the old slave he has conjured up by touching the bones wants him to use his writing skills to tell the story that the dead man will not/cannot write for himself: "The old slave has left me his bones, saying: carry the stories/memories and the time gathered together."[32] Writing, then, becomes the narrator's work of mourning for a slave he never knew in *L'esclave*, and the bones themselves, as relics of a secular sacrifice, assume a more important role in his emotional connection to the past than the particulars of his life story would have.

As a whole, Chamoiseau's novel suggests that mourning rituals reveal more about the sense of loss experienced by the bereaved than they convey specific details about the life of the deceased. The narrator mourns the imaginary slave by writing of his own obsession with the bones. Acting in accordance with what he supposes the dead slave would wish, the narrator of *L'esclave* "writes" an apocryphal text, *Toucher* (*To Touch*), excerpts of which appear as individual epigraphs at the start of each chapter. When considered together in isolation, the quotes from this supposedly larger apocryphal text read more like a poem than a work of prose:

To touch
Bones' still dream, of what has been and is no longer, and which yet persists
    upon awakening.
Bones' principle, mineral and living, opaque but organizing.
Bones' reflections, only imageless images of pregnancies and agonies.
Bones' mirror-brightness, total organic night of all living promises.
Bones' fertile cement, secret foundation of creations and re-creations.
Bones' memory, only perceiving trace of the works' forsaken.
Bones' shapeless shape, invincible intent of the creating desire.[33]

Each line constitutes one isolated bone, and together, they represent the slave's skeleton, much in the same way that all we have of history are isolated primary documents until historians compile and compare them, and give them meaning through narrative. While the verses/excerpts of the apocryphal *To Touch* are a meditation upon the metaphysical implications of the narrator's contact with the human remains, the plot of the novel *L'esclave* is an imaginative reconstruction of the fictional slave's life story, told as if the bones found in the forest were actually his. As the narrator imagines him, the old slave survived the treacherous Middle Passage crossing of the Atlantic and dies many years later, after he has run away into the tropical forest of Martinique.

The novel stages its own mini-exhibition about mourning practices when it displays the narrator's textual reliquary visually on the page. Unlike the quotes from Glissant, which appear alone and unattributed on the left page at the beginning of each chapter, the excerpts from the fictional narrator's text claim a position of privilege at the top of the right page preceding the text of each chapter, and include both the source and page number each time they appear. This level of bibliographic annotation constitutes a curatorial intervention into the text, which lends an implied authenticity to the apocryphal excerpts that is simultaneously denied to Glissant's real words, which appear without attribution. Thus, the novel equates mourning with either writing or reading.

The theory of mourning implicit within Chamoiseau's text is Creole in its emphasis on tangible art created within the Caribbean island itself: just like Mintah carved wooden figures, the narrator of *L'esclave* writes down his poetic musings and supposedly collects them within the apocryphal volume *Toucher*. The bones' exposed condition leads the narrator to assume that they had never been buried properly and, thus, were likely to belong to a runaway slave rather than to an Amerindian. His immediate response is to bury them symbolically, with words, rather than to cover them with dirt. Not only does this episode suggest that the bones have come to be at home on their rock in the island, but it also implies that by taking root in the narrator's consciousness, they have laid claim to his supposed Creole literary production: *Toucher*. Thus, through the vehicle of apocryphal metafiction, Chamoiseau portrays mourning for dead slaves as a communal experience, best accomplished by the reading/writing of fiction. Although not everyone can touch the skeletal remains of dead slaves in order to establish a physical connection between the past and the present, anyone can read a book about such an encounter between the living and the dead.

Another hybrid book that functions as a virtual reliquary is *Fortune's Bones: The Manumission Requiem*. An elegy commissioned by the Mattatuck Museum in Waterbury, Connecticut, and penned by the poet laureate of Connecticut, Marilyn Nelson, this book simultaneously presents and curates the elegiac poem as a contemporary act of mourning. Fortune was a slave who lived and worked on a small farm in Connecticut during the late eighteenth century. As the explanatory notes inform the reader, Fortune and his family belonged to "Dr. Preserved Porter, a physician who specialized in setting broken bones."[34] When Fortune died after an injury, Dr. Porter saw an opportunity to advance his scientific understanding of human anatomy by using Fortune's skeleton as a research and teaching tool. Thus, instead of burying him whole, Dr. Porter preserved Fortune's skeleton for his own, and his sons' edification, since all of them were physicians who had not previously had access to a complete set of human bones. Years later, a descendant of Dr. Porter donated the skeleton to the Mattatuck Museum. But it was not until the 1990s that historians, archaeologists, and anthropologists working in concert were able to piece Fortune's story together.

Following the precepts of new museology, the Mattatuck Museum made the entire process of the museum's history of display and the discovery of Fortune's identity the focus of their exhibition, including the episodes of mistaken identity, when the skeleton was called by the name "Larry," which had been inscribed upon one of the bones at some earlier time. The skeleton is accompanied by an explanatory text, as well as by a portrait painting, and a sculpture of what Fortune might have looked like—both of the latter were based on data uncovered through forensic science. There is a virtual gallery that also contains images and information about this exhibit.[35]

Fortune's tale has a synecdochic function within the museum—his story serves as an entry point for a larger exploration of the history of slavery in this local community, much in the same way that the anonymous human bones the narrator of *L'esclave* finds in the forest teach him something about the slave past of his island of Martinique. By commissioning this poem, both the Mattatuck Museum and the State of Connecticut, represented through the state Commission of the Arts, helped fund this project. Some have seen this as an opportunity to try to atone for the insult that Dr. Porter's preservation of Fortune's bones perpetrated against Fortune's memory. However, there is still no consensus about what, if anything, should be done with the skeleton. Some people favor burying Fortune, while others defend his continued exhibition because of his new pedagogical significance—instead of serving as an example of anatomy any longer, Fortune's bones now represent the complete disenfranchisement of slavery that did not extend enslaved persons the right to own even their bodily remains.

The book's title describes the genre of the poem as a "requiem," which it defines somewhat loosely as "words and music written to honor the dead."[36] As a whole, the book functions like a travelling version of the actual exhibit on display in a kiosk at the Mattatuck Museum and available online through its official Web page. The poem is printed on the right-hand pages, while the left-hand pages contain photographs documenting aspects of the exhibit as well as curatorial notes and annotations by Pamela Espeland, a professional ghostwriter and editor. Further amplifying this interdisciplinary project is the reference to the score Dr. Ysaye M. Barnwell composed to accompany the requiem.[37]

The requiem is divided into six distinct parts, each of which is a short poem in its own right. While the concept of the requiem is derived from the Latin mass tradition, Nelson creolizes this musical/lyrical genre through the use of vernacular terms for formal parts of the funeral mass. Nelson translates the "Introit" into a "Preface," but leaves the terms "Kyrie" and "Sanctus" in the original Greek and Latin. Nelson also adds a "lament," a genre of elegy usually associated with female mourners, and also incorporates Buddhist elements into the formal structure of the piece through the addition of a reassurance to the dead or dying slave that s/he is not his/her body. The refrain, "You are not your body,/you are not your bones. /What's essential about you/is what can't be owned,"[38] captures well the paradoxical situation the museum and the local community find themselves in regarding the most ethical thing to do with this skeleton. If Fortune's story is told and his individuality preserved against the cultural and historical amnesia that shrouded it for decades, his bones can have their own afterlife as historical artifacts interpreted for the general public through the self-referential museum display. Like the old slave's bones in the Martinican forest, Fortune's skeleton now belongs to his descendants.

Maryse Condé's novel *I, Tituba* imagines an entirely different interaction between the worlds of the living and the dead. In this text, the protagonist can summon the spirits of her ancestors at will, although it takes her a bit more effort to get them to appear when she lives in bondage in the United States than when she is on her own in the forest of her native Barbados. The novel functions as a mourning museum by showcasing three different grieving rituals that change depending on (1) the deceased, (2) the circumstances surrounding the deaths, and (3) the life and times of the mourner. Like the nameless African narrator of Deslauriers's *Middle Passage*, the eponymous first-person narrator of Condé's novel, Tituba, functions as a zombie or undead curator of her own life story, explaining to modern readers how she views her relationship to the dead. The novel portrays three different kinds of African-inspired mourning rites performed by its Barbadian characters: (1) the public commemoration of the deceased through popular song, (2) a private lament, and (3) the direct invocation of the spirits of the ancestors.

In describing these distinct ways of grieving for the loss of a slave character, *I, Tituba* suggests that slaves in the Caribbean colonies took steps, however small, to honor the lives of those who toiled alongside them and died. Through mourning, these bondsmen and women performed their humanity to themselves and each other, thus disproving the rhetorical fiction of their racial inferiority constructed by white, European capitalists and government agents to justify their ongoing subjugation. In its role as a mourning museum, *I, Tituba* argues that the lives of the present are enriched by their knowledge of the past and their appreciation of how the survivors of both the Middle Passage and the monotonous and exhausting toils of slavery marked the deaths of their companions, even as they themselves continued to endure the oppression of their own lives.

In keeping with the circular narrative pattern I have outlined in the previous discussion of Middle Passage novels, Tituba reveals in the concluding chapters that her entire first-person tale has been narrated from beyond the grave. The dead Tituba clamors to tell her own story, like the first-person narrator of Deslauriers's *Middle Passage*. However, the visual novel's Afrocentrism is expressed through the narrator's use of a collective first person, whereas Condé's Tituba is fiercely independent, perhaps owing to her New World origins. The story she tells is hers alone. Despite the obvious fact of the book's existence as a physical object in the material world, Tituba's ghost forcefully asserts that her tale constitutes an oral document for those who know how to properly honor their dead.

As discussed in chapter 1, Tituba reports that her own death has been commemorated through popular song in Barbados. She approves of this form of improvised public homage paid to her memory because it reaches out beyond blood ties and establishes kinship through a set of shared ideals. Tituba considers the song a fitting memorial to the struggle against oppression precisely because it outlasts the limitations of time and makes possible a connection both with later generations of slaves in Barbados and with her readers. Interestingly, Tituba does not include the lyrics of her memorial song within the text, thereby avoiding the awkwardness of seeming to mourn for herself.

Earlier in her narrative, Tituba had indeed included the lyrics of a mourning song she had composed to commemorate the untimely death of her first child. Having voluntarily given up her freedom as an adult living in Barbados to follow her husband, John Indian, into slavery in the American colonies, Tituba could not bear the thought of compromising their unborn child's future by giving birth to a slave who might be sold away from her at any minute. She decides to terminate her pregnancy, but has mixed feelings about killing the baby she so desperately wanted.[39] As part of the mourning process for her offspring, Tituba composes a song, "Lament for my lost child"; she commits it to memory, and softly sings it whenever she wants to commune with the spirit of her unborn child.[40] A secular apostrophe to the memory of the child she never met, the "Moonchild" poem takes the place of prayer in providing solace to Tituba. She shares the words of the song with her white master's children, who, unaware of their significance, hum along with it and therefore indirectly participate in the slave's ritual mourning. Later in the novel, Tituba sings her old lament to mourn not only her unborn child, but also the spirit of Hester Prynne's unborn baby who dies as a result of its mother's suicide in this instance of parodic rewriting and transworld identity.

These two occasions of interracial mourning, however unwittingly performed, are examples of the novel's ideology of reconciliation. They stake out a space for the reader to become involved in the work of mourning for these fictional slave characters about whom s/he knows much more than anyone has been able to establish about the many actual people who perished during the treacherous trip across the ocean from the waters off the coast of Africa and into a New World port. In yet another instance of the prevalence of interracial reconciliation as a running theme in the novel, Tituba's master, a Jewish merchant, who had recently lost his children in a fire from which he escaped himself, turns to Tituba in his time of crisis, instead of seeking solace within his faith. The merchant asks his slave, Tituba, to arrange for a brief conversation with his dead children to ensure that their souls are at peace.

Although, superficially, the ethnic identities of the two characters involved in this interaction would seem to indicate an overdetermined argument about the inherent parallels between the Middle Passage and the Holocaust, Condé's novel resists such easy pigeonholing. These two related examples of fictional characters seeking to establish dynamic interaction with the dead, rather than merely viewing them across an impassible barrier, prove that this novel considers successful mourning to be reciprocal, instead of entirely one-sided action. The grief of loss is the great equalizer in both the story and outside of it, in real life, and thus in its museum function, Condé's novel reaches out to the broadest possible audience to convey her message that we can all relate to death and dying.

Tituba's knowledge of herbs and potions plays a less sinister role in the novel's final portrayal of mourning, which, chronologically, takes place much earlier in her life story. She uses these natural products as a sacrificial offering to conjure up the spirits of her African ancestors at will— her mother, stepfather, and guardian—while she lives in Barbados and can do so, but with greater difficulty, in Salem Village, Massachusetts colony. The three different kinds of mourning depicted in *I, Tituba* are life-affirming, rather than death-centric, because they all grow out of the character's belief that death does not permanently sever the ties of kinship that unite individuals during their lifetime. Tituba's powers as a medium, and her ability to contact her family with ease in the Great Beyond, facilitate another sort of border crossing; she bonds physically and emotionally with her Jewish owner, Benjamin Cohen D'Azevedo, through their shared grief.

Caryl Phillips's *Crossing the River* also depicts rare moments in which people from different cultures, blacks and whites, improvise a fitting ritual to mark the passing of anonymous slaves. Phillips's novel emphasizes that both white and black characters occupy a hybrid space somewhere between the public and private realms of experience when they engage in such improvisational mourning practices. As mentioned in chapter 3, *Crossing the River* demonstrates its ideology of reconciliation through the depiction of a much-bereaved and guilt-stricken African father figure who wants to know how his children fare after he sells them into New World slavery, a fate tantamount to death. However, this first-person zombie narrator who addresses the reader from beyond the grave views the ongoing vibrancy of the many cultures of the African diaspora as living proof that the Middle Passage did not kill off African culture.

As a textual mourning museum, *Crossing the River* portrays the deaths and subsequent burials of two of the mythical African father's children, both of whom were enslaved in the United States. The first of these occurs in the vignette "The Pagan Coast." Nash Williams was an emancipated slave whose American master repatriated him to Liberia. Although technically a free man, Nash's correspondence with his master, Edward Williams, throughout his section of the novel signals his continued emotional subservience to the person he considers his spiritual father and who, literally, paid to make him free. In Liberia, Nash has trouble navigating the conflicting social spheres: those of the missionaries, expatriate Americans, and native inhabitants of the territory. After many years of living at a subsistence level, and the tragic loss of his American nuclear family, Nash "goes native": he abandons his plans to convert the Africans, takes on several local wives and has children with them, and builds an African compound for himself and his new family. He is brokenhearted, lives in poverty, and dies of an undisclosed illness.

When he stops receiving his favorite slave's missives, Nash's former master sets sail to Liberia to find out what happened. He learns of Nash's death from another of his former slaves, Madison, who guides Edward not to Nash's grave, as readers might logically expect but, instead, to where he spent his days, in his hut. This is no mere act of subterfuge on Madison's part. It underscores the fact that we can tell more about the dead by looking at how they lived than by gazing upon their memorials. Museum exhibits follow a similar logic as they combine and re-create specific aspects of everyday life to help their visitors connect in a very basic way with the familiar routines from the past. Mourning museums like the ones mentioned earlier regularly feature exhibitions of mourning customs that are set entirely within a domestic setting.

Despite arriving at Nash's residence, rather than his tomb, Edward's response is suitably funerary in nature. He covers his nose to guard from the stench he detects in the surroundings, and then breaks into a silent song. Compared to the popular song about Tituba in Condé's novel, the Christian hymn in this particular episode is an inappropriate memorial for Nash because he had renounced his Western faith as ineffectual. Furthermore, the silence of the performance, while symbolic of the one-sided nature of the communication between master and slave, is uncanny because of the incongruity inherent in the public performance of a grief felt privately. This scene illustrates how the impulse toward reconciliation in the context of slavery can go terribly wrong. It is nonetheless valuable as part of the novel's textual exhibit about "African" mourning practices.

A second, more positive, portrayal of mourning across racial and class lines takes place in the vignette "West," from *Crossing the River.* This section follows Martha, a runaway female slave character who decides to join a group of "colored pioneers"[41] as they make their way westward to California in hopes of eventually reuniting with her daughter, from whom she had been sold away. Because of her advanced age, as well as the hard treatment she suffered during her life in bondage, Martha's health deteriorates before she reaches her destination. Unable to care for her during the harsh winter, the caravan drops her off on the streets of Denver, Colorado, where a Good Samaritan gives her shelter and keeps her company as she agonizes and dies. This part of the novel presents the work of mourning as another act of witnessing that suggests that the most basic social contract is the implied promise that no one should have to die alone. Martha is too delirious in her agony to answer her bene- factress's questions and, thus, neither character learns anything concrete about the other's life. The unnamed white woman feels compelled to en- sure that Martha's body receives a proper burial: "She opened the door and looked in upon the small colored woman, who stared back at her with wide eyes. The unsuccessful fire in the pot-bellied stove was dead. The woman gently closed the door. Martha won't be taking any wash- ing today. And the woman wondered who or what this woman was. They would have to choose a name for her if she was going to receive a Christian burial."[42] Assisting the dead on their way into the afterlife is a basic duty that human beings feel they owe one another no matter what. To carry out that duty, the Good Samaritan follows the religious protocol laid out by her church or preacher.

By mourning for the dead, we claim some kinship to them. They enter our lives and consciousness, never to leave it again. Both Caribbean post- modern historical novels about slavery and bricks-and-mortar museums dedicated to the same topic walk a fine line between appropriating the sorrow the slaves felt for each other's passing, and commiserating with the pain of their loss. Reading about the risks slave characters take in order to ensure that someone receives a proper burial recalls the opening scene in Sophocles' *Antigone*, in which Oedipus's brave daughter con- fronts her uncle and declares herself willing to die if it means she can lay both her brothers' bodies to rest. By erecting monuments like cenotaphs, statues, mausoleums, museums, and even novels, the intellectual and political leaders of the various Caribbean islands hope to attract more heritage tourists to their shores.

Notes

Introduction

1. This law was named after its sponsor, Christiane Taubira, the deputy from French Guiana. The French name of the committee is Comité pour la Mémoire de l'Esclavage.

2. Bal, introduction to Bal, Crewe, and Spitzer, eds., *Acts of Memory*, vii.

3. Glissant eventually became fascinated by the figure of the runaway slave, or maroon, and returns to it explicitly in his novel *Quatrième siècle*, among other works.

4. "Chirac Names Slavery Memorial Day," BBC News, January 30, 2006, http://news.bbc.co.uk/2/hi/europe/4662442.stm.

5. Naipaul, *The Middle Passage*, 66.

6. Naipaul, *A Way in the World*, 30.

7. Faith Davis Ruffins of the Smithsonian Museum interprets these acts as indicative of a move toward "racial reconciliation" in "Revisiting the Old Plantation," 420.

8. Preziosi, "Brain of the Earth's Body," 83.

9. Alpers, "Museum as a Way of Seeing," 27.

10. Kirshenblatt-Gimblett, "Objects of Ethnography," 387–88.

11. Karp, "Culture and Representation," 14.

12. Carbonell, ed., *Museum Studies*, 7.

13. Ibid., 8.

14. For a description and analysis of Wilson's installation, see Corrin, ed., *Mining the Museum*.

15. The exhibition Kara Walker: My Complement, My Enemy, My Protector, My Love ran at the Whitney Museum from October 11, 2007, to February 3, 2008. The official Web site is still functional (http://www.whitney.org/www/exhibition/kara_walker/index.html).

16. Weil, *Making Museums Matter*, 212.

17. Ibid., 202.

18. More information on the Museum Management Program is available at http://www.nps.gov/history/museum/whoweare.htm.

19. Witcomb, *Re-imagining the Museum*, 13.

20. Kratz and Karp, "Introduction," 5.

21. Ruffins, "Revisiting the Old Plantation," 404.

22. UNESCO funded Andrew Hurley's translation of Edgardo Rodríguez Juliá's novel *La renuncia del héroe Baltasar* (published as *The Renunciation*) as one of its "Collection of Representative Works."

23. The PBS online virtual museum can be found at http://www.pbs.org/wnet/slavery/teachers/virtual.html.

1. Books as National (Literary) History Museums

1. Puerto Rico's fondness and nostalgia for colonial times are unusual sentiments in the Caribbean and Latin America, where Columbus is now more commonly regarded as a colonial tyrant, and his act of "discovery" is seen by many as a genocide of native peoples. The official Web site for the Museum of the Americas is http://www.prtc.net/musame/frame.htm.

2. Belcher, *Exhibitions in Museums*, 63.

3. In August 2008, I went to the Museum of the Americas in Old San Juan accompanied by my toddler son, William Carlos, and my aunt, Alma Blanco, who has lived her entire life in Puerto Rico and is well acquainted with Ricardo Alegría's scholarly reputation. Neither she nor any other member of my family had ever heard of this museum or of the Museo de Nuestra Raíz Africana. The three of us spent a few hours together in the African Heritage exhibition. During our visit, a few people came in and saw the exhibition, but no one other than my aunt and I spoke at all, making it hard for me to ascertain whether they were local museum visitors or tourists. My aunt and I had engaged the attendants in conversation in our native Puerto Rican Spanish, while I spoke English to my two-year-old son, who eventually grew tired of looking around. Thus, while my personal observation of the museum and its exhibitions yielded little in the way of audience analysis, the afternoon we spent there made for some interesting intergenerational bonding.

4. Quasi-official institutions face considerable obstacles as they try to serve an educational role. Their funding and their success depend upon the goodwill and generosity of the well-to-do, and yet their self-declared mission is to inform and educate those people with less access to, and investment in, literature and the fine arts. While their explicitly didactic mission cannot be dismissed too quickly, particularly in the specific context of the Puerto Rican myth of origin that tends to eclipse or efface the contribution of African slaves to the shaping of the island's culture and traditions, the limited reach of the museum as a cultural institution is a topic for analysis. The museum's reverent approach to history is in keeping with the expectations of its two largest constituencies, the cruise ship industry and the local schools, both of which expect this institution to

serve an explicitly didactic mission. This same conservatism limits the museum's potential appeal for, and impact upon, a broad local audience familiar with the island's history and more open to fresh or unconventional approaches that question accepted versions of the past.

5. Deetz, "A Sense of Another World," 376.

6. The translations are my own, and the original Spanish is Dr. Ricardo Alegría's text, which accompanies the display at the Museum of the Americas.

7. Duany, *Puerto Rican Nation on the Move*, 25.

8. There is also the possibility that Alegría dislikes the books, especially since Alejandro Cadalso, the historian who narrates each of the three "lectures" that constitute the parts of the Rodríguez Juliá's novel could be seen as a parody of Ricardo Alegría himself.

9. Henceforth, I will use a shortened version of the title, *La noche oscura*, to refer to Rodríguez Juliá's novel.

10. Irizarry, "Metahistoria y novela," 59.

11. In an interesting twist to the documentary nature of this story, Puerto Rican lawmakers cited the legend of Baltasar Montañez in law #60 of 2004, which sought to establish the second week in June as the "Semana del Hipismo Puertorriqueño/Week of Puerto Rican Horse Racing." For more information, see http://www.lexjuris.com/LEXLEX/Leyes2004/lexl2004060.htm.

12. McHale, *Postmodernist Fiction*, 16. McHale takes the term from Umberto Eco and expands both its context and meaning.

13. Bal, introduction to Bal, Crewe, and Spitzer, eds., *Acts of Memory*, xiii.

14. White, *Tropics of Discourse*, 13.

15. I will refer to Chamoiseau's and Condé's novels by shortened versions of their titles: *L'esclave* and *I, Tituba*, respectively.

16. Gaynor Kavanagh cites the rise of "the historical drama in television" as proof that the public in England has expressed interest in understanding the past through the lens of its own experience. He calls this "a more individualistic past" in "Melodrama, Pantomime or Portrayal?" in Carbonell, ed., *Museum Studies*, 350.

17. For a more detailed discussion of the many instances of "transworld identity," or intertextual borrowing of characters or historical figures in Arenas's novel, see William Luis, *Literary Bondage*.

18. Arenas, *Graveyard of the Angels*, 9.

19. Sommer discusses Villaverde's 1882 revisions to the 1839 version of *Cecilia Valdés*.

20. Baudrillard, *Selected Writings*, 169.

21. Chamoiseau, *L'esclave*, 17; emphasis in the original.

22. Ibid., 145.

23. Hirsch, "Projected Memory," 8.

24. Whitcomb, *Re-imagining the Museum*, 103.

25. Belcher, *Exhibitions in Museums*, 41.

26. Corrin, ed., *Mining the Museum*, 8.

27. Ibid.

28. "Entre-dire d'Édouard Glissant: *L'intention poétique* (1969) and *La folie celat* (inédit)."

29. Murdoch, *Creole Identity*, 212.

30. Bernabé, Chamoiseau, and Confiant, "In Praise of Creoleness," 886.

31. Benítez-Rojo, *The Repeating Island*, 59.

32. Dash, *The Other America*, 122.

33. Ibid.

34. Arenas, *Graveyard of the Angels*, 34.

35. McHale, *Postmodernist Fiction*, 123.

36. Arenas, *Graveyard of the Angels*, 94.

37. Luis, *Literary Bondage*, 244.

38. For a detailed comparative analysis of the paratexts of both the French and American versions of Condé's novels, see Lillian Manzor-Coats, "Of Witches and Other Things."

39. My argument about the novel's function as a national history museum considers only its explicit references to texts as literary artifacts. Thus, while other critics, like Manzor-Coats, read Hester Prynne's feminist project in Condé's novel as a parody of Monique Wittig's vision of a lesbian society in *Les guérrillères*, I will not assume that most readers would recognize the implied reference.

40. Condé, *I, Tituba*, 175; emphasis in the original.

41. Ibid., 144.

42. McBride, *Impossible Witnesses*, 5.

43. Barbados Museum and Historical Society, http://www.barbmuse.org.bb/index.php?option=com_content&task=view&id=34&Itemid=49.

44. Arenas left Cuba as part of the 1980 Mariel boatlift. By writing in exile, he also duplicates the conditions in which Cirilo Villaverde composed his masterpiece in the United States. Like Puerto Rico, Martinique is not an independent nation; it is considered an overseas department of France.

2. Art Museums: Visual (Inter)Texts

1. The digitized version of About Face can be accessed at http://www.chipstone.org/framesetspecialprojects.html.

2. *About Face: Toussaint L'Ouverture and the African American Image*, http://www.mam.org/exhibitions/details/aboutFace.php.

3. Nicole Ciccotelli, John and Mable Ringling Museum of Art, http://www.ringling.org/uploadedFiles/Programs/Educator_Programs/Resources/TeacherGuideLawrence.pdf.

4. According to the *Oxford Dictionary of Art*, François de Nomé (1593–1644) worked under the pseudonym Monsú Desidério, which he shared with

fellow artist Didier Barra (1590–1644). Lois Parkinson Zamora points out that
the painting featured in Carpentier's novel is also known by the following two
titles: *King Asa of Judah Destroying the Idols* and *King Asa of Judah Destroying the Statue of Priapus.*

5. My use of the term "interdisciplinary pastiche" is meant to expand on Ingeborg Hoesterey's notion that postmodernism inherently engages in a "conflation of genres" despite her own genre-specific discussion of postmodern pastiche
in *Pastiche* (2001). I share Dr. Hoesterey's comparative arts perspective on the
interaction between literature and art, but she groups each discipline separately
within her larger study of the minor genre, whereas I look at instances where the
two overlap within one textual medium.

6. Walvin, *Black Ivory*, 16.

7. For the most thorough account of the history of the *Zong* massacre, see
Shyllon, *Black Slaves in Britain*, 1974.

8. The historian Hugh Thomas names this event the "Africa Civilisation
Society" in *The Slave Trade*, 787; while Paul Gilroy calls the same meeting the
"World Anti-Slavery Convention" in *Small Acts*, 81.

9. Museum of Fine Art, Boston, online curatorial information on *Slave
Ship*, by Joseph Milord William Turner, 1840, http://www.mfa.org/collections/
search_art.asp?recview=true&id=31102. The note refers readers to the work of
A. J. Finberg for the full text of the poem.

10. Raiskin, "The Art of History," 65.

11. Only the reader is privy to both sides of this argument, since Mary Ellen
Pleasant shares her views about *The Slave Ship* with her Jamaican friend Annie
Christmas, but not with her hostess, Alice Hooper.

12. Cliff, *Free Enterprise*, 78.

13. Ibid., 71.

14. Thackeray's actual language is more ambivalent than this characteriza-
tion would suggest. In an article in *Fraser's Magazine* (quoted in Paul Gilroy,
Small Acts, 82), the British novelist wrote:

> the slaver throwing its cargo overboard is the most tremendous piece of
> colour that ever was seen. . . . The sun glares down upon a horrible sea of
> emerald and purple, into which chocolate coloured slaves are plunged, and
> chains that will not sink; and round these are floundering such a race of
> fishes as was never seen in the saeculum Pyrrhae . . . horrid spreading polypi,
> like huge, slimy, poached eggs, in which the hapless niggers, plunge and dis-
> appear. Ye gods what a "middle passage"!

Combined in Thackeray's assessment of the work are his obvious disapproval of
Turner's rather fantastic depiction of marine life and his horror at the fate of the
chained slaves. While he does not much care for Turner's palette, Thackeray's
tone and his final exclamation demonstrate that he, like Mary Ellen Pleasant,
was moved upon gazing at this painting.

15. Cliff, *Free Enterprise*, 73.

16. While Ruskin's critique of *The Slave Ship* in the first volume of *Modern Painters* (1843) celebrates mostly its use of color, in his private journal, Ruskin commented on the painting's foreground, especially as it related to the topic of human bondage: "Suspense about Slaver. My heart is all on eyes of *fish* now—it knew something of other kinds of eyes once, and of slavery too, in its way. Its slavery now is colder like being bound to the dead, as in old Spanish cruelty" (quoted in Gilroy, *Small Acts*, 82).

17. Gates Jr., *The Signifying Monkey*, 66.

18. Cliff, *Free Enterprise*, 180.

19. Raiskin, "The Art of History: An Interview with Michelle Cliff," 66.

20. See Dabydeen, *Hogarth's Blacks*; and Edgardo Rodríguez Juliá, *Campeche, o los diablejos de la melancolía*.

21. Dabydeen, "The Black Figure in 18th Century Art," http://www.bbc.co.uk/history/british/abolition/africans_in_art_gallery.shtml.

22. Dabydeen specifically points to the prostitute's bewildered-looking Jewish pimp and the young black servant boy in plate 2, along with one of Moll's fellow inmates, a black, pregnant prisoner in plate 4, as proof that Hogarth had a complex understanding of how heterogeneous British society became in the eighteenth century due to the international nature of commerce. This interpretation signals Dabydeen's intellectual allegiance to the black British cultural studies project, whose stated goal is to put the "black" in the Union Jack, to paraphrase the title of one of Paul Gilroy's books.

23. Dabydeen, *A Harlot's Progress*, 274.

24. In its portrayal of the uneven power dynamic that exists between white scribe and black ex-slave, *A Harlot's Progress* parallels or echoes two earlier American postmodern historical novels: William Styron's *The Confessions of Nat Turner* (1966) and Sherley Ann Williams's *Dessa Rose* (1986), both of which portray misguided white abolitionists who want to obtain the "true" confessions of enslaved people of African descent who have committed crimes against whites.

25. Mungo's first-person account of his life in England refers to the historical *Zong* massacre through a fictionalized newspaper account of the mass killing of slaves at sea for insurance purposes. However, the allusions to Turner's *The Slave Ship* in *A Harlot's Progress* are all implied, not explicit. Dabydeen calls his captain "Thiselwood" instead of Collingwood, and leaves the vessel unnamed. For details of the massacre, see *A Harlot's Progress*, 192–93.

26. According to María M. Alonso and Milagros Flores Román, the British invasion was led by Captain Abercromby, but the British forces were defeated by the Spanish army.

27. Campeche actually did a painting to commemorate the 1797 British invasion titled *Sitio de la ciudad de San Juan de Puerto Rico por los ingleses en el*

año de 1797. There was never a colony of New Venice. Edgardo Rodríguez Juliá discusses this painting at length in his monograph on Campeche.

28. Soto-Crespo, "The Pains of Memory," 452–53.

29. Soto-Crespo offers a compelling close reading of the image in Campeche's painting and mentions the offers he declined.

30. Edgardo Rodríguez Juliá explicitly contrasts Campeche's and Goya's artistic styles in his monograph.

31. My translation of Rincón, "Las imágenes en el texto," 27.

32. My translation of Rodríguez Juliá, *La noche oscura*, xi.

33. My translation of Rodríguez Juliá, *Campeche*, 7.

34. Ibid.

35. Ibid., 8.

36. Soto-Crespo, "The Pains of Memory," 474.

37. Ibid., 475. While he may indeed be referring to Campeche's paintings, the artwork discussed in the paragraph he cites from *The Renunciation* is clearly described as a drawing, not a painting.

38. Rodríguez Juliá, *The Renunciation*, 60–61.

39. Belcher, *Exhibitions in Museums*, 55.

40. *Explosion in a Cathedral* refers to several other paintings explicitly but does not dwell upon their significance.

41. Wall, "The Visual Dimension," 154.

42. The titles of Goya's paintings are *The Second of May 1808: The Charge of the Marmelukes* and *The Third of May 1808: The Execution of the Defenders of Madrid*.

43. Arenas, *Graveyard of the Angels*, 107.

44. Ibid., 108.

3. Ethnographic Museums: The Literary Diorama

1. Although key episodes in both volumes of Condé's epic novel take place in Jamaica, the island itself is never the final destination for members of the Traore family. Condé has a penchant for setting her novels in Caribbean islands other than her native Guadeloupe. For example, Barbados is the Caribbean setting for *I, Tituba*, as discussed in chapter 1.

2. See Wood, "The Diorama in Great Britain."

3. For American readers, these novels' concern with the negative impact of slavery on the black family unit resonates with Senator Daniel Patrick Moynihan's famous report for the U.S. Department of Labor, *The Negro Family: The Case for National Action* (1965). This document attributes the historical roots of the perceived instability of mid-twentieth-century African American family units to the separation of families practiced during the times of slavery in the United States.

4. Abraham Lincoln Presidential Museum and Library, *The Slave Auction*, http://www.lincolnlibraryandmuseum.com/pp.htm.

5. Parsons and Long, "Museum Pulls No Punches."

6. http://www.liverpoolmuseums.org.uk/ism/resources/museum_interpretation.asp.

7. http://www.diduknow.info/slavery/index2.html.

8. Clifford, *Routes*, 212–13.

9. Kirshenblatt-Gimblett, "Objects of Ethnography," 387.

10. Ibid., 387–88.

11. Since the plot of *Children of Segu* takes place after the end of the transatlantic slave trade and focuses primarily on the Islamic takeover of the Bambara kingdom and Segu within it, this novel will not figure further within this book.

12. A recent American analogue of this impulse can be found in Edward P. Jones's *The Known World*, winner of the 2004 Pulitzer Prize for fiction. This postmodern novel drew critical attention to black slave owners in the antebellum South, a topic rarely acknowledged in most American literary depictions of slavery.

13. Phillips's travel narrative *Atlantic Sound* clearly illustrates his negative view of the African diaspora.

14. Appadurai, *Modernity at Large*, 22–23.

15. Clifford, *Routes*, 201.

16. More information on the African Village exhibit is available at the official Web site for America's Black Holocaust Museum: http://www.blackholocaustmuseum.org/exhibits.html.

17. http://www.mpm.edu/exhibitions/permanent/eurovillage.php.

18. Chinosole, "Maryse Condé as Contemporary Griot," 597.

19. Condé, *Segu*, 3–4.

20. Condé's dedication of the novel to "my Bambara ancestress" signals that she, too, shares an interest in genealogy with her readers. The accompanying maps are useful tools for readers to have a real-world geographical context as a frame of reference.

21. Phillips, *Higher Ground*, 13. Among the things the translator tells the governor is the first mechanism through which slaves families are separated at the fort: men and children share one holding area, while women are isolated so as to prevent them from killing their offspring to spare them the horror and degradation of life inside the holding pens. This description is overdetermined because, while it may be historically accurate, it primarily echoes the key scene of Toni Morrison's *Beloved*, published just two years earlier, where the distraught mother tries to kill all four of her children to prevent them from being taken back to the plantation from which they had all escaped.

The slave fort on Gorée Island separated slaves by gender and by age. Children were not housed together with either men or women, according to the "Virtual Visit of Gorée Island" portal at http://webworld.unesco.org/goree/.

22. Phillips, *Higher Ground*, 60.

23. Ibid., 44.

24. Appiah, "Slavery: A Slow Emancipation."

25. Phillips, *Crossing the River*, 1.

26. This long-awaited reconciliation never actually takes place within the pages of the novel.

27. Phillips, *Crossing the River*, 68–69.

28. Between the title of the third section, "Crossing the River," and the two numbered subsections that follow, there is a fourth narrative segment called: "Journal of a voyage intended (by God's permission) in the *Duke of York*, snow, from Liverpool to the Windward Coast of Africa, etc., commenced the 24th August 1752" (emphasis in the original). This vignette mimics the captain's log of a slaving vessel. Since it addresses slavery more obliquely than do the other sections, it does not constitute a verbal diorama.

29. D'Aguiar, *The Longest Memory*, 125.

30. Ibid., 122.

4. Between Plantation and Living History Museum

1. Pattullo, *Last Resorts*, 193.

2. St. Kitts and Nevis closed their sugar plantations in 2005 because it was no longer an economically sustainable industry.

3. The Cinnamon Bay Plantation complex in St. John includes two cemeteries (http://www.nps.gov/history/nR/travel/prvi/pr44.htm). The Whim Museum belongs to the local government and is operated by the St. Croix Landmarks Society, but it still falls within the jurisdiction of the National Parks Service (http://www.nps.gov/history/nR/travel/prvi/pr50.htm).

4. The Web site for the Lopinot complex claims that it is "the former cocoa estate of the French count Charles Joseph de Lopinot, believed to be haunted by his ghost. It is now a museum dedicated to Trinidad's long history" (see http://www.trinidad-tobago.worldweb.com/Trinidad/Tunapuna/SightsAttractions/Museums/).

5. Dann and Seaton, *Slavery, Contested Heritage and Thanatourism*, 13.

6. Ibid., 16.

7. Eichstedt and Small, *Representations of Slavery*, 10.

8. Handler and Gable, *The New History in an Old Museum*, 18.

9. For the official museum press release on the "Follow the North Star" program, see http://www.connerprairie.org/press/viewrelease?id=56.

10. Pattullo, *Last Resorts*, 191.

11. hooks, *Yearning*, 42.

12. Ibid.

13. Arenas, *Graveyard of the Angels*, 98.

14. See Sharpe, *Ghosts of Slavery*, 2003. Sharpe also points out that Christiana supposedly runs away from the plantation shortly after this encounter.

15. Phillips, *Cambridge*, 73.

16. Ibid.

17. Ibid., 133.

18. Ibid., 147.

19. http://onmilwaukee.com/articles/streetsofold.html?page=1.

20. Readers can see pictures of the Freedom Center's slave pen exhibit online at http://www.freedomcenter.org/exhibits/slave-pen.html.

21. Rothstein, "Museum Review."

22. Crane, "Memory, Distortion, and History," 323.

23. D'Aguiar, *The Longest Memory*, 83.

22. Eichstedt and Small, *Representations of Slavery*, 10.

5. World Heritage Sites: The Fortress

1. Pattullo, *Last Resorts*, 192.

2. Ibid.

3. Malraux, *The Voices of Silence*, 15.

4. Phillips, *Higher Ground*, 16.

5. Hartman, *Lose Your Mother*, 163.

6. See "World Heritage," http://whc.unesco.org/en/about/.

7. See "National History Park—Citadel, Sans Souci, Ramiers," http://whc.unesco.org/en/list/180.

8. Trouillot, *Silencing the Past*, 35.

9. James, *The Black Jacobins*, 155–56.

10. Trouillot, *Silencing the Past*, 46.

11. Until September 25, 2008, this information was available online at "Parc National Historique La Citadelle" on the Lonely Planet Web site. The same text may be purchased as a PDF file at http://www.lonelyplanet.com/shop_pickand-mix/previews/caribbean-is-5–haiti-preview.pdf. Currently, the description of the Citadel available through the main Lonely Planet Haiti Web site describes this fort as follows: "The magnificent Citadelle la Ferrière is the mother of all Caribbean forts—a true castle perched high on a mountain and the master of all it surveys. Built in the early years of independence, it's a monument to the vision of a short-lived king, whose ruined palace of Sans Souci sits below, looking like something from a tropical Hollywood adventure movie" (http://www.lonelyplanet.com/haiti/northern-haiti).

12. http://www.discoverhaiti.com/sights_cap_012000.htm.

13. Gauthier, lenouvelliste.com, August 9, 2007.

14. Soirélus, lenouvelliste.com, February 14, 2008.

15. "The Slave Route: UNESCO Culture Sector," http://portal.unesco.

org/culture/en/ev.php-URL_ID=25659&URL_DO=DO_TOPIC&URL_SEC-TION=201.html.

16. Kirshenblatt-Gimblett, *Museum Frictions*, 171.

17. Ibid., 187.

18. http://www.discoverhaiti.com.

19. Trouillot, *Silencing the Past*, 31–32.

20. Ibid., 34.

21. Carpentier, "Prologue," 75. All subsequent quotations from the prologue will refer to this translation.

22. Haitian writers have reclaimed their native landscape by developing their own conceptions of how magical realism applies to them. Jacques Stéphen Alexis and Jacques Roumain have both articulated their own visions, but my reading of Carpentier's text sees it as a product of a Cuban imagination, not an accurate reflection of Haitian life.

23. Carpentier, "Prologue," 78.

24. Mackandal was a one-handed slave who led a large-scale poisoning campaign against several plantations.

25. Despite its traditional structure, *The Kingdom of This World* does not correspond to Lukács's specifications in *The Historical Novel*, primarily because Carpentier's text is not a work of realism but, rather, heralds the beginning of a new narrative style, *lo real maravilloso* (the marvelous real), which Carpentier defines in the prologue to the novel, cited previously.

26. Carpentier, *Kingdom of This World*, 123.

27. Ibid., 170.

28. Ibid., 173.

29. Carpentier was a public supporter of Fidel Castro and his revolution. He moved back to Cuba once the political situation settled down, in order to work for the government. Until his recent illness, Castro's favored attire when appearing in public was his green fatigues uniform. In *Explosion in a Cathedral*, Carpentier employs a similar narrative strategy when he traces the movement of the guillotine in the New World as it accompanies one of the protagonists, Victor Hugues.

30. Carpentier's critique does not include Cuba, since he was an ardent supporter of Castro.

31. Antonio Benítez-Rojo remarks upon this very feature of Rodríguez Juliá's prose in his reading of *La noche oscura*; he calls attention to "the insolent and sometimes demented baroqueness of [the novel's] language" (244) and discusses Rodríguez Juliá in the context of other contemporary practitioners of what he terms the "neobaroque": Cubans Lezama Lima, Severo Sarduy, Reinaldo Arenas, Fernando Ortiz, Nicolás Guillén; Puerto Rican Luis Rafael Sánchez; and, of course, Colombian Gabriel García Márquez.

32. In *Explosion in a Cathedral*, Carpentier traces the origins and after-

maths of the Haitian Revolution from the perspective of Cuban witnesses to the French battle to reimpose colonial control throughout the islands in the Lesser Antilles.

33. Wagenheim and Jiménez de Wagenheim, *The Puerto Ricans*, 47.

34. http://whc.unesco.org/en/list/266.

35. http://www.nps.gov/archive/saju/morro.html.

36. http://www.gotopuertorico.com/puerto-rico-fort-san-felipe.php.

37. Benítez-Rojo, *The Repeating Island*, 334.

38. González points out that by the time the events in *La noche oscura* take place in the 1770s, the Spanish Crown had already acknowledged the strategic importance of El Morro Castle (see González, "La subversión de la historia," 125).

39. Baralt, *Esclavos rebeldes*, 16.

40. Ortega, *Reapropriaciones*, 155.

41. Both *La noche oscura* and *The Kingdom of This World* portray the intersection of the supernatural and the human in the context of Caribbean religious practices. Ti-Noel learns to shift his shape by watching Mackandal do so during a vodun ritual in Carpentier's novel. Rodríguez Juliá's texts make repeated references to the presence of armies of angels or devils that interfere with human political affairs. However, no prelate ever calls upon God to keep his minions in order in Rodríguez Juliá's texts. In fact, the priest characters rarely pray or say mass. Thus, supernatural events within these novels only amount to the interference of the fantastic, rather than the divine.

42. The novel itself is structured as three distinct public lectures delivered by a Puerto Rican historian who is disavowing his previously published research because of new documents that he has miraculously uncovered after decades of neglect.

43. Although Rodríguez Juliá does not make a reference to it in his novels, Jamaica did experience a large-scale slave rebellion around this time, led by a slave named Tacky in 1760 (see Gaspar, *A Turbulent Time*).

44. Rodríguez Juliá, *The Renunciation*, 19.

45. Ibid., 56.

6. Mourning Museums: Diasporic Practices

1. Tacky's monument is located in St. Mary's Parish, Jamaica (see http://www.jnht.com/heritage_site.php?id=169).

2. An image of the mausoleum erected in memory of Dessalines in Port au Prince, Haiti, can be found at http://thelouvertureproject.org/index.php?title=Image:Dessalines_tomb.jpg.

3. Photos of the fortress Christophe constructed, the Laferrière Citadel, are available at http://www.galenfrysinger.com/henri_christophe.htm.

4. Bennhold, "158 Years Later, France Recalls End of Slavery."

5. Dann and Seaton, *Slavery, Contested Heritage and Thanatourism*, 24.

6. Valère is a Martinican sculptor. Photos of the memorial are at http:// www.laquenette.com/situation/memorial/index.htm.

7. Reinhardt, *Claims to Memory*, 141.

8. When HBO acquired the distribution rights to this film, it commissioned Walter Mosley to adapt, not translate, Chamoiseau's French text into English. The cable network has aired *Middle Passage* regularly during February, which is designated African American history month in the United States.

9. Slavery museums in the United States, like the National Underground Railroad Freedom Center in Ohio, include exhibits about ongoing human rights crises that require the visitors' urgent attention. When informing its audience about opportunities for continued activism and opposition to repression world-wide, museums risk equating past and current human rights crises so much that past events lose their specificity for contemporary audiences.

10. See "Freedman's Village," http://www.arlingtoncemetery.net/freedman. htm.

11. Museum of Funeral Customs in Illinois: http://funeralmuseum.org/in-dex-2.html; National Museum of Funeral History in Houston: http://nmfh. org/; Museum of Mourning Arts in Pennsylvania: http://www.fieldtrip.com/ pa/02595800.htm; and Mourning Museum in Virginia: http://www.gravegar-den.org/museums.htm.

12. Holloway, *Passed On*, 1.

13. After the 1990 passage of the Native American Graves Protection and Repatriation Act (NAGPRA), museums in the United States containing funerary objects or human remains belonging to groups such as Native Americans have had to restrict public access to these materials.

14. There is no agreement among historians about the correct figure of deaths during the Middle Passage. All the reputable figures number in the millions, but the range only widens from there.

15. Ruffins, "Revisiting the Old Plantation," 412–13.

16. Eventually, the bodies of 419 eighteenth-century slaves were unearthed during this excavation (http://www.africanburialground.gov/ABG_AnAfrican-AmericanHomecoming.htm).

17. The official Web site reports that scientists and historians were granted access to the slaves' remains for research purposes.

18. The amended 1991 Memorandum of Agreement between the General Services Administration (GSA) and the Advisory Council on Historic Preservation (ACHP) had stipulated that such steps be taken, following the guidelines set forth in the National Historic Preservation Act of 1966. This information was published in the National Parks Service Draft Management Recommendations Report, available through the portal of the African Burial Ground Web site at http://www.africanburialground.gov/ABG_FinalReports.htm.

19. Stanton, "Rites of Ancestral Return."

20. Ruffins, "Revisiting the Old Plantation," 414.

21. National Park Service, *Draft Management Recommendations*, 9, http://www.africanburialground.gov/Report/Chapter7.pdf.

22. Ruffins, "Revisiting the Old Plantation," 417.

23. Walter Mosley has made no public comment about what methods he used to guide him during the adaptation of Chamoiseau's text, or why this process should not be described as a translation. This is not the place for a detailed analysis of the differences between the two texts, especially since I have been unable to determine whether the French subtitles available on the DVD of the film correspond to Mosley's English text or to Chamoiseau's original script.

24. Crew and cast bio, *The Middle Passage*, DVD, directed by Guy Deslauriers (2000; HBO, 2003).

25. The hypermasculinity of this particular account of slavery is compounded in the American voice-over by the choice of actor cast to lend his vocal talents, Djimon Hounsou, whose breakthrough role was as the slave leader Cinque in Steven Spielberg's own Middle Passage movie, *Amistad* (1997). The same year Deslauriers's film premiered, Hounsou played a Roman slave in the Hollywood blockbuster *Gladiator* (2000).

26. Dialogue quoted from the film.

27. This novel dramatizes the *Zong* massacre that resulted in the deaths of 132 slaves, and that Turner commemorated in his painting *The Slave Ship*, discussed in chapter 2.

28. D'Aguiar, *Feeding the Ghosts*, 209.

29. Ibid., 208.

30. Ibid., 229.

31. Ibid., 230.

32. Chamoiseau, *L'esclave*, 146.

33. Each epigraph appears on a different page, listed here in order: 17, 33, 59, 69, 83, 121, 141.

34. Nelson, *Manumission Requiem*, 12.

35. "Fortune's Story," http://www.fortunestory.org/fortune/.

36. Nelson, *Manumission Requiem*, 8.

37. Dr. Ysaye M. Barnwell's music, http://www.myspace.com/ysayembarnwell.

38. Nelson, *Manumission Requiem*, 27.

39. The background of slavery makes it possible for Condé to be correct on both sides of the abortion debate—Tituba clearly regards her fetus as a child, but nonetheless *chooses* to have an abortion rather than let him or her grow up to be a slave.

40. Condé, *I, Tituba*, 55.

41. Ibid., 87.

42. Ibid., 94.

Bibliography

Alonso, María M., and Milagros Flores Román. *The Eighteenth Century Caribbean and the British Attack on Puerto Rico in 1797*. San Juan, P.R.: National Park Service, Department of the Interior, Publicaciones puertorriqueñas, 1997.

Alpers, Svetlana. "The Museum as a Way of Seeing." In *Exhibiting Cultures: The Poetics and Politics of Museum Display*, edited by Ivan Karp and Steven D. Lavine, 25–32. Washington, D.C.: Smithsonian Institution Press, 1991.

Anderson, Benedict. *Imagined Communities: Reflections on the Origins and Spread of Nationalism*. 1991. Rev. ed. New York: Verso, 2000.

Appadurai, Arjun. *Modernity at Large: Cultural Dimensions of Globalization*. Minneapolis: University of Minnesota Press, 1996.

Appiah, Kwame Anthony. "Slavery: A Slow Emancipation." *New York Times Magazine*, March 18, 2007.

Arenas, Reinaldo. *La loma del ángel*. Barcelona: Dador, 1987. Translated by Alfred J. MacAdam as *Graveyard of the Angels*. New York: Avon, 1987.

Bailey, Anthony. *Standing in the Sun: A Life of J. M. W. Turner*. New York: Harper Collins, 1997.

Bakhtin, Mikhail. *Dialogic Imagination: Four Essays*. Edited by Michael Holquist and Vadim Liapunov. Translated by Vadim Liapunov and Kenneth Brostrom. Slavic Series. Austin: University of Texas Press, 1982.

Bal, Mieke. Introduction to Bal, Crewe, and Spitzer, eds., *Acts of Memory: Cultural Recall in the Present*, vii–xvii.

Bal, Mieke, Jonathan Crewe, and Leo Spitzer, eds. *Acts of Memory: Cultural Recall in the Present*. Hanover: University Press of New England, 1999.

Baralt, Guillermo A. *Esclavos rebeldes: Conspiraciones y sublevaciones de esclavos en Puerto Rico (1795–1873)*. Río Piedras: Ediciones Huracán, 1981.

Bauer, Marilyn. "Images in Limestone." Cincinnati.com, August 1, 2004. http://www.cincinnati.com/freetime/nurfc/J8_historyinlimestone.html.

Baudrillard, Jean. *Jean Baudrillard: Selected Writings.* Edited by Mark Poster. Stanford: Stanford University Press, 1988.

Belcher, Michael. *Exhibitions in Museums.* Washington, D.C.: Smithsonian Institution Press, 1991.

Bell, Madison Smartt. *All Souls Rising.* New York: Pantheon, 1995.

Benítez-Rojo, Antonio. *The Repeating Island: The Caribbean and the Postmodern Perspective.* Translated by James E. Maraniss. 2nd ed. Durham, N.C.: Duke University Press, 1997.

Benjamin, Walter. "The Work of Art in the Age of Mechanical Reproduction." In *Illuminations,* by Benjamin, translated by Harry Zohn, 217–51. New York: Schocken Books, 1968.

Bennhold, Katrin. "158 Years Later, France Recalls End of Slavery." *International Herald Tribune,* May 11, 2006. http://www.iht.com/articles/2006/05/10/news/slaves.php.

Bernabé, Jean, Patrick Chamoiseau, and Raphael Confiant. "In Praise of Creoleness." *Callaloo* 13, no. 4 (1990): 886–909.

Boime, Albert. *The Art of Exclusion: Representing Blacks in the Nineteenth Century.* Washington, D.C.: Smithsonian Institution Press, 1990.

Bradley, David. *The Chaneysville Incident: A Novel.* New York: Harper and Row, 1981.

Brathwaite, Edward Kamau. *Middle Passages.* New York: New Directions, 1994.

Cabrera, Lydia. 1940. *Cuentos negros de Cuba.* 2nd ed. Madrid: Ramos, Art. Gráf., 1972.

Carbonell, Bettina Messias. "Introduction: Museum/Studies and the 'Eccentric Space' of an Anthology." In Carbonell, ed., *Museum Studies,* 1–17.

———, ed. *Museum Studies: An Anthology of Contexts.* Malden, Mass.: Blackwell, 2004.

Carpentier, Alejo. *El reino de este mundo.* Madrid: Editorial Seix Barral, 1983. Translated by Harriet de Onis as *The Kingdom of This World.* New York: Farrar, Straus and Giroux, 1989.

———. *El siglo de las luces.* México: Planeta Mexicana, 1992. Translated by John Sturrock as *Explosion in a Cathedral.* Minneapolis: University of Minnesota Press, 2001.

———. "Prologue." *Review: Latin American Literature and the Arts* 47 (1993). Reprinted in *Cubanísimo,* edited by Cristina García. New York: Vintage, 2002.

Carretta, Vincent. *Equiano the African: Biography of a Self-Made Man.* Athens: University of Georgia Press, 2005.

———. "Olaudah Equiano or Gustavus Vassa? New Light on an Eighteenth-Century Question of Identity." *Slavery and Abolition: A Journal of Slave and Post-Slave Societies* 20, no. 3 (1999): 96–105.

Cassuto, Leonard. *The Inhuman Race.* New York: Columbia University Press, 1996.

Césaire, Aimé. *La tragédie du roi Christophe.* Paris: Présence africaine, 1963.

———. *Toussaint L'Ouverture: La révolution française et le problème colonial.* Paris: Présence africaine, 1962.

Chamoiseau, Patrick. *L'esclave vieil homme et le molosse.* Paris: Gallimard, 1997.

———. *Solibo Magnifique.* Paris: Gallimard, 1988.

———. *Texaco.* Paris: Gallimard, 1992.

Chinosole. "Maryse Condé as Contemporary Griot in *Segu.*" *Callalloo* 18, no. 3 (1995): 593–601.

Ciccotelli, Nicole. "Jacob Lawrence: Three Series of Prints: Genesis, Toussaint L'Ouverture, Hiroshima." *Special Exhibition Teacher's Guide.* John and Mable Ringling Museum of Art. http://www.ringling.org/uploadedFiles/Programs/Educator_Programs/Resources/TeacherGuideLawrence.pdf .

Clarke, Austin. *Pig Tails 'n Breadfruit.* New York: New Press, 1999.

———. *The Polished Hoe.* New York: Amistad, 2004.

Cliff, Michelle. *Abeng.* 1984. New York: Plume, 1995.

———. *Free Enterprise.* New York: Dutton, 1993.

Clifford, James. *Routes: Travel and Translation in the Late Twentieth Century.* Cambridge: Harvard University Press, 1997.

Coleridge, Samuel Taylor. "The Rime of the Ancient Mariner." 1798. In *The Poems of Coleridge*, 186–209. New York: Oxford University Press, 1960.

Coll y Toste, Cayetano. *Leyendas y tradiciones puertorriqueñas.* Río Piedras, P.R.: Editorial Cultural, 1975.

Comité pour la Mémoire de l'Esclavage. *Mémoires de la traite négrière, de l'esclavage et de leurs abolitions.* Report prepared for the prime minister of France, April 12, 2005, 87–114. http://www.comite-memoire-esclavage.fr/IMG/pdf/Rapport_memoire_esclavage.pdf .

Condé, Maryse. *The Land of Many Colors and Nanna-Ya.* Translated by Nicole Ball. Lincoln, Neb.: Bison Books, 1999.

———. *Les dernières rois mages.* Paris: Éditions Mercure de France, 1992. Translated by Richard Philcox as *The Last of the African Kings.* Lincoln: University of Nebraska Press, 1997.

———. *Moi, Tituba, sorcière . . . noire de Salem.* Paris: Éditions Mercure de France, 1986. Translated by Richard Philcox as *I, Tituba, Black Witch of Salem.* New York: Ballantine Books, 1992.

———. *Ségou: Les murailles de terre.* Paris: Éditions Robert Laffront, 1984. Translated by Barbara Bray as *Segu.* New York: Penguin, 1987.

———. *Ségou: La terre en miettes.* Paris: Éditions Robert Laffront, 1985. Translated by Linda Coverdale as *The Children of Segu.* New York: Viking, 1989.

Conrad, Joseph. *Heart of Darkness*. 1902. New York: Penguin Classics, 1994.

Corrin, Lisa G., ed. *Mining the Museum: An Installation by Fred Wilson*. Baltimore: Contemporary and New Press, 1994.

———. "*Mining the Museum*: Artists Look at Museums, Museums Look at Themselves." In Corrin, ed., *Mining the Museum*, 1–22.

Courlander, Harold. *The African*. New York: Crown, 1967.

Crane, Susan A. "Memory, Distortion, and History in the Museum." In Carbonell, ed., *Museum Studies*.

Cugoano, Quobna Ottobah. *Thoughts and Sentiments on the Evil of Slavery*. Edited by Vincent Caretta. New York: Penguin, 1999.

D'Aguiar, Fred. *Feeding the Ghosts*. New York: Ecco Press, 2000.

———. *The Longest Memory*. New York: Pantheon, 1995.

Dabydeen, David. "The Black Figure in 18th Century Art." *British History: Abolition of the Slave Trade 1807*. BBC. http://www.bbc.co.uk/history/british/abolition/africans_in_art_gallery.shtml.

———. *A Harlot's Progress*. London: Jonathan Cape, 1999.

———. *Hogarth's Blacks: Images of Blacks in Eighteenth Century English Art*. Athens: University of Georgia Press, 1987.

Dann, Graham M. S., and Robert B Potter. "Supplanting the Planters: Hawking Heritage in Barbados." In Dann and Seaton, eds., *Slavery*, 51–84.

Dann, Graham M. S., and A. V. Seaton, eds. *Slavery, Contested Heritage and Thanatourism*. New York: Routledge, 2002.

Dash, J. Michael. *The Other America: Caribbean Literature in a New World Context*. New World Studies. Charlottesville: University of Virginia Press, 1998.

Deetz, James. "A Sense of Another World: History Museums and Cultural Change." In Carbonell, ed., *Museum Studies*, 375–80.

Delany, Martin A. *Blake, or The Huts of America*. Edited by Floyd J. Miller. Boston: Beacon Press, 1971.

Derrida, Jacques. *Demeure: Fiction and Testimony*. Translated by Elizabeth Rottenberg. Stanford: Stanford University Press, 2000.

———. *The Gift of Death*. Translated by David Wills. Chicago: University of Chicago Press, 1995.

———. *The Work of Mourning*. Edited by Pascale-Anne Brault and Michael Naas. Chicago: University of Chicago Press, 2001.

Deslauriers, Guy, dir. *The Middle Passage*. DVD. 2000; HBO, 2003.

Diegues, Carlos, dir. *Quilombo*. Copacabana Filmes, 1986.

———. *Ganga Zumba*. Copacabana Filmes, 1963.

Douglass, Frederick. *The Heroic Slave*. In *Three Classic African American Novels*, edited by William L. Andrews. New York: Signet, 1990.

———. *Narrative of the Life of Frederick Douglass, An American Slave, Written by Himself*. Edited by John Blassingame. New Haven: Yale University Press, 2001.

Duany, Jorge. *The Puerto Rican Nation on the Move: Identities on the Island and in the United States.* Chapel Hill: University of North Carolina Press, 2002.

Durix, Jean-Pierre. *Mimesis, Genres, and Postcolonial Discourse: Deconstructing Magical Realism.* New York: Palgrave Macmillan, 2001.

Eco, Umberto. *The Role of the Reader: Explorations in the Semiotics of Texts.* Bloomington: Indiana University Press, 1979.

Eichstedt, Jennifer L., and Stephen Small. *Representations of Slavery: Race and Ideology in Southern Plantation Museums.* Washington, D.C.: Smithsonian Institution Press, 2002.

Eliot, T. S. "Tradition and the Individual Talent." In *Selected Prose of T. S. Eliot,* edited by Frank Kermode, 37–44. New York: Farrar, Straus and Giroux, 1975.

Everett, Susanne. *History of Slavery.* Edited by John Man. Secaucus, N.J.: Chartwell Books, 1996.

Finberg, A. J. *The Life of J.M.W. Turner, R. A.* Oxford: Clarendon Press, 1961.

Flower, Sir Henry. "Local Museums." In Carbonell, ed., *Museum Studies,* 315–17.

Freud, Sigmund. *On Murder, Mourning and Melancholia.* Translated by Shaun Whiteside. New York: Penguin Classics, 2005.

Gaines, Ernest J. *The Autobiography of Miss Jane Pittman.* New York: Dial Press, 1971.

Garret, Graham W. "The Mirror of Nature." *Beaver* 75, no. 6 (1996): 11.

Gaspar, David Barry. *A Turbulent Time: The Haitian Revolution and the Greater Caribbean.* Blacks in the Diaspora. Bloomington: Indiana University Press, 1997.

Gates, Henry Louis, Jr. *The Signifying Monkey: A Theory of African-American Literary Criticism.* New York: Oxford University Press, 1988.

Gauthier, Jean Gady. "Vers la rehabilitation du parq historique national." lenouvelliste.com, August 9, 2007. http://www.lenouvelliste.com/article.php?PubID=1&ArticleID=47039 .

Gilroy, Paul. *The Black Atlantic: Modernity and Double Consciousness.* Cambridge: Harvard University Press, 1993.

——— . *Small Acts: Thoughts on the Politics of Black Cultures.* New York: Serpent's Tail, 1994.

Glissant, Edouard. *Le monde incrée.* Paris: Gallimard, 2000.

——— . *Le quatrième siècle.* Paris: Gallimard, 1967.

——— . *L'intention poétique.* Paris: Gallimard, 1997.

——— . *Monsieur Toussaint.* Paris: Éditions du Seuil, 1961.

——— . "Pour un centre National à la mémoire des esclavages." *Libération,* May 9, 2008. http://www.liberation.fr/tribune/010180372–pour-un-centre-national-a-la-memoire-des-esclavages.

González, Rubén. "*La noche oscura del Niño Avilés*: La subversión de la historia." *Revista de crítica literaria latinoamericana*, 13, no. 25 (1987): 121–29.

Haley, Alex. *Roots*. New York: Doubleday, 1976.

Handler, Richard, and Eric Gable. *The New History in an Old Museum: Creating the Past at Colonial Williamsburg*. Durham, N.C.: Duke University Press, 1997.

Hartman, Saidiya. *Lose Your Mother: A Journey along the Atlantic Slave Route*. New York: Farrar, Straus and Giroux, 2007.

Hawthorne, Nathaniel. *The Scarlet Letter*. Orchard Park, N.Y.: Broadview Press, 2004.

Hirsch, Marianne. "Projected Memory: Holocaust Photographs in Personal and Public Fantasy." In *Acts of Memory: Cultural Recall in the Present*, Edited by Mieke Bal, Jonathan Crewe, and Leo Spitzer, 3–23. Hanover: University Press of New England, 1999.

Hoesterey, Ingeborg. *Pastiche: Cultural Memory in Art, Film, Literature*. Bloomington: Indiana University Press, 2001.

Holloway, Karla FC. *Passed On: African American Mourning Stories*. Durham, N.C.: Duke University Press, 2003.

hooks, bell. *Yearning: Race, Gender, and Cultural Politics*. Boston: South End Press, 1990.

Hufbauer, Benjamin. *Presidential Temples: How Memorials and Libraries Shape Public Memory*. Lawrence: University Press of Kansas, 2005.

Hutcheon, Linda. *A Poetics of Postmodernism: History, Theory, Fiction*. New York: Routledge, 1988.

International Museum of Slavery. "Slaves' Stories." http://www.diduknow. info/slavaery/index2.html.

Irizarry, Estelle. "Metahistoria y novela: *La renuncia del héroe Baltasar* de Edgardo Rodríguez Juliá." *La Torre* 3, no. 9 (1989): 55–67.

Jacobs, Harriet. "Incidents in the Life of a Slave Girl." 1861. In *The Classic Slave Narratives*, edited by Henry Louis Gates Jr. New York: Signet Classics, 2002.

James, C. L. R. *The Black Jacobins: Toussaint L'Ouverture and the San Domingo Revolution*. 2nd ed. New York: Vintage Books, 1989.

Johnson, Charles, Patricia Smith et al., eds. *Africans in America: America's Journey through Slavery*. San Diego: Harvest Book, Harcourt Brace, 1998.

Jones, Edward P. *The Known World*. New York: Amistad, 2003.

Karp, Ivan. "Culture and Representation." In Karp and Lavine, *Exhibiting Cultures*, 11–24.

Karp, Ivan, Corinne A. Kratz, Lynn Szwaja, and Tomás Ybarra-Frausto. *Museum Frictions: Public Cultures/Global Transformations*. With Gustavo Buntinx, Barbara Kirshenblatt-Gimblett, and Ciraj Rassool. Durham, N.C.: Duke University Press, 2006.

Karp, Ivan, and Steven D. Lavine, eds. *Exhibiting Cultures: The Poetics and Politics of Museum Display*. Washington, D.C.: Smithsonian Institute Press, 1991.

Kavanagh, Gaynor. "Melodrama, Pantomime or Portrayal? Representing Ourselves and the British Past through Exhibitions in History Museums. In Carbonell, ed., *Museum Studies*, 348-55.

Kincaid, Jamaica. *My Brother*. New York: Farrar, Straus and Giroux, 1998.

———. *A Small Place*. New York: Plume, 1989.

Kirshenblatt-Gimblett, Barbara. "Objects of Ethnography." In Karp and Lavine, eds., *Exhibiting Cultures*, 386–443.

———. "World Heritage and Cultural Economics." In Karp, Kratz, Szwaja, and Ybarra-Frausto, eds., *Museum Frictions*, 161–202.

Klein, Herbert S. *African Slavery in Latin America and the Caribbean*. New York: Oxford University Press, 1986.

Kratz, Corinne, and Ivan Karp. "Introduction: Museum Frictions: Public Cultures/Global Transformations." In Karp, Kratz, Szwaja, and Ybarra-Frausto, eds., *Museum Frictions*, 1–31.

Kreamer, Christine Mullen. "Shared Heritage, Contested Terrain: Cultural Negotiation and Ghana's Cape Coast Castle Museum Exhibition 'Crossroads of People, Crossroads of Trade.'" In Karp, Kratz, Szwaja, and Ybarra-Frausto, eds., *Museum Frictions*, 435–68.

Kreps, Christina F. *Liberating Culture: Cross-Cultural Perspectives on Museums, Curation and Heritage Preservation*. New York: Routledge, 2003.

Lamming, George. *In the Castle of My Skin*. 1953. Ann Arbor: University of Michigan Press, 1994.

———. *Natives of My Person*. 1972. Ann Arbor: University of Michigan Press, 1991.

Leantes, Cesar. *Los guerrilleros negros*. Havana: Unión de Escritores y Artistes de Cuba, 1976.

Leone, Mark P., and Barbara J. Little. "Artifacts as Expressions of Society and Subversive Genealogy and the Value of History." In Carbonell, ed., *Museum Studies*, 363.

Luis, William. *Literary Bondage*. Austin: University of Texas Press, 1990.

Lukács, Georg. *The Historical Novel*. Translated by Hannah and Stanley Mitchell. Lincoln: University of Nebraska Press, 1983.

Malraux, André. *The Voices of Silence*. Translated by Stuart Gilbert. Bollingen Series no. 24. Princeton, N.J.: Princeton University Press, 1978.

Manzor-Coats, Lillian. "Of Witches and Other Things: Maryse Condé's Challenges to Feminist Discourse." *World Literature Today* 67, no. 4(1993): 737–44.

McBride, Dwight A. *Impossible Witnesses: Truth, Abolitionism, and Slave Testimony*. New York: New York University Press, 2001.

McHale, Brian. *Postmodernist Fiction*. New York: Methuen, 1987.

Melville, Herman. *Bartleby and Benito Cereno*. New York: Dover Thrift Editions, 1990.

———. *Moby Dick*. 1851. Hertfordshire, England: Wordsworth Classics, 1992.

Menton, Seymour. *La nueva novela histórica de América Latina*. San Diego: Fondo de cultura económica, USA, 1998.

Michaels, Walter Benn. *The Shape of the Signifier: 1967 to the End of History*. Princeton, N.J.: Princeton University Press, 2004.

Milne, Lorna. "The *Marron* and the *Marqueur*: Physical Space and Imaginary Displacements in Patrick Chamoiseau's *L'esclave vieil homme et le molosse*." In *Ici-là: Place and Displacement in Caribbean Writing in French*, edited by Mary Gallagher, 61–82. Amsterdam: Rodopi, 2003.

Miller, Arthur. *The Crucible: A Play in Four Acts*. 1953. New York: Penguin, 2003.

Mitchell, Margaret. *Gone with the Wind*. 1936. New York: Macmillan, 1975.

"'Monsù Desiderio.'" In *The Oxford Dictionary of Art*, edited by Ian Chilvers, Harold Osborne and Dennis Farr. New York: Oxford University Press, 2004. *eNotes.com*. 2006. http://www.enotes.com .

Montejo, Esteban and Miguel Barnet. 1966. *Biografía de un cimarrón*. Havana: Editorial Letras Cubanas, 1980.

Morrison, Toni. 1987. *Beloved*. New York: Knopf, 1998.

Murdoch, H. Adlai. *Creole Identity in the French Caribbean Novel*. Gainesville: University Press of Florida, 2001.

Naipaul, V. S. *The Middle Passage: Impressions of Five Societies—British, French and Dutch—in the West Indies and South America*. 1962. New York: Vintage, 1981.

———. *A Way in the World*. New York: Vintage International, 1995.

National Park Services. *Draft Management Recommendations for the African Burial Ground*. http://www.africanburialground.gov/Report/Chapter7.pdf.

Nelson, Marilyn. *Fortune's Bones: The Manumission Requiem*. Asheville, N.C.: Front Street, 2004.

Ortega, Julio. *Reapropriaciones: Cultura y nueva escritura en Puerto Rico*. Río Piedras, P.R.: Editorial de la Universidad de Puerto Rico, 1991.

Ortiz, Fernando. *Contrapunteo cubano del tabaco y el azúcar*. Havana: J. Montero, 1940.

Parsons, Christi, and Ray Long. "Museum Pulls No Punches." *Chicago Tribune*, April 19, 2005.

Patterson, Orlando. *Die the Long Day*. New York: Morrow, 1972.

———. *The Sociology of Slavery: An Analysis of the Origins, Development and Structure of Negro Slave Society in Jamaica*. Rutherford, N.J.: Fairleigh Dickerson University Press, 1967.

Pattullo, Polly. *Last Resorts: The Cost of Tourism in the Caribbean*. New York: Cassell, 1996.

Pender, Rick. "What I Saw at the Freedom Center." *CityBeat: Cincinnati's News and Entertainment Weekly* (2004). http://www.citybeat.com/2004–08–18/cover2.shtml.

Petry, Anne. *Tituba of Salem Village*. 1964. New York: Harper Trophy, 1991.

Phillips, Caryl. *Atlantic Sound*. New York: Vintage, 2001.

———. *Cambridge*. New York: Vintage, 1993.

———. *Crossing the River*. London: Bloomsbury, 1993.

———. *Higher Ground*. New York: Vintage, 1995.

Preziosi, Donald. "Brain of the Earth's Body: Museums and the Framing of Modernity." In Carbonell, ed., *Museum Studies*, 71–84.

Prince, Mary. "The History of Mary Prince, a West Indian Slave." 1831. In Gates, *Three Classic Slave Narratives*, 249–322.

Raiskin, Judith. "The Art of History: An Interview with Michelle Cliff." *Kenyon Review* 15, no. 1 (1993): 57–71.

Reinhardt, Catherine A. *Claims to Memory: Beyond Slavery and Emancipation in the French Caribbean*. New York: Berghahn Books, 2006.

Rhys, Jean. *Wide Sargasso Sea*. 1966. New York: Norton, 1992.

Rincón, Carlos. "Las imágenes en el texto: Entre García Márquez y Roberto Bolaño: De la alegoría del tiempo al universo de las imágenes." *Revista de crítica literaria latinoamericana* 28, no. 56 (2002): 19–37.

Robotham, Rosemarie, ed. *Spirits of the Passage: The Transatlantic Slave Trade in the Seventeenth Century*. New York: Simon and Schuster, 1997.

Rodríguez Juliá, Edgardo. *Campeche, o los diablejos de la melancolía*. San Juan: Instituto de cultura puertorriqueña, 1986.

———. *La noche oscura del Niño Avilés*. 1984. Río Piedras: Editorial de la Universidad de Puerto Rico, 1991.

———. *La renuncia del héroe Baltasar: Conferencias pronunciadas por Alejandro Cadalso en el Ateneo Puertorriqueño, del 4 al 10 de enero de 1938*. San Juan: Editorial Antillana, 1974. Translated by Andrew Hurley as *The Renunciation*. New York: Four Walls Eight Windows, 1997.

Rothstein, Edward. "Museum Review: Slavery's Harsh History Is Portrayed in Promised Land." *New York Times*, August 18, 2004.

Ruffins, Faith Davis. "Revisiting the Old Plantation: Reparations, Reconciliation and Museumizing American Slavery." In Karp, Kratz, Szwaja, and Ybarra-Frausto, *Museum Frictions*, 394–434.

Rushdy, Ashraf H. A. *Neo-Slave Narratives: Studies in the Social Logic of a Literary Form*. New York: Oxford University Press, 1999.

Ruskin, John. *Diaries of John Ruskin*. Edited by Joan Evans and J. H. Whitehouse. Oxford: Clarendon Press, 1956.

———. *Modern Painters*. Vol. 1, *Of General Principles and of Truth*. 1843. New York: Booksurge, 2000.

Savary, Claude, and Gilles Labarthe, eds. *Mémoires d'esclaves*. Geneva: Musée d'ethnographie, 1997.

Scarboro, Ann Armstrong. Afterword to *I, Tituba*, by Condé, 187–225.

Schwarz-Bart, André. *La mulâtresse Solitude*. Paris: Éditions Seuil, 1972.

Scott, Ridley, dir. *Gladiator*. Dreamworks, SKG, 2000.

Seaton, A. V. "Guided by the Dark: From Thanatopsis to Thanatourism." *International Journal of Heritage Studies* 2, no. 4 (1996): 234–44.

Shakespeare, William. *The Tempest*. Edited by Barbara A. Mowat and Paul Werstine. Folger Shakespeare Library. New York: Washington Square Press, 1994.

Sharpe, Jenny. *Ghosts of Slavery: A Literary Archaeology of Black Women's Lives*. Minneapolis: University of Minnesota Press, 2003.

Shepherd, Verene, and Hilary McD. Beckles, eds. *Caribbean Slavery in the Atlantic World*. Kingston: Ian Randle, 2000.

Shyllon, F. O. *Black Slaves in Britain*. Oxford: Oxford University Press, 1974.

Soirélus, Lima. "Haïti veut se mettre à l'heure du turisme mondial." lenouvelliste.com, February 14, 2008. http://www.lenouvelliste.com/article. php?PubID=1&ArticleID=54230.

Sommer, Doris. *Proceed with Caution, When Engaged by Minority Writing in the Americas*. Cambridge: Harvard University Press, 1999.

Sophocles. *Three Theban Plays: Antigone, Oedipus the King, Oedipus at Colonus*. Translated by Robert Fagles. New York: Penguin Classics, 1999.

Soto-Crespo, Ramón E. "'The Pains of Memory': Mourning the Nation in Puerto Rican Art and Literature." *MLN* 117, no. 2 (2002): 449–80.

Spielberg, Stephen, dir. *Amistad*. Dreamworks, SKG, 1997.

Stanton, Junious Ricardo. "Rites of Ancestral Return: Tribute Honors African Remains." *Chickenbones: A Journal for Literary and Artistic African-American Themes*, October 4, 2003. http://www.nathanielturner.com/ritesofancestralreturn.htm.

Stowe, Harriet Beecher. *Uncle Tom's Cabin*. Edited by Elizabeth Ammons. New York: Norton, 2004.

Styron, Susana, dir. *Shadrach*. Millennium Films, 1998.

Styron, William. *The Confessions of Nat Turner*. New York: Bantam, 1981.

Tanzilo, Bobby. "Streets of Old Milwaukee Delights New Generation." March 31, 2007. OnMilwaukee.com.

Taubira law. Loi no. 2001–434 du 21 mai 2001. http://www.ldh-toulon.net/ spip.php?article575.

Thomas, Hugh. *The Slave Trade: The Story of the Atlantic Slave Trade: 1440–1870*. New York: Simon and Schuster, 1997.

Tibbles, Anthony. "Interpreting Transatlantic Slavery: The Role of Museums." http://www/liverpoolmuseums.org.uk/ism/resources/museum_interpretation.asp.

———, ed. *Transatlantic Slavery: Against Human Dignity*. Liverpool: Liverpool University Press, 2005.

Trouillot, Michel-Rolph. *Silencing the Past: Power and the Production of History*. Boston: Beacon Press, 1995.

Twain, Mark. *The Adventures of Huckleberry Finn*. New York: Penguin Classics, 2002.

UNESCO. "International Year to Commemorate the Struggle against Slavery and Its Abolition." General Conference, Paris, 2003. http://unesdoc.unesco.org/images/0013/001312/131242e.pdf.

United States Department of Labor, Office of Policy Planning and Research. *The Negro Family: The Case for National Action*. Office of Policy Planning and Action, U.S. Department of Labor, 1965. http://www.dol.gov/oasam/programs/history/webid-meynihan.htm.

Villaverde, Cirilo. 1882. *Cecilia Valdés, o La loma del ángel*. Caracas, Venezuela: Biblioteca Ayacucho, 1981.

Wagenheim, Kal, and Olga Jiménez de Wagenheim. *The Puerto Ricans: A Documentary History*. Rev. ed. New York: Markus Wiener, 2002.

Walcott, Derek. "A Frowsty Fragrance." *New York Review of Books* 47, no. 10 (June 15, 2000) : 58.

Walker, Alice. *The Color Purple*. 10th anniversary ed. New York: Harcourt, Brace, Jovanovich, 1992.

Walker, Dionne. "Richmond, Va., Unveils Slavery Memorial." Associated Press. March 30, 2007. http://abcnews.go.com/US/wireStory?id=2997140 .

Wall, Catherine E. "The Visual Dimension of *El siglo de las luces*: Goya and *Explosión en una catedral*." *Revista Canadiense de Estudios Hispánicos* 13, no. 1 (1988): 148–57.

Walker, Margaret. *Jubilee*. Boston: Houghton Mifflin, 1966.

Walvin, James. *Black Ivory: A History of British Slavery*. London: Harper Collins, 1992.

Weil, Stephen E. *Making Museums Matter*. Washington, D. C.: Smithsonian Institution Press, 2002.

Whitcomb, Andrea. *Re-imagining the Museum: Beyond the Mausoleum*. New York: Routledge, 2003.

White, Hayden. *Metahistory: The Historical Imagination in Nineteenth-Century Europe*. Baltimore: Johns Hopkins University Press, 1973.

———. *Tropics of Discourse*. 1978; repr., Baltimore: Johns Hopkins University Press, 1985.

Williams, Sherley Anne. *Dessa Rose*. New York: Morrow, 1986.

Wilson, Fred. *Mining the Museum: An Installation by Fred Wilson*. Edited by Lisa G. Corrin. Baltimore and New York: Contemporary and New Press, 1994.

Wolfe, George C. *The Colored Museum: A Play*. New York: Grove Weidenfeld, 1988.

Wood, R. D. "The Diorama in Great Britain in the 1820s." *History of Photography* 17, no. 3 (1993): 284–95. Also available online at http://www.midley.co.uk/.

Wordsworth, William. "To Toussaint L'Ouverture." In *The Collected Poems of William Wordsworth*, 363–64. London: Wordsworth Editions, 1995.

Zamora, Lois Parkinson. "Magical Ruins/Magical Realism: Alejo Carpentier, François de Nomé, and the New World Baroque." In *Poetics of the Americas: Race, Founding and Textuality*, Edited by Bainard Cowan and Jefferson Humphries, 63–103. Baton Rouge: Louisiana State University Press, 1997.

Index

New World Studies

Vera M. Kutzinski, *Sugar's Secrets: Race and the Erotics of Cuban Nationalism*

Richard D. E. Burton and Fred Reno, editors, *French and West Indian: Martinique, Guadeloupe, and French Guiana Today*

A. James Arnold, editor, *Monsters, Tricksters, and Sacred Cows: Animal Tales and American Identities*

J. Michael Dash, *The Other America: Caribbean Literature in a New World Context*

Isabel Alvarez Borland, *Cuban-American Literature of Exile: From Person to Persona*

Belinda J. Edmondson, editor, *Caribbean Romances: The Politics of Regional Representation*

Steven V. Hunsaker, *Autobiography and National Identity in the Americas*

Celia M. Britton, *Edouard Glissant and Postcolonial Theory: Strategies of Language and Resistance*

Mary Peabody Mann, *Juanita: A Romance of Real Life in Cuba Fifty Years Ago* Edited and with an introduction by Patricia M. Ard

George B. Handley, *Postslavery Literatures in the Americas: Family Portraits in Black and White*

Faith Smith, *Creole Recitations: John Jacob Thomas and Colonial Formation in the Late Nineteenth-Century Caribbean*

Ian Gregory Strachan, *Paradise and Plantation: Tourism and Culture in the Anglophone Caribbean*

Nick Nesbitt, *Voicing Memory: History and Subjectivity in French Caribbean Literature*

Charles W. Pollard, *New World Modernisms: T. S. Eliot, Derek Walcott, and Kamau Brathwaite*

Carine M. Mardorossian, *Reclaiming Difference: Caribbean Women Rewrite Postcolonialism*

Luís Madureira. *Cannibal Modernities: Postcoloniality and the Avant-garde in Caribbean and Brazilian Literature*

Elizabeth M. DeLoughrey, Renée K. Gosson, and George B. Handley, editors, *Caribbean Literature and the Environment: Between Nature and Culture*

Flora González Mandri, *Guarding Cultural Memory: Afro-Cuban Women in Literature and the Arts*

Miguel Arnedo-Gómez, *Writing Rumba: The Afrocubanista Movement in Poetry*

Jessica Adams, Michael P. Bibler, and Cécile Accilien, editors, *Just Below South: Intercultural Performance in the Caribbean and the U.S. South*

Valérie Loichot, *Orphan Narratives: The Postplantation Literature of Faulkner, Glissant, Morrison, and Saint-John Perse*

Sarah Phillips Casteel, *Second Arrivals: Landscape and Belonging in Contemporary Writing of the Americas*

Guillermina De Ferrari, *Vulnerable States: Bodies of Memory in Contemporary Caribbean Fiction*

Claudia Sadowski-Smith, *Border Fictions: Globalization, Empire, and Writing at the Boundaries of the United States*

Doris L. Garraway, editor, *Tree of Liberty: Cultural Legacies of the Haitian Revolution in the Atlantic World*

Dawn Fulton, *Signs of Dissent: Maryse Conde and Postcolonial Criticism*

Nick Nesbitt, *Universal Emancipation: The Haitian Revolution and the Radical Enlightenment*

Michael G. Malouf, *Transatlantic Solidarities: Irish Nationalism and Caribbean Poetics*

Maria Cristina Fumagalli, *Caribbean Perspectives on Modernity: Returning the Gaze*

Vivian Nun Halloran, *Exhibiting Slavery: The Caribbean Postmodern Novel as Museum*